The Game Narrative Toolbox

Learn how to create compelling game storylines.

Four experienced narrative designers from different genres of game development have banded together to create this all-inclusive guide on what it's like to work as a writer and narrative designer in the video game industry. From concept to final testing, *The Game Narrative Toolbox* walks readers through what role a narrative designer plays on a development team and what the requirements are at every stage of development. Drawing on real experiences, authors Tobias Heussner, Toiya Kristen Finley, PhD, Ann Lemay, and Jennifer Brandes Hepler provide invaluable advice for writing compelling player-centered stories and effective dialogue trees to help readers make the switch from writing prose or screenplay to interactive.

Thoroughly revised, the Second Edition includes updated content reflecting the industry's latest developments. In addition to revised and updated chapters, this new edition features two additional chapters covering more advanced topics that are applicable to the lessons learned from the original chapters.

Accompanying every chapter are exercises that allow the reader to develop their own documentation, outlines, and game-dialogue samples for use in applying for industry jobs or developing independent projects.

Introducing The Focal Press Game Design Workshops

The Focal Press Game Design Workshops was created as a means to bring real-world experience and practicality to both game design students and professionals. The books in this series are developed with strong foundational pedagogy and accompanied with robust learning resources for both students and instructors, including video tutorials, test materials, practical exercises and more.

This series is continually being developed to match common game design and development curriculum so it can be utilized in different programs and at different levels.

The Game Narrative Toolbox
Tobias Heussner, Toiya Kristen Finley, Jennifer Brandes Hepler, Ann Lemay

The GameMaker Standard
David Vinciguerra, Andrew Howell

Unity 3D and PlayMaker Essentials: Game Development from Concept to Publishing
Jere Miles

The Game Narrative Toolbox, Second Edition
Tobias Heussner, Toiya Kristen Finley, Jennifer Brandes Hepler, Ann Lemay

Series Editor **Heather Maxwell Chandler** is a veteran game producer with experience at Activision, EA, and Ubisoft. She's also the founder of Media Sunshine, Inc., (www.mediasunshine.com) a company that provides game production contract services to developers, publishers, and vendors. She has contributed to the production of *Apocalypse, Civilization: Call to Power, Heavy Gear 2, Sacred 2: Fallen Angel*, and eight games in the *Ghost Recon* series. She's the author of *The Game Production Handbook*, Third Edition*, The Game Localization Handbook*, Second Edition and *Fundamentals of Game Development*.

The Game Narrative Toolbox

Second Edition

**Tobias Heussner, Toiya Kristen Finley, PhD,
Jennifer Brandes Hepler, Ann Lemay**

CRC Press
Taylor & Francis Group
Boca Raton London New York

CRC Press is an imprint of the
Taylor & Francis Group, an **informa** business

Second edition published 2024
by CRC Press
2385 Executive Center Drive, Suite 320, Boca Raton FL 33431

and by CRC Press
4 Park Square, Milton Park, Abingdon, Oxon, OX14 4RN

CRC Press is an imprint of Taylor & Francis Group, LLC

© 2024 Tobias Heussner, Toiya Kristen Finley, Jennifer Brandes Hepler, Ann Lemay

First edition published by CRC Press 2015

Library of Congress Cataloging-in-Publication Data
Names: Heussner, Tobias, author. | Finley, Toiya Kristen, author. | Hepler, Jennifer
    Brandes, author. | Lemay, Ann, author.
Title: The game narrative toolbox / Tobias Heussner, Toiya Kristen Finley, PhD,
    Jennifer Brandes Hepler, Ann Lemay.
Description: Second edition. | Boca Raton : CRC Press, 2024. | Series: Focal press game
    design workshops | Includes bibliographical references and index.
Identifiers: LCCN 2023005849 (print) | LCCN 2023005850 (ebook) |
    ISBN 9781032439051 (hardback) | ISBN 9781032438962 (paperback) |
    ISBN 9781003369332 (ebook)
Subjects: LCSH: Video games—Design. | Video games—Programming. |
    Video games—Authorship.
Classification: LCC QA76.76.C672 H48 2024 (print) | LCC QA76.76.C672 (ebook) |
    DDC 794.8/1536—dc23/eng/20230515
LC record available at https://lccn.loc.gov/2023005849
LC ebook record available at https://lccn.loc.gov/2023005850

ISBN: 978-1-032-43905-1 (hbk)
ISBN: 978-1-032-43896-2 (pbk)
ISBN: 978-1-003-36933-2 (ebk)

DOI: 10.1201/9781003369332

Typeset in Times
by Apex CoVantage, LLC

Access the Instructor and Student Resources:
www.routledge.com/9781032438962

Contents

Preface to the Second Edition

Great stories are timeless and universal. Just ask *Assassin's Creed: Odyssey* and the inspiration it took from three-thousand-year-old Greek mythology and epic poetry. Game genres, on the other hand, evolve rapidly.

When we first wrote this book, mobile games were a new emerging market, dominated by story-light titles like *Angry Birds*, and our information on writing for mobile focused in part on answering the question of whether mobile games had any need for stories at all. But since 2021, mobile games now make up the majority of game spending, at 52 percent, and have become over a ninety-two-billion-dollar market.[1] And with thousands of cloned match-three and farming games out there, many companies have bet on narrative as the thing that will set their particular product apart.

So, whether you are picking this book up for the first time this year, or you've studied our original words until your copy is dog-eared and broken-spined, you will find new, relevant information below for today's game-writing marketplace, including a chapter on visual novels—story-heavy, gameplay-light, often romance-focused mobile games that have exploded into an enduringly popular new genre—and the new idea of "Games as a Service," the need for open-world games that provide ongoing content and living worlds for players to return to again and again. Both of these genres have a strong need for constant new and engaging content to keep players in their app or game, ensuring continued demand for professional writers and narrative designers.

And with the pandemic trapping so many people in their homes for so long, the gaming audience has expanded like never before, as have opportunities for developers. Most game companies now are far more remote-work-friendly than they used to be, which opens freelance or full-time-remote possibilities for narrative designers, even with companies on the other side of the world. So, sit down, pull up a chair, and see what you can learn about designing great narratives for games of all genres.

Note

1 Jeffrey Rousseau, "Newzoo: Mobile Game Revenue Generated $93.2bn in 2021," *GameIndustry.biz*, last modified January 20, 2002, https://www.games-industry.biz/newzoo-mobile-game-revenue-generated-usd93bn-in-2021.

Acknowledgments

The authors of *The Game Narrative Toolbox* would like to especially thank all the companies who supported this project by giving their permission to use screenshots and artwork from their projects. To Brian Kindregan, Chris Avellone, Cori May, Rhianna Pratchett, and Tom Jubert, thanks for sharing your insights into the narrative-design process. To Tonia Laird, we're so appreciative of your storyboard example and are grateful you could help us demonstrate the collaborative effort between narrative designers and artists. A special thanks goes to Cameron Harris. Your thoughtful suggestions helped to bring the writers of this book together. We're also grateful to the staff at Focal Press for their support and the opportunity to write *The Game Narrative Toolbox*. Special thanks to Sean, Caitlin, and Heather for their feedback during the production and their help in shaping this book you now hold in your hands.

Ann: There are so many folx in the industry I am thankful for that I have befriended, worked with, and learned from over the years that the list would be endless. Every time I see your faces or your words, be it online or in person, I am reminded of all the good things. A special callout to Ceri Young, Anne Farmer, Jo Berry, and all those who have supported me through thick and thin and helped me become a better writer and a better person—love y'all. Also, much appreciation and love to my husband, Eric, who supported me (and made sure I actually ate) while I worked on this book. A huge shout-out to my team at WB Games Montréal—what a stellar bunch you all are. Last but not least, I would also like to thank Gary Corriveau and Patrick Naud, who believed in me and gave me my first shot at game writing all those years ago. I remember.

Jennifer: I would like to thank Daniel Erickson, Alex Freed, Brent Knowles, David Gaider, Hall Hood, and all the other talented writers and designers at BioWare that I learned so much from. A big thanks to my current team at Thought Pennies (doubling up on Daniel and Alex!) for letting me put all this stuff into practice on such a huge project. Thanks in addition to my husband, Chris, who has shared this whole crazy thirty-year writing journey with me, my children, Beverly Rowan and Shane (who are now old enough to read these acknowledgements), and my amazingly supportive mom, Sue Brandes, without whom I would never have been able to do any of this. My work is, always, in loving memory of my father, Larry Brandes, who told me I could do anything and was as shocked as I was any time he was wrong.

Acknowledgments

Toiya: Thanks to Lakeview for their never-ending support (and for putting up with me) during my early career as a freelancer in this industry, to the fabulous alpha females Nikko and Selene (now both playing together beyond the Rainbow Bridge) for staying up with me till early in the morning as I worked on the first edition of this project, and to Cleo for being a constant, calming presence as I worked on the second. To Wendy Despain, Tom Abernathy, Richard Dansky, Evan Skolnick, and Andrew Walsh: Thank you for encouraging me when I was a fledgling who showed up at GDC and GDC Online, and for letting me know that I actually had a clue about this whole game-writing thing. To Anna Megill, Eddy Webb, C.J. Kershner, and Michelle Clough: Thank you for being a support system and perception check as I've evolved in my skills and career. To Rob Miles, Carl Varnado, Dennis Mathews, Kevin Gillis, and Cornell Wright: Thank you for teaching me the fine art of networking and that it's more about community than collecting contacts. I never would have gotten this far without you. Finally, my deep gratitude goes to my mother, Myra, for her relentless support. God, thanks for giving me to her.

Tobias: I would like to thank Jesus Christ for everything, Charis, my wonderful wife and helper, for her support and encouragement, and my children, Ruben, Esther, and Ruth, who always remind me to see the world with a kid's eyes. I would also like to thank Brian Kindregan, Chris Avellone, and Mateusz Pohl for their support for this book project, as well as the IGDA Special Interest Group Writing, who welcomed me and helped me to get connected and learn about this wonderful craft. Finally I'd like to thank my church and my friends for their support and encouragements. God bless you all.

Authors

Tobias Heussner is an experienced game content/narrative designer and producer, who started developing games in high school. He has worked on more than 25 published titles ranging from AAA PC games to console, handheld console games and Free2Play browser games. His areas of expertise include game content design, game narrative design/writing, game system design, and game production.

Toiya Kristen Finley, PhD has nearly 30 years of experience as a writer and editor in several media. In games, she has worked as a game designer, narrative designer, game writer, editor, narrative consultant, and diversity consultant (or some combination of the six) on several AAA, indie, social, and mobile games for children and general audiences, including *Destiny 2* and visual novels for Ubisoft and *Chapters* apps. With Tobias Heussner, she cofounded the Game Writing Tutorial at GDC Online and served as an instructor. Her books include *Narrative Tactics for Mobile and Social Games: Pocket-Sized Storytelling*; *Freelance Video Game Writing: The Life & Business of the Digital Mercenary for Hire*; and *Branching Story, Unlocked Dialogue: Designing and Writing Visual Novels*.

Jennifer Brandes Hepler got her start in tabletop game development, working for well-known properties such as *Shadowrun* and *Paranoia* before detouring to Hollywood to work on CBS Television's *The Agency*. She was a senior writer and narrative designer at BioWare, on the *Dragon Age* franchise and *Star Wars: The Old Republic* and more recently at Pixelberry Studios on *Choices: Stories You Play* and *Storyloom*. She is currently the Writing Director at Thought Pennies Entertainment.

Ann Lemay joined the video game industry in 1997. Over the years, she's taken on the role of game designer, narrative designer, and writer on a wide range of AAA projects. She has worked at many companies, including Ubisoft, BioWare, and Microids. Ann is currently a Narrative Director at WB Games Montréal where she leads a team of very talented writers, narrative designers, and voice designers on *Gotham Knights*.

Introduction

When you sit in a movie theater watching the explosion-packed opening of a modern action movie, you're giving up your right to know exactly what's going on in favor of pulse-pounding excitement. What does it matter if you know who these people are, as long as you can tell that they're on a helicopter, piloted by a demon, that's packed with C4 and plummeting into the heart of an active volcano?[1]

Moviegoers know that whatever questions are still plaguing them at the end of the opening spectacle will be answered later, and they're willing to wait a little to find out what it all means. But writers for video games do not have that luxury. Despite working for an audience that generally loves a good explosion even more than film buffs, game writers can't count on that audience willingness to go along for the ride.

While screenwriters only have to equip their audience to answer a single question after every scene—"What happened?"—game writers must make sure players also know "What do I do next?" and "Why does it matter?"

The difference between stories for games and stories for movies is that games are, by definition, interactive. They don't have "viewers," they have "players," and players play an active role. It is their actions in gameplay—and, in some genres, their choices in dialogue—that drive the plot forward. This means that *not knowing what to do next is the single biggest sin in interactive writing.* Yet striving too hard to be clear can easily shoot you over the line into boring, repetitive, expository, and pedantic.

It is this balance of clarity vs. adrenaline, narrative momentum vs. player agency, that requires narrative designers. More than mere dialogue writers who, criminally, are still sometimes brought in at the end of game projects to just "add the words," narrative designers are ideally involved with a game's development from the earliest stages.

So, What Are We Doing Here?

During the course of this book, you will be taken through the game-development process step by step, from the initial pitch, through documentation, production, and playtesting, and learn the role a narrative designer can play throughout the process. By following along with the provided exercises, you will build a portfolio of game-development documents and samples, suitable for inclusion with job applications or as the jumping-off point for developing independent projects. By using this toolbox of tips and tricks from working professionals, you will ensure that you make the best use of games as a medium and avoid common beginner mistakes.

The authors have over fifty years of game-development experience between them, in Europe, Canada, and the United States, and on games ranging from social media, to action, to MMOs[2] and RPGs.[3]

Every genre of games has distinct requirements for narrative, and few narrative designers have worked in all genres. In *The Game Narrative Toolbox*, each author will primarily (though not exclusively) focus on writing for a particular genre: Tobias Heussner will be talking about MMOs; Toiya Kristen Finley will address indie, social, and mobile games; Ann Lemay will discuss the action-adventure genre; and Jennifer Brandes Hepler will focus on single-player RPGs. Since the first edition, all of the writers have done additional work in new fields (some of which didn't exist yet at the time!), leading to the addition of new sections on the growing fields of visual novels and open-world games. Other types of games will be addressed where possible, in interviews with other writers active in that field.

And now a little background, so you'll know who we all are as we impart our wisdom . . .

Toiya Kristen Finley

There's no one way to become a narrative designer. With every narrative designer and game writer you talk to, you'll hear a different story as to how they got that first job. My path to becoming a narrative designer started as I was playing *Shenmue II*. I had been thinking about a game I wanted to make. I'd thought up gameplay, the plot, its dramatic tensions, and its resolution. But I worried my ideas were a little too crazy. Maybe a game like that couldn't exist. *Shenmue II* proved to me that the kind of games I wanted to make *were* possible. The world could be dynamic, and the NPCs[4] living in it could have interesting lives of their own. They didn't have to simply exist to be at the service and mercy of the player-character.

This gave me the confidence to pursue game writing. I'd been writing for almost my entire life. I had a variety of publications in fiction, creative nonfiction, and academic writing; I'd been editing all kinds of writing; and, at the time, I was working on a doctorate in literature and creative writing. Still, I knew absolutely nothing about game writing— or the game industry in general. At that time, I thought writers came up with everything: the story, the gameplay, and the mechanics. They were "writing" everything, right? What I didn't realize is that I was thinking about games like a narrative designer. I wanted to be one, but I didn't even know the term.

I had no idea how to go about finding a writing job in games. With a little bit of Google-fu, I found Black Chicken Studios, an indie developer working on their first game, *Academagia: The Making of Mages*. I started off as a lore writer and also got to work as an assistant game designer. About a year later, a developer asked if I could help design a mobile game for their client. Although I was the game designer, I wrote the story and created character types as well. I had taken on the responsibilities of a narrative designer, and I still didn't know it.

It finally clicked for me while I was working on my next project, a Facebook RPG (remember those?). Since then, I've worked on everything from social RPGs and mobile games for children; *Insecure: The Come Up Game* as a developmental editor; visual novels as a writer and editor for NBCUniversal, Ubisoft, and the *Moments* and *Chapters* apps; *Destruction AllStars* as a writer; *Destiny 2* as an editor; several projects as a diversity and narrative consultant; and a number of fantastic games that will sadly never be published.

How I became a narrative designer is neither usual nor unusual. Film writers have become narrative designers. Comic book writers have become narrative designers. Tabletop-RPG designers and writers also have careers in narrative design. You can now study narrative design in school, or you can bring to video game projects your valuable experiences writing for other media.

There have never been so many opportunities for narrative designers. From AAA[5] developers to independent individuals doing all of their own art, music, and code with visual coders and no-code platforms, people realize players want and expect great stories. Whether you want to work on big-budget titles or casual mobile games, you will find that developers are looking for your help.

Jennifer Brandes Hepler

I am an avid tabletop gamer and began writing for pen-and-paper RPGs before I even graduated college. I have had the opportunity to work on several very popular titles, including *Shadowrun*, *Paranoia*, *Earthdawn*, and *Legend of the Five Rings*. I was actually under deadline for my *Shadowrun* sourcebook, *Cyberpirates*, the day I graduated; I went to commencement in the morning, came home, took off the cap and gown, and finished writing a chapter that afternoon.

I subsequently spent several years in Hollywood, working on CBS Television's *The Agency* and developing many other projects, the bulk of which ended up being game adaptations. When I was approached by BioWare, I happily accepted a job working at one of the most story-oriented video game studios in the business, and spent eight amazing years as a senior writer on epic games such as *Dragon Age: Origins*, *Dragon Age II*, *Dragon Age: Inquisition*, and *Star Wars: The Old Republic*. After leaving BioWare, I left the industry for a time to work on game-style educational simulations to teach better, more empathetic communication skills to doctors, teachers, social workers, and parents.

I returned to games to work in visual novels, a format I love, heading up several projects on *Choices: Stories You Play*, the brief and lamented *Storyscape*, and multiple launch titles for Pixelberry Studios's visual novel creation tool, *Storyloom*. I am currently the writing director at Thought Pennies, building the writing team and processes for an unannounced large-scale social RPG.

In my various roles at different companies, I have seen hundreds of submissions from aspiring narrative designers and helped launch quite a few careers. And in that time, I have seen people make the same mistakes over and over. And not just the newcomers. On any given day in a narrative review, we would usually hit one or more of the triumvirate of game-narrative deadly sins: a passive player-character, confusing goals, or unconvincing NPCs.

Interactive writing can be *hard*. How do you tell a story when you don't know who the protagonist is? How do you keep a flow of information over the course of six questions which can be asked in any order . . . or not at all? And how do you ensure that players can always answer that all-important question: What do I do next?

I have spent almost twenty years learning the best way to answer those questions. Now I'm ready to help you learn which answers work for you.

Ann Lemay

I was raised on *Star Trek* and *Star Wars*, have been an avid *Transformers* fan since the original series, and have been reading science fiction and fantasy novels for as long as I can remember. My first memories of playing video games include titles such as *Night Stalker* and *Frogger* on my Intellivision II (which, yes, I still own), and later *Zelda* and *Shadowgate* on the Nintendo Entertainment System (NES). I leapt at the chance to make video games when Ubisoft established itself in Montréal in 1997, and have been in the game industry ever since. Before taking up the role of writer in 2005, I was a game designer. And before that, a graphic designer, and before that, a community manager. Having had the good fortune to learn a variety of roles early on during the establishment of the Montréal game community has been a boon to me as a writer, giving me insight into what the needs of other disciplines are, and how to complement them best while advocating for narrative.

I've worked on a wide variety of games (*F1 Racing Championship*, *High School Musical: Sing it!*, *Naruto: Rise of a Ninja*, *Your Shape: Fitness Evolved*, *Mass Effect 3*, *Mass Effect: Andromeda*, *Discovery Tour by Assassin's Creed: Ancient Egypt*, *Assassin's Creed Origins* and *Gotham Knights*, among many others) as well as various multimedia projects, including an alternate reality game (*Still Life*) and the *Assassin's Creed Encyclopedia*. As this second edition goes to print, I am now at WB Games Montréal as a narrative director, working with a team of incredibly talented people. There is nothing quite like finding the right crew of people to work with.

As a writer, my tasks on my projects encompassed the roles of both writer and narrative designer. While many tend to define the role of writer as "person who writes dialogue," I have found it is a prescriptive and limiting way to describe the goals I would set for myself in being a good writer on a game. As well, the definitions of "writer" and "narrative designer" can vary widely from company to company. In my personal view, to be a good writer in games is to strive to be a good narrative designer.

As a narrative director, my job is to empower a team of writers, designers, and voice designers and to make sure they are given the tools to perform their jobs with excellence. As a director, it's not my job to write the game, but rather, it's my job to make sure my team's work is going in the direction we need it to go in for the project, and that their writing is the best version of what it can be. I am an advocate for the narrative of the game and the work my team does, and also, I enable and help to communicate with the teams we collaborate with as well, as we all strive to bring a story to life in an interactive medium.

I have been making games since 1997. My experience covers many genres from teams small to large. My contribution to this book will focus more on practical-experience advice, rather than theory. Specifically, I will note what you should expect as a junior narrative designer joining a team, be it big or small, and will detail how you can ensure that you are contributing to the best of your abilities while learning as much as you can.

Tobias Heussner

Where do I start . . . ? Let's see. Well, when I was a child, I loved games. Okay, that's not a surprise, is it? My favorite toys were LEGO and Playmobil. I spent hours playing with the sets and using them to dive into fantasy worlds. It didn't take long before I started to invent games around those fantasy universes, which mostly ended up being bad luck for my family because they had to play them with me.

In high school, I bought my first box of a game called *The Dark Eye*, which could best be described as being the German version of *Dungeons & Dragons*. Soon my friends and I found ourselves deep in the worlds of fantasy, fighting thieves, orcs, and dragons.

Back then, making or writing for games was not on my agenda. Instead, I planned to go into medical science, maybe researching immunizations against killer viruses such as Ebola. But something went wrong with this plan. As the years passed, I wrote my first game concepts—still in high school, still not considering game design as a profession but slowly getting into computer programming. It was in 1998 that I started my first group for game development and met other game professionals for the first time. Most people today can't imagine how game development looked back then, but in the whole area of Berlin, there were maybe a hundred professional game developers, and teams were rarely larger than twenty members. Today, most teams are at least twice as big, and there are more *studios* than there used to be people working in the business in the entire capital of Germany. With this group, I developed my first storyline and game concepts while finishing high school and attending university to study computer science. Yes, my life had changed. No longer did I want to be a scientist; from now on, I was going to be a game designer.

In my free time, I got deeper into roleplaying and also started to attend and organize live roleplaying events, which were a good learning experience for me as a narrative designer. In 2005, I was hired by a company called Radon Labs to work first on edutainment games, the famous German horse games, then later on an AAA RPG called *Drakensang: The Dark Eye*. I was back in the fantasy world that had ignited my passion for roleplaying games. Even though we had many challenges to overcome, it was a very fun experience to take this world that had existed for so many years in our heads and turn it into virtual reality.

I started studying feature film writing, then left university to fully focus on game development. Together with Radon Labs, I developed a sequel to *Drakensang: The Dark Eye*, before Radon Labs closed its doors, and I went on to Bigpoint to create *Drakensang Online*. I ended up working on *Drakensang Online* for several years as a level designer, which included a lot of narrative-and game-design tasks. In my free time, I worked on several screenplays, short stories, and projects, as well as spent time learning different technologies (something I consider important for any narrative designer), and joined the Independent Game Developers Association (IGDA) and its Game Writing Special Interest Group.

In 2011, Toiya and I organized the first Game Writing Tutorial Day at the Game Developers Conference (GDC) Online and enjoyed sharing what we had learned over the years with many other talented folks. In 2013, I was elected to become the chair of the Special Interest Group and was happy to serve the game-writing community in this position.

Due to my more technical background, I'll try to serve as the voice of "design" in the chapters, with a focus on the technical and design sides of game narrative. So, I'll be talking about level design and scripting, things that might or might not fall under the narrative-design umbrella, depending on your studio. It's not always necessary for narrative designers to understand level design and scripting, but it never hurts!

With this book, I, and the other writers, want to invite you on a journey to experience the typical day-to-day life of a narrative designer during a game-development production cycle. We hope we can share with you some secrets and challenges and inspire you to start mastering this amazing craft!

Notes

1 Not an actual movie opening.
2 Massively multiplayer online: A group of genres where hundreds of players play together in the same game world/scenario while being connected via online functionalities.
3 Roleplaying game: A genre where players act out the roles and take on the responsibilities of characters within the game.
4 Non-player character: A character within an interactive story that is not controlled by any player.
5 An AAA game is one that aims for the highest market and industry standard, similar to a blockbuster in Hollywood.

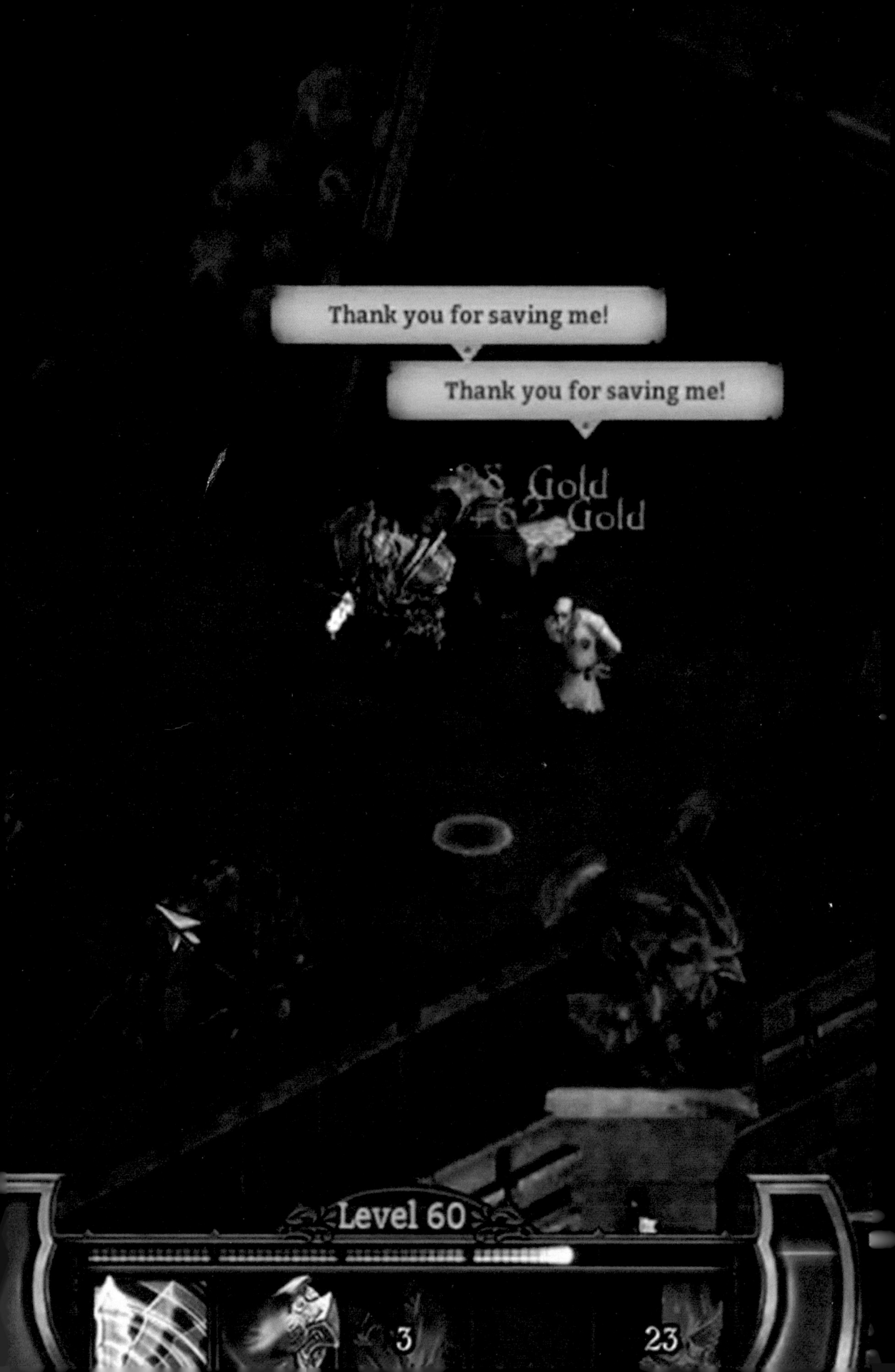

What Is Narrative Design?

What is narrative design, and what does a narrative designer do? This is one of the most discussed questions among industry professionals right now. While the Introduction gave you a chance to learn about the goals of this book, this chapter invites you to take a look into the world of narrative design and the responsibilities of a narrative designer.

IN THIS CHAPTER, YOU WILL LEARN TO . . .

- Define narrative design.
- Recognize the responsibilities of a narrative designer.
- Step into the role of a narrative designer.

To begin, here are the definitions for narrative design and narrative designer that will be used throughout the book:

> Game Narrative Design is the art of telling a story in a computer, console, or mobile game using the techniques and devices available. It is the art of using gameplay and the sum of visual and acoustic methods to create an entertaining and engaging experience for players.

DOI: 10.1201/9781003369332-1

A game narrative designer is the champion of an interactive story, works in the field of narrative design, and combines the roles of a writer with those of a game designer. Working with other departments (programming, game design, level design, art, sound, etc.), the narrative designer organizes and integrates the story into the game using the available mechanics, designs, and assets.

A WORD REGARDING TERMS

Terms in the game industry are normally, and unfortunately, not as defined as would be helpful. Some studios use a term one way, while others use it another way. What you call your tools isn't so important. It *is* important that you understand how they work. Throughout the book, whenever using a term, the book will give you a short definition for how it uses this term. This definition may not be the same as what you learned at school or in your studio. Still, the underlying principles should be the same and should be clear. So, please don't be confused if, for example, "mechanics" are called "systems" in your environment, or if you use the term "logline" instead of "high concept."

As mentioned before, the industry at this point uses a number of definitions for those two terms. To give you a short look into how differently developers view the role and field, here are personal definitions and experiences.

Jennifer Brandes Hepler (AAA In-House Writing Director)

"What is narrative design?" is a surprisingly hard question to answer. Nothing in the games industry is standardized, so people whose function is narrative design may be called different things at different companies. Titles I've seen personally include: writer, game writer, game story writer, narrative designer, and quest designer. But because of the casual nature of the industry, nothing particularly prevents a company from calling their narrative designer "senior story woodchuck supreme," or using the title "narrative designer" for the guy who cleans the bathrooms.

So, for the purposes of this book, I see the "narrative designer" as being someone who:

- works as an integrated part of a game development team
- is the primary designer of and advocate for the story in the game being developed;
- is the primary writer for all documentation involving the game narrative, from initial pitch through postproduction;
- designs the world, characters, and plotlines for the game in development;
- writes the dialogue for the game;
- remains involved as an advocate for the story throughout testing and postproduction, including dialogue recording.

It is the "design" part of narrative design that makes this role different than a "writer," although they share many responsibilities, and the terms are often used interchangeably. But if narrative designers were the same as writers, then anyone with a good grasp of dialogue and a background in film could easily make the switch into game writing, as the jobs would be functionally the same.

This is, in my experience, not the case. Everyone I know who has worked as a narrative designer has seen other writers with film or novel backgrounds who couldn't make the switch. Most often, there are two main reasons for this. Either the writer:

- can't give up control over the story to allow the player to be in the driver's seat;

or

- can't give up the freedom of being the sole creator and work as part of a multidisciplinary team.

These are both my key factors in being a narrative designer for games. A game story is not like a movie, or book, or play, in which your characters say only what you want them to say and go only where you want them to go. Players love the freedom in games to wander off the narrative path, whether for brief side quests, hundreds of hours of open-world exploration, or to forgo the narrative altogether in competitive multiplayer games. In some games, often those which take pride in being "story driven," there isn't a single, linear narrative at all. Instead, players' choices in gameplay and dialogue lead to distinct branching middles and endings.

As a narrative designer, you must plan a story that leaves players room to make these choices and also convinces them they are truly holding the reins. To do this, a good narrative designer must not only have mastered the craft of story and interactive dialogue but also should understand the other disciplines involved in creating a game.

A narrative designer should understand the craft of level design, in which game designers and environment artists lay out landscapes that encourage players to create emergent stories from the settings, creatures, and treasures they provide. Narrative designers should have a basic grasp of systems design, understanding the powers, moves, weapons, and abilities that will be available for the player to use in the course of the story. Narrative designers must understand what audio needs their game has, as spoken dialogue must be written more sparsely than read dialogue; whether their game will be localized (translated into other languages); and what their art and animation limitations are (dialogue for a fully cinematic, romantic cutscene is written very differently than if that same scene is conveyed only through still 2D portraits).

DEVELOPMENT ROLES IN AAA GAME DEVELOPMENT

These roles may have different titles at different companies, but for big-budget games, they will usually exist in some form:

Executive producer: In charge of the overall project. The buck stops here.

Creative director: The holder of the overall concept and creative vision for the project.

Lead designer: In charge of the creative vision for narrative and gameplay.

Lead artist: In charge of the creative vision for the visual look of the game.

Level designers: Handle the nuts and bolts of executing the gameplay; design individual levels in the game.

Systems designers: Create game systems, including combat, crafting, mini games, etc.

Animators/cinematic designers: Animate both gameplay and cutscenes.

Artists: Create art for levels (environment artists), characters (character artists), and initial concepts for any new creatures or assets (concept artists). There are also artists who specialize in making sure all this art works within the constraints of the engine and code available (tech artists).

Tools programmers: Program the software tools in which designers and artists create their work.

Gameplay programmers: Create the engine in which the game occurs.

Audio programmers: Make the music, sound effects, and spoken dialogue work in the game.

Quality assurance and testers: Playtest the game repeatedly until it's not as broken.

To sum it all up, to me, a good narrative designer has to:

- **Have good organizational and communication skills**. As the go-to person for documentation on the team, you must be able to easily and concisely use words to communicate ideas to people who don't like to read words.
- **Develop an intimate understanding of the overall game**. As a narrative designer, you must understand the gameplay experience intended on your project and use the story to best enhance that experience for the player. Writing *Hamlet* when the project is supposed to be *Leisure Suit Larry 42* won't get you any points, no matter how great the writing is.
- **Have an ear for dialogue**. Like movies and TV, video games are a visual and auditory medium, which means that even if you spend 75 percent of your time crafting the plot of the game, the part that will be recognized immediately as "writing" is dialogue. If your strengths as a writer are in penning long, poetically descriptive passages, game-writing is probably not for you . . . although the rise of visual novels as a genre has given game writing a new use for prose skills (see Chapter 10)
- **Be a team player**. In AAA game development, a team requires engine programmers, tools programmers, physics programmers,

technical artists, concept artists, character artists, environment artists, audio specialists, animators, cinematic designers, level designers, systems designers, combat designers, and voice actors. Of all of those specialties, narrative design tends to be the smallest. Even at the most story-driven companies, the ratio is usually something like twenty artists, to fifteen programmers, to ten designers, to one writer. So, it's key to understand that while your role is to advocate for the story in the game, that story is important only *as a part of the game*, not as something precious in its own right. If it doesn't serve the needs of the game, the story goes. If you're not comfortable with that, then narrative designer won't be the role for you.

Ann Lemay (AAA In-House Narrative Director)

Regardless of the functional tasks and duties (the nature of the position has a wide range of variances from one company to another), ultimately a narrative designer's focus, in my mind, will always center upon two very important things:

- **To advocate for story among the team and across disciplines**. It will be your charge to not just convey what the story is to the team but also to ensure their investment in the narrative focus.
- **To be a nexus of information at all times**. You have answers, are able to come up with the answers (and the right ones with the time and work needed to find them, not just making things up on the spot to look good), or know who has the answers for those who have questions as they pertain to narrative and story on all levels.

If you succeed at the above, the act of writing dialogue will happen at some point during production. But the reality is that a lot more happens on a project before you ever get to start stuffing lines in a character's mouth, and most of that involves talking to other people and working out what you want to do as well as where and how you want to take it. And then ripping it up and doing it all over again. As a narrative designer and/ or writer, iteration is your best friend. This grows exponentially when you're working on a game—and with a team. Clear communication and an ability to bring a group of people with different priorities to become invested in the narrative work are crucial to the role.

WORK EXPERIENCES: ANN LEMAY

"Writer" means something more than a wrangler "stringing words together in a generally pleasing fashion." It means the following, as well:
- Understanding the mechanics of the jobs of your colleagues on your project, so that you can speak their language enough to have a point of commonality, and so you can support each other in your work. For example:

- Know what game design is, but also know what the game design on *your* game is.
- Know your game designers as well, because when things change, you need them to think it's normal to *tell* you that things have changed.
- You want them to feel that narrative can bring enough to gameplay that consulting with you will make their jobs easier, and the end result of their work is better for it.
- The above example centers on gameplay because it's the obvious one. But when programming is making your tools, you, really want to bribe the tools guys with all the cookies in the world. They are actively making your job easier or harder with every string of code they output.
- Understanding that storytelling is more than "just words" (yes, I went there). It's also about setting, and pacing, and environmental narrative, and gameplay, and all the feelings you can evoke when you mesh everything that makes a game together into a whole.

If you can't work with other disciplines, if you can't or won't understand other disciplines in order to make sure your writing enhances them, just as you ensure that your writing is enhanced *by* them . . . your work will never be as good as it could be, or as it should be.

Toiya Kristen Finley (Narrative Designer, Game Writer, Game Designer, Editor, and Consultant of AAA, Indie, and Mobile Games)

When I was first introduced to the narrative design and game writing community, there was a lot of debate about the concept of "narrative designer." Some said it was a role separate from the responsibilities of the game writer. Others said it was synonymous with being a writer. I listened to industry veterans hash out definitions and engage in ongoing conversations in newsgroups, on message boards, and at conferences. With all of the opinions on what narrative design was and what it was not, my understanding was fuzzy at best.

I didn't have a grasp on narrative design until I found myself unwittingly doing it. Working as the game designer and writer on a Facebook RPG, I wasn't just coming up with the game mechanics and the story. I needed to make sure that the mechanics and the story worked in tandem with each other. The story needed to be reflected in the gameplay. The world needed to express the game's mechanics. The gameplay needed to showcase the world and its characters. Now I needed to come up with a main storyline that would make good use of the mechanics. That story needed to be broken down into missions and objectives that would not only make sense for the world in which the game took place but also make sense for the game's genre. Crafting and waiting hours (and sometimes days) for items to be completed needed logical worldbuilding to explain why the process took so long. Even the items players could collect to craft into weapons would say something about the state of the world and the characters that would use them. I'd heard that narrative designers "champion the story," but I didn't realize that responsibility was making sure that the story and world embodied the gameplay and mechanics.

My understanding of narrative design and its multifaceted definition continues to evolve. The best way I can describe it simply is to say that narrative design = story delivery: narrative design delivers aspects of story, world, and characters across all parts of the game, whether those parts of the game are traditional story, gameplay and mechanics, animation and art, UI, or music and sound design.

My role as a narrative designer combines my skills as both a game writer and a game designer. As a narrative designer, I make sure to integrate story into gameplay, and vice versa. I discovered I was a narrative designer when working on the game design and story at the same time. But it doesn't matter whether the story is developed along with the game's mechanics, the mechanics are designed first, or the story is created first. I need to understand worldbuilding, story development and pacing, character creation and development, and dialogue. I need to understand how these story elements will engage the player in the game and how the player might interact with the story through the mechanics.

How narrative design is implemented will vary from game to game. With some games, the gameplay must remain the focus. Sometimes the gameplay and story will have equal weight. And with some games, like the late, lamented Telltale's titles, the gameplay is at the service of the story. Every game is going to be different and have different aesthetics to give players diverse experiences. As narrative designers, it's up to us to work closely with game designers and game writers (if we aren't serving in these capacities ourselves) to determine what the right relationships between story and gameplay will be for each project.

Tobias Heussner (Game Content/ Narrative Designer, Producer)

Narrative design for me is the combination of writing and game design with the goal to tell a story in a computer game. It is not the sum of both fields, but rather the area where both fields overlap in the quest of story creation.

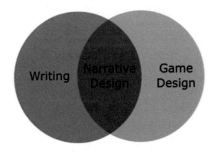

Narrative design is writing a great story and dealing with the question of how this story can be told to the player by just using the tools resulting from the game's mechanics. It asks the questions:

- How can this story be interactive?
- How can the players influence the plot to create their own, unique story?
- Which game-mechanic obstacles can be used to portray the story obstacles of the player-character?
- What is the story the player will experience?

Besides these main responsibilities, narrative design includes a high amount of planning and management because narrative design is not only the creation of the story but also the art of communicating this story to the rest of the development team. It keeps everyone united under one vision when it comes to all narrative-related content. Especially in big teams, it doesn't help the project if the artists design beautiful steampunk assets, the level designers block medieval castles, the game designers design mechanics for futuristic mechs, and the programmers are busy with implementing everything that is needed to ride dinosaurs. It is the second main objective of narrative design to unite everyone on the team under one story vision and to keep it consistent throughout the game's development and all eventual following sequels and add-ons.

Finally, narrative design, in my experience, can include a very practical, hands-on side, which is the task to implement story content into the game by using various tools, such as level and quest editors, Microsoft Excel, or whatever else is used. This side may involve learning a scripting language and usually requires some expertise from other fields such as level design, art production, and programming. This final part is not always the responsibility of a narrative designer, but it can be, especially in smaller teams. For example, I'm currently working (while writing this) as a senior producer, and I'm overseeing the project's story part, including the work done by content design and level design.

So, based on my experience, narrative design is the art and mastery of developing, telling, and implementing a story in an interactive environment.

What Role Does a Narrative Designer Play on a Game Development Team?

And what are the actual responsibilities of a narrative designer? Before going into more details here, it may be good to say again that, at this point, the position of a writer is often confused with the responsibilities of a narrative designer. On some teams, writers are called narrative designers too, and on others, there is a difference. From the perspective of discussing narrative design, a narrative designer is not the same as a writer. Especially on bigger projects, one cannot live without the other—both are equally important. In a way, you can see the writer as like a 2D concept artist and the narrative designer as a 3D artist who brings the concept to life. While a writer is not usually a narrative designer, the narrative designer can also be a writer. So, on small teams, both roles may be combined into one position.

Here is a short example: Developer A, an expert writer, writes a wonderful script for an amazing cutscene. But without anyone bringing it into the game, it will be nothing more than a collection of words in a document. This is where Developer B, the narrative designer, enters the scene. B takes the script, just in a similar way as a 3D artist takes the concept from a 2D artist, and plans all the elements that need to be developed to bring this script into the game. B will look for assets that are needed and plan their production with the different departments, talk with programmers to get the features needed into the game, and evaluate the script against the overall story and story experience presented in the game to the player. B would also rewrite the script if necessary and could be fully involved in the writing process. One cannot really live without the other, unless both roles are combined in one person. Just as the 2D and 3D artists have different roles, both are needed. So, writers and narrative designers are developers with different responsibilities.

Here again is the definition for "narrative designer," to demonstrate why a narrative designer is a writer with additional responsibilities, and why a narrative designer is not just another fancy name for "game writer": a Game Narrative Designer is the champion of an interactive story, works in the field of narrative design, and combines the roles of a writer with that of a game designer. Working with other departments (programming, game design, level design, art, sound, etc.), the narrative designer organizes and integrates the story into the game using the available mechanics, designs, and assets.

So . . .

A Game Narrative Designer Is the Champion of an Interactive Story . . .

The narrative designer is the go-to person on the team for all story aspects of the game. The narrative designer either knows the answer or knows who knows the answer. Also, the narrative designer is the one person on the development team who knows the story best and can evaluate which part happens when in the overall context. It is also important for a narrative designer to be able to keep the big picture in mind because, as narrative designer, one is not only responsible for writing material but also for keeping everything consistent. It doesn't matter if you write the perfect cutscene for a scene with dinosaurs when you're actually working on a space shooter.

. . . Combines the Roles of a Writer with That of a Game Designer . . .

The narrative designer is a combination of two roles to form a new role. The narrative designer is a writer and a game designer, but not all writers or game designers are narrative designers. Also, more specialized writers may be better at writing than a narrative designer. On the other hand, they will lack the game-design skills required to bring the story to life via the rules of a game.

A narrative designer is usually involved in the writing process and needs to understand the rules and conventions of creative writing, fiction, and screenwriting. The narrative designer needs to understand the use of storytelling devices, how they were used in the past, and what makes an excellent story. One of the most important exercises for narrative designers is to write and constantly improve their writing skills.

The narrative designer has to understand the discipline of game design because, besides writing content just like a writer, a narrative designer also needs to be able to implement and communicate this content with the devices of a game. To do so, a narrative designer needs to understand content design, which includes level design, asset and audio production, as well as system design, which includes everything about game mechanics.

Beginners often ask whether they need to be able to use level editors and be familiar with a scripting language. There is no easy answer to this question, and it depends on many different aspects. The biggest of these aspects is how the studio for whom you want to work defines your role. If you just want to work in the role of a writer, then you don't have to learn scripting or level design. On the other hand, it doesn't hurt to be familiar with the tools of the trade, and you would be able to integrate your content quickly. It can help you a lot if you want to grow into another role later in your career. If you want to become a narrative designer, understanding level-design and content-production tools becomes a requirement at some studios because your focus is on how to tell the story in the game, not just how to write it. Understanding those tools doesn't mean you need to be an expert in using them, nor that you need to know every little aspect, but you should be able to understand the basic concepts and limitations that come with a certain technology. At studios that are just starting up and do not already have proprietary tools, narrative designers may also be intimately involved in the development of narrative tools, working closely with programming and cinematics to figure out and write documentation to decide what sort of tools are needed to let writers write dialogue that will play in-game and function in cutscenes.

So, yes, if you want to become a narrative designer, you may have to learn how to design a level, and maybe even know how to script. Again, this could be a requirement, but it's not always the case. There are many very good narrative designers who can't script, and they still do an awesome job. On the other hand, there are also those who are able to script, and they too do an awesome job. In the end, it really depends on you and your goals whether you learn to script or not. But, in general, the more you know, the more likely it is you'll have an easier time communicating your ideas with a team.

. . . and Organizes and Integrates the Story

Writing and game design are the two main areas of expertise a narrative designer needs to understand. On top of these two areas, a narrative designer often has a lot of management and communication tasks related to the story content of the game, so it is good for a narrative designer to understand and be able to use methods of project planning and management. Being a good communicator and being a team player are two essential skills that every narrative designer needs, and it is impossible to be a narrative designer if you can't communicate your story, or if you can't work together with other disciplines of game development.

Integration can be writing the text into the game with any tool developed or used for this reason. Or, as mentioned earlier, this means actually using methods of level and game design.

Again, on some teams, narrative designers do not have to be level designers; on others they do. But don't worry—no one expects a narrative designer to be a perfect level designer or scripter.

Most of what you generally need to know will be covered in this book, as well as taking a look at how narrative design can be implemented in certain genres, including types of games some developers think don't have any story. Social and mobile games will serve as examples for this topic.

But first, there's another important issue—being a key provider of information and a strong communicator for members of your team.

How Can You Help Your Team? On Being a Nexus of Information

Communicate. Your job is to not just advocate for the story but also to get everyone else on board with it too. (Or, at least, not to actively hate it.) But there's more to this than meetings or emails. In fact, it's important to remember that people may not read emails. Your best bet will always be to talk to people, either at their desk or via a Zoom call (with cameras on).

There's nothing like stopping briefly by someone's desk or initiating a casual Zoom conversation to check on how their work is going and asking if they need anything from you to maintain healthy lines of communication. If questions or uncertainties are brought up, then you can easily find out what needs to be clarified and make sure every other department is on the same wavelength.

Joining a Team as a Junior Writer

Depending on the team, project, and company you join, your experience as a junior writer will vary, likely to extremes. As such, there are some things to keep in mind as you begin your career as a game-industry writer.

Odds are fairly high that, as a junior writer, you will not be involved in the initial creation or design of a given project, particularly if you are part of a writing team, as opposed to being the sole writer on the project. This is entirely normal. In fact, a junior being involved in high-level work (usually reserved to core leads, directors, and sometimes even high-level executives) is not the norm—not to say it can't happen, but you shouldn't be surprised if it doesn't.

That doesn't mean you won't be allowed to see the documentation for pitches and concepts once they are ready, nor that you will not be asked for feedback. In fact, very often, giving feedback is an excellent way to learn, and being

Once that is done, send a brief email (bullet points are your friends) to confirm what was discussed. Email confirmation afterwards is important and helps to make sure all are in agreement with the verbal discussion, and is useful if the talking points need to be referred to later on and as an aide-mémoire for all involved:

- Discuss.
- Confirm.
- Iterate.

TABLE 1.1 Sample Domains of a Writer and a Narrative Designer

	Writer	Narrative designer
Overall story/plot development	×	×
Iteration response	×	
Iteration tracking		×
Establish/watchdog tone	×	×
Writing content	×	×
Planning and implementing content		×
History and backstory development	×	
Mission flow design		×
Story-related VO writing	×	
Story-related VO/MoCap planning, data preparation, casting, and participation		×
VO implementation/verification		×
Narrative tools planning		×
Narrative scope tracking/ scheduling		×
Edit/polish written content	×	
Narrative submissions/approvals		×

A Note on Clarity and Being Succinct

You'll have noticed the use of bullet points and lists already. People don't have time to read walls of text and novel-length pitches, and some people just don't enjoy reading. Even when in a studio that is entirely story centric, throwing around endless documents isn't the best way to get your idea or concept across. Or anything really. You need to:

- Be clear.
- Be succinct.
- Be organized in how you convey information.
- Update.

Here's what you want to look at for any email or document you send with important information, or even any confluence page you set up:

- **Point of contact**: If it's you, fine, but in case it's not, make sure to list this first.
- **Short summary of the story, mission, or what have you**: Keep it high level. Absolutely critical data only.
- **Bullet-point list**: Include this after if needed, and in short form (one sentence per bullet-point list of other pertinent points).
- **Other topics**: Sometimes you'll have sections for other disciplines or other topics depending on the nature of the document. Organize those to death. And organize again.
- **Links leading to more in-depth topics that support/enhance/ expand on the topic at hand**: Geek out all you want in those. If people hit the "more information page" link, they've been duly warned, and you can throw all you want at them there (as long as it's clear and well organized too).
- **Edit, edit, edit**: If you are blessed by the gods and thus fortunate enough to work with editors, this is where you taunt everyone you know who doesn't, and ask your editor to review and fix your content so that it's even clearer and more succinct, to the endless joy of your team.

Remember: You may not mind reading a novel, but you aren't your target audience. Everyone else on your team is, and your documents aren't the only ones they have to read:

- Make the information simple and accessible.
- Make yourself available for questions.
- Update your content. (Also known as "iterate." You will never get away from that concept.)

Make sure all the additional information is available should it be requested.

As stated before, and to demonstrate that narrative design is not just a topic for AAA production, here's a bit about . . .

Narrative Design in Social, Mobile, and Indie Games

Early social, mobile, and indie games mostly weren't story oriented. But as the field has exploded since the first edition of this book, story has quickly become the major way that mobile games without new gameplay innovations seek to distinguish themselves. Even in games where players are not making major decisions to affect the story or communicating with NPCs via dialogue trees, narrative design can

a part of this initial development process will help hone your knowledge base for when your turn comes—which it will, as writing pitches for missions and quests should definitely be a part of your workload, whether you're a junior writer or not.

The ideal situation for a writer new to the industry is to be part of a writing team, as this will give you a space to learn with readily available mentors. Often, new writers who have just joined a team are assigned what some might consider to be "small stuff." Here's the thing—the "small stuff" may not be the highly creative, critical-path dialogue writing you would want to work on, but it is nonetheless just as important to the final version of the game. It needs to be done, and it needs to be done well. Things such as data pad entries, diary pages, abilities descriptions, ambient conversations, one-liner barks, and onomatopes—all of this is a huge part of the gameplay experience as a whole. Without it, the quality of the game will suffer.

And if it's done in a perfunctory way, players will either notice or just plain not care. Writing the "small stuff" well can be incredibly rewarding, particularly when players notice and discuss what they've seen. Any page for a video game on the TV Tropes wiki is an example of how much players pay attention to detail, and how good they are at extracting even the most seemingly insignificant content from a game.

There are many things that will be out of your control. But in the end, what you want to bring to a team, the attitude you display, and the level of your ability to learn—those are entirely up to you. And the more open you are to writing anything that is asked of you, the more quickly you will become a trusted senior writer who is sought after to work on more critical storylines.

give players helpful information by reinforcing a gameplay feature with little or no text. Great narrative design can make a non-story-oriented game more entertaining and give players little insights into the game's world. In an increasingly crowded and competitive marketplace, adding a little extra entertainment value can make a game stand out.

With games on a smaller screen and games heavily focused on gameplay, it might be easier to think of the game's *space*, not the game's *world*. There's a finite space to work in. How can you add "bits of story" to that space? These can be strong visual or audio clues. They're unique to the game and its gameplay. Popular mobile and social games with good narrative design use visuals and sound effectively.

KingsRoad

On some maps, the bodies of massacred townspeople lie on the roads and in yards. Player-characters (PCs) must track down the enemy NPCs who killed the victims. In this case, a detail about the world (there's a menace taking over towns and killing innocent people) adds to the level design—enemy NPCs are usually found in the vicinity of the bodies.

Clicking on some NPCs who are taken hostage and bound "frees" these NPCs. Before they run off to safety, they'll give player-characters a few coins to show their gratitude. This is basically a way for the player to loot gold. However, player-characters directly interacting with the NPCs by freeing them offers players gratitude, not just loot, and demonstrates the positive, heroic impact the player-characters are having on the world and its inhabitants.

Tiny Wings

The bird dreams of being able to fly. When soaring long distances, the bird shouts an excited "Yeehoo!" Lifting up into the clouds—achieving the dream of "flight"—will gain players more points based on a multiplier. The bird's characterization, a desire to be able to fly, is reflected in the game's sound, animation, and mechanics.

Among Us

This multi-platform social game pits at least one imposter player against crewmate players who must suss out their enemy before the imposters kill them. On a variety of maps, the crew finishes tasks (mini games) of different lengths, while the imposters fake tasks to look like crew members, sabotage systems to keep the crew from finishing their tasks, and kill all of the crewmates before players can catch them and jettison them from the ship or base.

Screenshot from *KingsRoad* developed/published by Rumble Entertainment and protected by United States and international copyright law. © Rumble Entertainment

Screenshot from *KingsRoad* developed/published by Rumble Entertainment and protected by United States and international copyright law. © Rumble Entertainment

Learn to Pick Your Battles

All companies and teams have their cultures. While everyone has narrative elements and creative concerns that are dear to them, learning which battle to pursue is a critical part of preserving one's energy and sanity in the game industry. It is a process that has to be started over again every time you change companies or teams. It's a normal and important one.

Know your allies. Learn to pick your battles.

And remember that, particularly when it concerns diversity in games, sometimes, as exhausting as the fight may be, the end result can be the best reward you've ever imagined. Just be wary not to burn yourself out in the process—being able to fight another day is important. If you end up leaving the industry due to burnout, that won't help anyone, least of all you. Remember to take care of yourself.

Among Us is all about the gameplay and social interactions, but the environments, tasks, and controls emphasize the narrative that the players must maintain their ships/bases in order to survive. For example, players must take their ID cards and swipe them through the card reader during the aptly named "Swipe Card" task. Players literally drag the card through the reader; if they do it too quickly or not fast enough, they will fail. The controls mimic the motion of swiping a card and create the same frustrations of having to do it over again. The task also provides a little bit of characterization. Players pull the ID card out of a bifold wallet with a picture window. The picture reveals the crewmate has a family wearing the same silly suits.

Triple Town

The dreaded bear tiles antagonize the town and serve as obstacles. When bears come near townspeople, the townspeople scream in terror and run away. The townsfolk's reactions through sound and animation remind players that those seemingly adorable bears are a nuisance.

Don't Starve

When player characters wander into dark areas at night, they're subject to attack and can be killed. If player characters are in the dark for too long, lines of dialogue will pop up over their heads. The lines of dialogue suggest increasing nervousness and convey whether danger is imminent or not:

> It's so dark!
> What was that?!
> OW! Something bit me!

With the last line of dialogue, players will know they've taken hit points. Each line of dialogue is also accompanied by a sound effect portraying the player-character's anxiety.

***

Characters, worldbuilding, and stories may not be as developed in certain types of social, mobile, and indie games. But the concepts and ideas in this book will still help with the narrative design of these kinds of non-story-oriented games. Keep the game genre and players' expectations in mind. They don't need a lot of story or character development. Quick, little details will do for games that are all about the gameplay. These details, or "bits of story," work best when they highlight or reinforce gameplay or specific mechanics.

To determine how you're going to incorporate story through narrative design, think about the gameplay and its mechanics. If you don't have a story already, can you think of a scenario to fit the gameplay? Some things to consider when adding "bits of story":

Among Us's "Swipe Card" task. "Swipe Card," Among Us Wiki, accessed October 6, 2022, https://among-us.fandom.com/wiki/Swipe_Card. © InnerSloth LLC.

- What are the player-character's motivations, and can these be communicated through the mechanics?
  - *Among Us*'s crewmate player-characters are trying to survive and remove the imposter(s). Finishing their tasks helps them survive and discover the identity of the imposters.
- Are there other characters with motivations?
  - The bear tiles serving as obstacles to town construction in Triple Town growl at players.
- What's going on in the world?
  - Bears are trying to take over as players try to construct their towns in *Triple Town*. The townspeople's animations show they're afraid of the bears.
- How can you use sound, animation, and other visual clues to tell players something about the world and characters?
  - In *Don't Starve*, very short lines of dialogue text and sound effects suggesting anxiety let players know their unnerved player characters have wandered too far into the dark filled with monsterly terrors.

As a narrative designer, you can integrate story into any game genre. The techniques this book discusses will help you come up with a plan for narrative design, share it with your team members, and get everyone excited about the story content, even if they don't see how narrative design can benefit the game at first.

Work Experiences: Tobias Heussner

Before I started working as a producer, I worked for several years on browser-based action-RPG MMOs as a level designer. This project did not have the role of a narrative designer, and the responsibilities were shared between the writers and level designers. As part of our normal design process, it was the level designer's responsibility to come up with a first sketch of a new map and the quest's concept for this map based on the agreed-upon background. This background information was provided by the writing department and included a very rough set of information on the overall storyline for this area, as well as some information as to how it related to the maps/regions around it. Once this concept was complete, the designer sat together with the writing team to discuss the individual quests and how they contributed to the game in general. Also, in this step, the team talked about ways the questlines could be improved.

As soon as this step was completed, the level designer started to build the map, starting with a rough layout, and then iterating it until it was ready for final polish by an artist. The designer also implemented the gameplay mechanics, such as spawn areas and interactive objects.

Finally, it was the designer's responsibility to implement the quests and provide the empty-but-functional quest files for the writing team that wrote the final quest texts and assigned names to all creatures and objects in an area.

This was our workflow, and I hope you can easily see how the role of a narrative designer was shared between the writers and level designers. While the writers took care of the written content, which could be a responsibility of the narrative designer, the level designers implemented the content into the game, which would be the game-design side of narrative design.

One of the biggest challenges for narrative design on this project was that all quest texts were limited to 255 characters. Almost no other devices for storytelling were present. At the point where I was involved, the project had no in-game cutscenes and very limited ways to trigger specific animations or interactions. Also, the overall content was highly optimized to ensure fast downloads and quick access to the game from a browser, regardless of the available bandwidth. So, in such a scenario, it was important from a narrative-design perspective to understand what stories could be told via text only and how they could be implemented in such a way that they would not interfere with the fast action gameplay of a hack 'n' slay action RPG.

So, my personal learnings:

- Design quests around collect-and-kill mechanics that quickly reward the player every few minutes and hide long grinding periods.

- Use talk-to or breadcrumb quests to develop deeper storylines and connect the characters of the world with each other.

- Keep the story information on a more shallow and generalized level due to short attention spans and the need for quick and clear communication.

- Use names of items, objects, and encounters to reflect the different cultures present in the game.

- Avoid long and complex storylines that involve the completion of several questlines.

- Use each questline to tell its own little story, which by itself can be embedded in a bigger storyline.

- Use well-known archetypical graphics and sounds to portray certain backgrounds and themes. For example: fire and lava for dragons or gothic architecture for undead.

- Focus on visual effects, such as decals and particles, together with specific light settings to create the required atmosphere.

Stepping into the Role of the Narrative Designer

This book defines "narrative design" and "narrative designer" in the following ways:

> Game Narrative Design is the art of telling a story in a computer, console, or mobile game using the techniques and devices available. It is the art of using gameplay and the sum of visual and acoustic methods to create an entertaining and engaging experience for the players.

> A game narrative designer is the champion of an interactive story, works in the field of narrative design, and combines the roles of a writer with that of a game designer. Working with other departments (programming, game design, level design, art, sound, etc.), the narrative designer organizes and integrates the story into the game using the available mechanics, designs, and assets.

The duties of a narrative designer on a project can cover a wide range of practical tasks:

- Working on worldbuilding.
- Writing the high-level story concept.
- Writing character profiles.
- Writing placeholder dialogue iterated upon until it is finalized dialogue.
- Writing cinematic scenes (including descriptions/actions).
- Writing things such as codex entries, diaries, letters, etc.
- Naming all the things.
- Writing descriptions of weapons/items/abilities.
- Writing barks (the dreaded "find twenty ways to have this character say 'Hi!'").
- Writing blurbs for marketing.
- Writing live events or alternate reality games (ARGs) as part of promotional events.

- Providing communication between various disciplines at all times.
- Iterating. Over and over and over again. . . .
- Etc. (This word is deceptive. "Etc." can cover more than the above, when least expected. Usually on Monday mornings or Friday evenings.)

Suffice it to say, being ready to apply oneself to anything which may involve words or storytelling, or the promotion of good communication in one way or another, is an invaluable tool in the narrative designer's arsenal. Flexibility is paramount, particularly when starting off as a writer in the industry. The willingness to provide text for anything that is needed on a project can be literally job saving.

Exercises

Now that you have reviewed what narrative design is, what the daily
responsibilities of a narrative designer are, and how to step into the role
of a narrative designer, you're invited to participate in the first exercises.

Each chapter will end with some exercises that challenge you to put the
learned material into practice. Throughout the book, you're encouraged
to work on your own story and move it through a simplified
development process. If you complete all of the exercises, you will
have a full set of game documentation and dialogue samples for your
portfolio, or a jumping-off point for beginning development on your
own indie game. The samples included with the exercises are not
meant to be perfect solutions, but rather examples that communicate
what will be expected as a minimum for a particular exercise.

Exercise 1.1
Imagine you are working in HR and looking for a narrative designer.
How would your job description read on half a page?

Exercise 1.2
You're a narrative designer, and you're looking for a job. How would
you advertise yourself in less than half a page?

Samples

The following samples show possible solutions for the exercises in this chapter. They're not to suggest the perfect answers but give you ideas for how to answer the questions.

Sample 1.1

The narrative designer will be the champion of the story and will focus on the quality of the story, narrative, plot, and the player's journey throughout the game. The ideal candidate has mastered interactive storytelling techniques, is familiar with the dynamic of game stories, and is able to implement story elements via scripting and design. The role includes a high level of collaboration with other departments and the ability to clearly communicate with the art, design, and programming departments. Occasionally, the narrative designer will have to contribute and support the marketing department with high-quality material, and they will be responsible for the management and communication of writing-related outsourcing.

Responsibilities

- Act as the go-to person for the story and story-related assets.
- Write and design content and copyedit materials.
- Manage and keep the lore and story documentation up to date.
- Implement story content into the game, including eventually scripting prototypes of interactive elements.
- Work with external writing resources to help translate their material to become game-relevant.
- Work with the other departments to ensure consistency of the story and the storytelling devices.
- Support the marketing department with high-quality, game-related materials.

Sample 1.2

My name is Tobias Heussner, and I'm a game content/narrative designer. I have more than twenty years of professional experience within the game development industry. My areas of expertise are in game content design (including narrative design, quest/mission design, level design) and game system design (including game mechanic design, combat design, encounter design, rule design). I am very enthusiastic about all aspects of games, especially the development of engaging storylines and interesting characters. I love to sit together with other team members and develop interesting plots, discussing ways to ensure that all disciplines have one vision and can enrich the story with their expertise.

My favorite multiplayer game universe is *World of Warcraft*. With its multilayer story setup, it allows many players to build a world together and enjoy adventures. On the single-player side, the storylines I have most enjoyed are *Mass Effect* and *StarCraft II*.

In the past, besides my work in the computer game industry, I studied screenwriting for feature films and worked on several novels. I also took classes in computer science to better understand the technical side of programming and to improve my skills in communicating with programmers and software engineers. Most recently, I took classes in business administration, literature, storytelling, and the history of Jerusalem during the time between the First and Second Temples. I also took a class on leadership principles.

Besides my studies, I also use the Game Narrative Summit to improve my skills, and I was a speaker at the Game Developers Conference Online's (GDC Online) Game Narrative Summit in the past. I cofounded the Game Writing Tutorial Day and also spoke at the Game Developers Conference (GDC) in San Francisco as part of a Q&A panel for new writers.

The Concept

"I'm hooked. I have to see how this turns out!"

Isn't this something you'd like to hear when pitching your new idea to your development team, or to an executive?

The concept phase is when the development of a new game, game part, or story starts. In this phase, the initial idea around which everything else is built is formed. As a narrative designer, your role in the concept phase can range from developing the concept, to writing the pitch document for an idea developed by someone else on the team, to actually being the one in the room with executives, trying to sell them on the project. Normally, your expertise as a writer is requested so that the final pitch will be well written and can be easily communicated to others. So, knowing the ins and outs of pitching is a key skill for every narrative designer, regardless of what needs to be pitched.

DOI: 10.1201/9781003369332-2

Pitching a new project or part of a game like a mission is not only pitching an interesting storyline or content. Pitching in game development means presenting an idea for an interactive experience, and this requires that narrative designers understand some basic game-design terms, such as **mechanic**, **core mechanic**, and **dynamic**, especially since as a narrative designer you'll work collaboratively with other designers who focus on these elements of the game. Plus, the full pitch document for a new game most likely will not be written just by you but by a team of professionals from various areas of game design and development.

Play, Don't Tell

Similar to "Show, don't tell" from the movie business, this catchline works for all your content. One of the most important points in the concept phase is to understand gameplay and its relation to the narrative design. System designers[1] and producers[2] will normally ask not only for great stories but also for *how the player will interact with those stories*. It is important to understand that in most decisions, gameplay usually takes priority.

Some games will have a stronger focus on story than others. Depending on the importance of story, the amount of influence you have on the actual rules will vary. In games driven by the story (also known as narrative- or story-driven games) you, as the narrative designer, will most likely be more involved in system design, maybe even helping develop narrative and other gameplay systems yourself. The systems designer will require your input and feedback more frequently on the designed systems to deliver the best possible experience.

As a narrative designer, you do not need to be an expert system designer. However, as you wish for the game designers to understand you, it is just as important that you understand them.

Even the best idea is worthless if it can't be communicated. Do not assume that others will make the effort to understand you. Instead, like a good salesman, sell your idea in a way they understand and in a way that shows you honor their craft and expertise. The readers of your pitch need to be able to connect to your idea to evaluate, give feedback, and green-light it. If they don't understand it, they most likely will not tell you. Instead, they'll pass on it and forget about it. And this is not what you want. So, the best way for you to avoid this

THREE IMPORTANT GAME DESIGN TERMS

Critical Path

The **critical path** is the collection of all the missions, narrative, and gameplay elements which are required to complete the game.

For example: In the original *Super Mario Bros.*, players need to complete at least the following levels when they use the shortcuts to save Princess Peach: 1–1, 1–2, 4–1, 4–2, 8–1, 8–2, 8–3, and 8–4.

Mechanics

Mechanics are the rules of a game and represent the things players can do.

In *Super Mario Bros.*, you need to jump, run, collect, and fire. This is a very simplified view of the game, but all the things mentioned are the *mechanics* of the game.

Dynamics

Dynamics are the things players do with the mechanics, and how they try to optimize or use them to maximize their chance to win. In *Super Mario Bros.*, players invented new terms and tactics to achieve the fastest play through time. One of them is the "Ricochet Jump," hitting a block while jumping and bouncing back to kill an enemy. Many dynamics are invented in multiplayer scenarios because the social aspect of multiplayer gaming gives a lot of room for new dynamics and player creativity.

is to learn the basics of their world and language. This will help you get the pitch into the green-light process. Also, by understanding them, you can learn and grow in your own craft.

The two most fundamental aspects of game design are mechanics and dynamics. They are the lifeblood of each game, and in one way or another, they are what system designers use during their day to bring the game to life.

For a narrative designer, now it is important to understand that a mechanic causes certain dynamics. Those dynamics can be used to tell the story and involve the player in the experience.

Because mechanics are designed by the development team, the team usually has complete control over them. Dynamics, on the other hand, are "invented" applications of the rules and are made up by the players. They usually can't be controlled directly. To better understand what dynamics may be created through a certain mechanic, you can ask yourself what would happen if you tried to break the rules that are established by the mechanics to gain an advantage.

For example, take an MMO with an open-PvP[3] setting and a mechanic allowing players to hunt and kill each other anywhere. The dynamic that can develop is players forming groups or raiding bands that protect their members and hunt players outside the group. Depending on the goals in the narrative, you can now use this dynamic to tell a story about the group dynamics in the world, and how the world became so violent that no one can survive on his or her own.

But what if you don't want a certain dynamic to come up? While it is true that dynamics can't be controlled directly, they can be controlled indirectly by introducing new mechanics addressing an unwanted element.

In the above example, it can be very frustrating for new players to join this MMO setting because they may not be part of a group right away. So, what kind of mechanic can you or the system designers now introduce to give those players a chance of survival and still keep most of the original dynamic intact?

A possible solution can be to introduce cities as safe havens and city guards as strong NPCs to prevent fighting in cities. Skilled players may still overtake a city by killing all guards, but with this mechanic, the likelihood of PvP in all cities is reduced. This gives new players a place of peace to evaluate their options before heading into more dangerous areas. Also, it gives you another chance to draw them deeper into your world by a narrative that makes this situation a part of the world's story. This is how mechanics and dynamics generally work together.

You, as a narrative designer, can help to create a great gaming experience by providing the right context for the mechanics and dynamics. The work of a narrative designer can explain from a fictional-world point of view why things are the way they are.

A last word needs to be addressed on the concept called "Core Mechanics" or "The Road." All the mechanics that define the core idea of the game, and thus are the heart of it, belong in this category. Nothing added to the game should ever block or hinder these mechanics because it would damage not only the overall feel of the game but also the core idea. Having the mindset of not blocking the road is extremely important for narrative designers in all phases of development, but especially during the concept phase. Often, story is not a core mechanic, and it exists to make the game more enjoyable. In these cases, none of the narrative content should interfere with the gameplay designed by the development team. Sometimes it helps to see yourself as a gardener who makes a road prettier, but the road will always remain what it was before—a straight path to get from A to B.

For example, in *Diablo III*, the player fights hordes of monsters while the story is told via audio files (lore books, etc.), which players can activate when they want. They can continue fighting while listening to the story. This is action-oriented "on-demand storytelling," and it shows how a strong core mechanic—killing monsters—is enriched, but not blocked by narrative content.

It is crucial to keep these underlying game mechanics in mind while preparing to make your pitch.

The road only (aka only core mechanics).

The road with good narrative content.

The road blocked with too much content.

The High Concept, aka the One-Liner

The **high concept**, also known as the **one-liner**, is a very helpful tool to develop your pitch. The term "high concept" or "logline" was developed in the early 1970s in Hollywood for movie productions. In general, it describes the idea of condensing your whole story (or whole game in this case) down to one or two sentences. This is usually very helpful because it shows that you have a clear vision of your project, and it can serve as the core vision during the development phase. And, most importantly, it's easy to communicate and remember.

You can use a high concept to introduce a pitch for an entire game (as it is presented here), or for any individual scenario, mission, questline, etc. To help get familiar with how to pitch a high concept effectively, try getting together with your coworkers or teammates and pitching the high concepts for your favorite games:

- "Use FPS[4]-style shooting to create tunnels that let you travel to and from anywhere. Use these tunnels to escape a physical and psychological prison."[5]
- "Journey into the ruins of an underwater colony dedicated to Ayn Rand and fight the monsters who remain there, as you learn what happened in the disaster that destroyed it."[6]

You can also take a look at the available high concepts from movies or other games for better understanding.

TABLE 2.1 Game Genres, Mechanics, and Narrative Focus

Genre	Common Core Mechanics	Good Narrative Focus/Techniques
First-person shooter	Aiming, shooting, dodging	Fast paced, action-oriented, moment-to-moment storytelling with fast beats. Keeping longer story parts for breaks between the action.
Tactical strategy game	Resource management, unit movement, tactical combat	Event-based storytelling that tells story elements as they happen in the game. Short cutscenes at the beginning and end of a map.
Real-time strategy game	Resource management, unit building, base building	Little, dialogue-like story pieces during the mission when a certain event happens. Main story parts as (interactive) cutscenes between the missions.
Roleplaying game	Questing, exploration, combat	Complex, slow-paced storylines that can be connected and are enriched by deep character plots. Story is always present and drives the gameplay.
Simulation	Management, use of . . .	Depends on the kind of simulation but, in general, is limited to short, non-distracting plots happening on the sidelines.
Platformer	Jumping	Story is told with an overall objective as well as a level-based narrative which is mostly presented through environmental narrative.
Action adventure	Exploration, combat	Mixed paced (slow and fast parts) around the challenges the player-character faces. It can be enriched by a protagonist's in-depth, personal story.
Action RPG	Combat, questing, item gathering	Fast-paced, action-oriented on-demand storytelling as the player fights through the world. Story pieces are kept short and quick, just like the other gameplay elements. Some longer parts can be told in the breaks between the action.
Sandbox game	Constructing, exploration, combining	The story builds around the exploration of the player-character as part of the world in which he/she lives and interacts.
Adventure	Puzzle solving, exploration	Generally slow-paced storytelling, strongly relying on the puzzles and the environment. Combination of different complexity within the puzzles to create depth and progression.

One-Liner Comparison and One-Liner Description

As with many terms in game development, the term "high concept" is used in many different ways in the industry. To avoid any confusion with terms you may hear or be taught by others, *The Game Narrative Toolbox* uses the following descriptive terms and definitions for the two most commonly used forms of written "high concepts":

The one-liner as a description: A one- or two-sentence description of the core idea of a game that does not compare your idea with an existing one. It summarizes the mood and shows your creativity.

31

The one-liner as a comparison: A short (ideally one- to two-sentence) description of a game which includes elements such as genre, protagonist, comparable game, goal, and type of game world.

The One-Liner as a Description

The one-liner description is a short description of a game which highlights your idea's creativity and captures the project's mood. It avoids using comparisons to emphasize the uniqueness of your idea. It demonstrates why someone would want to make this product and why players would want to buy it, as opposed to picking up something that's already been made.

As mentioned earlier, the one-liner description is one of two major forms for writing down a high concept, and all development should start with using either this form or the one-liner comparison to summarize the idea. This summary will become the golden thread of your project, and everything should be linked to it. It can also easily be shared within thirty seconds and memorized. These will both be beneficial later during the production when quick decisions have to be made, or when the project needs to be pitched to an always-busy executive.

A good way to start with your one-liner description is to write down your idea in as few sentences as possible. From there, start thinking about it, and shorten it until only one or two sentences are left.

During this revision process, it can be very helpful to think about what is unique and what is familiar in your description. Karl Iglesias proposed this for screenwriting, and it works equally well for game pitches and game-related one-liner descriptions. So, a good one-liner description always has a unique element and a familiar element. The unique element shows what is new, and the familiar element helps to connect it with something people already know. This connection helps them to better envision and understand your idea and its uniqueness.

Usually, the unique element is the part of your idea no one has done before, or at least not in this way. To find this idea, you may want to ask yourself, "What is new?" or "What makes this game unique?"

The familiar element is something you can relate to, for example, emotions or definitions. Questions to find this element can be "How can one relate to this idea?" or "Is it understandable?"

Here is a possible one-liner description for *Spec Ops: The Line*:

Play a soldier on a rescue mission to find a lost soldier while facing post-traumatic stress disorder.

In this case, the familiar element is "Play a soldier on a rescue mission" because it is so commonly used in action games and other story-based media. The unique element is "while facing post-traumatic stress disorder," as it is rarely addressed in game stories.

Using the same principles for your own one-liner descriptions today may result in a clearer vision and a one-liner description that gets higher-level attention during pitches.

Finally, here are some don'ts for your one-liner descriptions that may prove to be useful:

- **Consider carefully whether to use comparisons (covered below)**. If you use comparisons to other media within your core vision, you risk making a product that is not unique. Using sentences like "It is like X mixed with Y" can be a red flag that you might be proposing something that's been made before.
- **Avoid being too general**. If you are too general, you'll miss the chance to communicate the beauty of your unique idea.
- **Don't complicate it**. A one-liner description should help to communicate your idea, not confuse others.
- **Avoid nonmainstream terms**. You never know who's reading your pitch and if they will be able to understand these terms.
  - For example, without looking in a dictionary, do you know right away what a vision clearance engineer does? Instead of using "vision clearance engineer," it would be better and clearer if you use the more common term for this job, which is "window cleaner."
- **Never use any potentially insulting terms**. Again, you don't know who will be reading your concept, and you surely don't want to unintentionally insult the executive who is supposed to sign a development deal.

Those are the basics for a good one-liner description. At this point, you may have noticed that you can use it not only for the big vision of the whole game but also for every single piece of it. You can write one-liner descriptions for almost everything. For, say, a character, or a quest, or a region, or a specific mechanic.

However, because these one-liners focus on your inspiration, rather than the practical aspects of how to create, market, and sell a game, they tend to be of more use internally than externally. When pitching to executives, investors, or other outside gatekeepers who must approve your idea before it goes into production, you want to use a pitch that makes it clear where your project sits in the market, what its gameplay is, who its audience is, and what other games it might be similar to. These "one-liner comparisons" expand upon the idea from your one-liner description, but with an eye toward marketing and sales.

The One-Liner as a Comparison

In Hollywood, one-liner comparisons are where you get the oft-ridiculed "*The Terminator* meets *The Secret of NIMH*, with a dog!" kind of pitch from. But these comparisons to existing properties, while limiting, do spark an immediate understanding and (ideally) excitement in the listener. That is something that a one-liner description, such as "It's about a dog who gets given human intelligence by a secret government agency, and then goes back in time on a murderous rampage," can't do so easily.

When pitching a game, your one-liner comparison needs to address the genre of game, general type of gameplay, and a hint of what the game world will be like, if not the actual story. It can also include a more explicit comparison to existing games, particularly if you're working on a sequel or other project that is deliberately building on an existing audience ("This will be just like *Call of Duty*, but set in the modern world . . .").

Most executives are looking for some variant on the following Mad Lib:

> A [GENRE OF GAME] (*optional similar to [GAME]*) with a [TYPE OF CHARACTER] who [ACCOMPLISHES A GOAL] in [TYPE OF GAME WORLD].

Here are a few tips for the development of a one-liner comparison:

- **Pick well-known examples**. The better your audience knows your examples, the easier it will be for them to envision what you are trying to communicate. That's why it is better to pick well-known examples rather than unknown ones.
  - For example: More people know Super Mario than Alex Kidd, even though both are originally characters from platformers.
- **Try to show the uniqueness of the idea**. Even when you compare your idea to an existing property, you still want to show that the idea hasn't been made before.
- **Use the optional [game] to clarify the idea**. Mentioning another game can be useful if it helps to show how the final product will feel. Keep in mind, however, that the idea still needs to be unique, and the comparison should not just be a fancy way to describe your example game. If you're working on a sequel of any sort, providing an explanation of how your project differs from the original game is essential.
- **Try to stick to formula as best you can**. It's what most people expect and are familiar with. Sticking close to the formula avoids discussion about the form of your presentation and keeps everyone focused on the idea.

By that standard, *Mass Effect* becomes "A third-person shooter with a fully voiced character who learns about an ancient alien conspiracy in the far future." *Dragon Age: Origins* is "A western RPG similar to *Baldur's Gate* with a customizable character who must defeat an ancient evil in a dark-fantasy world." *Skyrim* is "An open-world RPG, even larger than *Oblivion*, with a customizable character who can be and do anything, while fighting off a flood of dragons in a war-torn fantasy world." *Return of the Obra Dinn* is "A puzzle game starring an early-nineteenth-century investigator with a magic pocket watch who deduces the unknown fates of a doomed ship's passengers and crew." And *Until Dawn* is "An interactive creature feature in which multiple player-characters try to survive the night on a lonely, snowy mountain."

For a sample fictional RPG, try "A Japanese-style RPG similar to *Final Fantasy* with an emotionally scarred heroine who must journey into the dreams of her enemies in a modern-day fantasy world."

Jazzing It Up

Those sentences aren't likely to set anyone's heart on fire, though, so part of the art of the pitch is to combine that kind of clarity with a glimpse of what will be fun about the finished product. When pitching *Mass Effect*, the concept team wanted to evoke the feel of the 1980s space-fantasy epics they had grown up with. For *Dragon Age: Origins*, it was BioWare fans' nostalgia for the much-loved 1998 *Baldur's Gate* series.

Both of those concepts make their intended audience very clear. For example, the abovementioned fictional RPG can try to reach out to alienated teenagers who feel no one understands them. For such an audience, a game which gives them the powers to be invisible, to spy on other people's inner lives, and to know what someone is thinking might be very appealing. With that in mind, the pitch can be modified from the basic concept into more of an actual, original pitch:

> Journey into the darkest dreams and secrets of everyone in your high school in this Japanese-style RPG about a shy girl who finally gets the power to take on her bullies . . . while unravelling the mysteries of her own past.

Not the most commercial concept, perhaps, but it has a clear audience, and it establishes its genre, its concept, something about the protagonist, and something about the story all in under forty words.

Presenting Your Pitch

The next part of the pitch is the hardest for a lot of writers because it's the part where your words can't stand on their own. No one sells or makes a game without having to get in front of a room and tell someone (usually a lot of someones) what their game is about and why they think it's so great. And that's a problem for a lot of writers, no small percentage of whom became writers *because* they're terrible at talking to people.

There are a lot of books and videos out there about how to be a better public speaker (and clubs like the Toastmasters which allow you to practice public speaking). But start with the following tips:

- **Be relaxed**. Game companies are very informal places. The minute you step back from that informality, you become stiff, and that makes

Making the Pitch

A short disclaimer has to be given here: If you're in a large studio, the only way you're likely to pitch a concept for a new game is if you're already a lead writer. Which means you've worked your way up through the ranks for years already and won't need this book. But if you're working in the indie scene and trying to raise money or coordinate with your artist and programmer friends, writing an effective pitch is key to communicating your vision. And even as a junior writer in a large studio, you'll need to be pitching story ideas for individual quests and storylines. So, knowing how to write an effective pitch is a key skill for narrative designers at every level.

The most important thing in a pitch, especially if you're trying to launch a new project, is, as mentioned before, to have a single, defining idea that can be expressed in a sentence and is easily remembered by anyone who hears it.

the people watching you uncomfortable. It helps to be seated (say, at a conference table, working the keyboard for your PowerPoint projection), instead of standing in front of the room. Your pitch will go over best if it feels like you're just hanging out with some cool people, telling them about this awesome game you played.

- **Use visuals**. Game companies are usually made up of roughly 25–50 percent artists, and many executives and producers may have worked their way up through the art side. This means there are a lot of visual thinkers in your audience, and they will react better to what you're saying if you give them specific images to cement the ideas in their minds. If you have concept art for your project, use that. If not, even images from the web can help give you a visual focus (just make sure to clearly mark them as external, where you got them from, and who is the copyright holder). PowerPoint is a great tool for this. By preparing slides to flip every few minutes, you keep the meeting moving, even if you have a lot to say.
- **Use humor**. This is the logical combination of the last two points. If you can't find a good visual for something in your story, try something that's a surprising contrast, or a cartoon that expresses the need in the current market for what you're pitching. Again, gamers are casual, and humor goes a long way to make your pitch feel like you understand *fun* (essential for a game creator).
- **Don't get bogged down in the details**. A pitch meeting isn't the time to discuss specific scenes or individual combat abilities. This is the time to hit the high points: What is the game? What will it feel like to play? What will you accomplish by the end? And what need does it meet in the audience that no other game is currently doing?
- **Reiterate**. In your final slide, always return to your initial pitch. Even if you've avoided most irrelevant details, you never know when someone is going to get weirdly fixated on the kind of monster you talked about in the climactic scene and forget the overall concept. If you end back where you started, you keep people's questions focused on where you want them to be: Your idea. (And if you take questions after your pitch, restate the concept again before you actually wrap up and leave the room.) Just like you'll see later in the chapter about dialogue, the only thing people actually remember is the last thing you say.

Writing the Pitch

Soon after or maybe even before the presentation, you'll start writing down the pitch. Writing the pitch can and will have many different forms, depending on things like company culture, workflows, and your personal experience. All narrative designers have written pitches in both PowerPoint and Word, and pitches that include gameplay information and those without it.

A pitch doc is not a novel; it is a marketing document intended to present a vision of a complex experience in the simplest and most exciting form possible. It will also form the basis for the eventual Game Design Document (GDD), which is the technical documentation of the intentions of the game design team. At this stage, however, technical information should be given only in broad strokes ("an FPS using the Unreal Engine, with shooting, jumping, and grappling mechanics"), not full details ("when grappling, press A to hold the enemy down for one to six seconds, while doing two points of damage per second . . .") Remember, many people in your studio may not even be willing to read more than one page of a pitch doc.

So how can you solve this problem and write a good pitch?

- **Keep it short**. A pitch longer than eight pages is too long. It's better to keep it at two to five pages (including a cover page) or even shorter.
- **Keep it visual**. You can use tons of pictures, even from the Internet (but pay attention to the next point) to portray your idea.
- **Beware quotes and references**. If you use any text or material besides your own, make sure to mark and quote correctly. Material on the Internet is normally not "free to use." You can use it internally, but you may have to rewrite or remove it once you need to show it to someone outside your studio.
- **Try alternative techniques**. You can use techniques such as One-Page Design,[7] Prototyping, and Journeys.
  - **One-page design** is the idea to include all essential information on exactly one page (which can be as big as you can print it) and to keep it highly visual by using visuals wherever possible. For example, you can use a center mock-up and explain ideas via callouts. It's also a great way to pitch characters and locations. Please have a look at the presentation from Stone Librande for more on this technique.
  - **Prototyping** requires a technology which can be easily modified to show or create a playable version of the idea. Sometimes a mod for an existing product can be developed, or you can develop an analog, paper-based prototype to be played with pen and dice. The basic idea is to have something playable.
  - **Journeys** indicate a kind of presentation where you lead your audience through the interactive experience with different slides. In a way they can be compared to choose-your-own-adventure books and similar interactive stories. They mix the traditional presentation style with the idea of interactivity.

Throughout the game industry, you'll hear about a lot of different document types when it comes down to writing the pitch. The two most common that you'll use in your field as a narrative designer are the game pitch doc and the narrative pitch doc.

"Dumb it down. Players are stupid!"

This is something you hear more than you might imagine. This kind of mentality is tricky and can sometimes permeate all the work that is done, whether people realize it or not (often not). If anyone tries that argument on you, figure out if they mean "make it clearer" or "dumb it down." If it's the latter, just nod politely and move on, because it is a dangerous mentality to underestimate your audience.

As to the former point, wanting to ensure a clear narrative to allow for a certain understanding of a story is a justifiable argument, allowing for varying levels of complexity when taking into account the genre of the game and what the audience itself expects or wishes to see in it. But, as to the latter point, taking shortcuts or making a story overly simplistic based on an argument that denigrates your player base is a shortcut to enabling your own laziness as a developer. And this, make no mistake, will eventually become a crutch that will result in substandard work.

Players will poke holes in the science of the universe of your game, will spot details and make connections you'd never dreamed of (and wish you had), and will remember every single detail of your game's lore, right down to the commas and the em dashes. Players are *smart*. Never underestimate them.

Your goal should always be to make things *clear* to the player, to present a consistent and seamless narrative— never to presume the player is stupid.

Write *to* your players, not *down* at them.

The Game Pitch Doc

Publishers, developers, investors, or potential partners might ask you to send a pitch document, by which they usually mean a game pitch doc, to give them a sense of your project and vision. The purpose of this written pitch is to keep the conversation going. No matter whom you're pitching to, you want the game's pitch to get you a meeting, or at least a second look. Games are rarely sold or invested in at the pitch stage. What a great written pitch will do is tell the interested parties that your project should be taken seriously, and they should consider supporting you in making it. Unlike the high-concept pitch, the game pitch doc should ideally be one page (plus a cover page), not longer than a page and a paragraph, and single spaced. You don't want to get into too much detail. Think about simply giving them the gist.

The Essential Parts of the Game Pitch Doc

First, include the game's title, genre, platform, and audience. These should be in one line each at the beginning of the document:

> **Title**: *Pokey and Pia's Pie Adventures*
> **Genre**: Endless Runner
> **Platform**: Android/iOS
> **Audience**: Children ages 7–10
> **One-liner description or one-liner comparison**: You can use both or just one, but you should include it in your document

Don't worry if you don't have a title yet. Whoever reads the pitch won't be concerned with that. You can simply put "Untitled Endless Runner," for example, instead. The title, genre, platform, and audience give a quick "snapshot" of the game and provide the most general information. A publisher may be looking for a game for kids. The audience information tells her to keep reading. An investor will note that the game will have a much smaller budget than a console game from the platform information. A developer looking for a hidden-object game might lose interest when he sees "Endless Runner."

The rest of the pitch should have a paragraph per section. You can also use bullet points to highlight features and draw attention to key details you feel are important, like specific mechanics or important storylines:

> **Story**: Who are the player-characters and important NPCs? What is the game's main storyline and conflict? The more narrative-driven the game, the more information you want to give here.
> **Gameplay**: How would you describe the game's gameplay? What are its mechanics?
> **Gameplay innovations/KSPs**[8]: What makes this game stand out from others in its genre?

Example of gameplay: Describe a scenario so your audience can see how the gameplay and story work together. Think of a challenge players will face and what they might do to complete it. Is it a puzzle or a part of a level? Will the player-character have to make an important decision? What abilities will players use? Will they use any skills? Did you highlight key mechanics, characters, or plot points in other sections? You'll want to explain how these come together in the gameplay scenario.

If someone requests additional information, be sure to include it!

Keep in mind that you don't have to have everything figured out. You might still be working on the story or gameplay elements. You will likely collaborate with game design for gameplay elements. Aspects of a game change all of the time before and during development. Anyone reading your pitch won't expect you to be describing a finished product.

On *The Game Narrative Toolbox's* website, https://routledgetextbooks. com/textbooks/9781138787087/, you'll find a template for the one-page design pitch as well as a Word template for the traditional game pitch doc.

The Narrative Pitch Doc

The narrative pitch doc is very similar to the game pitch doc, and most of what was mentioned in this section applies for the narrative pitch as well.

The big difference is that the narrative pitch doc focuses only on the narrative part of the game. Thus, information that was required for the game pitch doc, such as gameplay innovations, example of gameplay, platform, audience, and genre, are not included in this document. It is assumed that all those things are covered in the game pitch doc.

On the other hand, the narrative pitch doc requires elements such as the one-liner and introduces new elements such as the fluff text, the setting, story integration, and other story-specific elements. Most of these elements should explain themselves, except maybe the following two:

Fluff text: This is a short sentence taken out of your story world, such as a dialogue line, which captures the mood and atmosphere of your story. It should help the reader to understand and feel your story.

Story integration: This part focuses on your idea of how you want to integrate the story into the game. Do you want to use audio? A quest system? Which game mechanic is used for which story element, and so on? While it is still important to keep the document short, you want to at least give your audience an idea of how you plan to tell your story. If you can't explain the integration of your story, then you should consider a different medium for it, or rewrite it so that it can be told via gameplay.

The Dream Catcher

date
SAMPLE FOR THE NARRATIVE DESIGN TOOLBOX

Genre

JRPG

Platforms

Windows PC, Playstation 4 and XBox One

Setting

The game takes place in a stylized, manga-like modern Asian setting, mixed with Tim Burton-style fantasy elements when showing the dream world.

One-Line Comparison

A Japanese-style RPG similar to Final Fantasy, with an emotionally scarred heroine who must journey into the dreams of her enemies in a modern-day fantasy world

One-Line Description

A young girl fights with her self-esteem and her emotions, while traveling into her enemies' dreams to save her world.

Story

Kiyoko, a 17-year-old student from Okinawa, moved recently with her parents to Kyoto. Not used to the high-paced, fashion-oriented city life, she struggles to find friends and a social life in her new home. Often she escapes to Umekoji Park, to be on her own and live in her books and daydreams. Life was so different back in Okinawa and her problems just got worse when she met Akemi, the most popular boy in school.

But as the game begins, Kiyoko learns that her daydreams can have teeth, as she and Akemi become trapped inside an elaborate revenge fantasy Kiyoko has concocted against Akemi's vicious girlfriend. Now trapped in the dream world, Kiyoko will have to find Akemi and escape the fantasy she herself has created. And their problems don't end once they're back in school. The dreams follow them, their emotions taking form to haunt their waking hours, until Kiyoko starts to wonder if she'll ever be able to escape.

Example of Gameplay

The player as Kiyoko is in the school yard as she runs into Akemi, who waves at her and asks her over for a chat. During the conversation he asks if she's seen his girlfriend Hitomi, who's been missing since yesterday. While they talk the player can see in the background that a shadow, Kiyoko's personified jealousy, passes by, carrying someone in a bag. With the "X-Button" the player can interrupt the conversation and start hunting the shadow to its hideout. If she decides not to interrupt the conversation, she will have to find more clues before finding the shadow and having the chance to defeat her own jealousy in a turn-based boss fight. During the fight all skills are based on emotions instead of a magic system. The player for example can "cast Delight" if an enemy hits her with an "Anger spell". All in all the mechanics and visuals of this project are built around the themes of emotions, dreams and consequences.

Gameplay in short

- Final Fantasy-like turn-based combat system
- Exploration of both known and unfamiliar worlds that change with the choices of the player
- Random events during the story make every playthrough unique
- Dialogues with multiple options allow players to influence the outcome of dialogue
- Quicktime events during dialogues allow "spontaneous" actions

Gameplay Innovations / KSPs

- A world that shows how dreams and reality blend
- Decisions have visual consequences
- Multiple endings
- Emotion-based combat system
- Multiple ways to solve tasks

Target Audience

Teenage girls ages 14 to 20, with an interest in anime/manga.

ON WRITING THE PITCH—CULTURAL REFERENCES AND SHIPS IN THE NIGHT

It is important to remember that not everyone shares the same cultural reference points. A movie that may be obviously known to everyone from your point of view may in fact be entirely out of someone else's cultural framework, which can be a tricky thing to account for as more people see your pitch. While a one-liner comparison can use cultural shortcuts to pass itself off in a convenient shorthand, it's also a potentially dangerous thing to do, one which can result in a very carefully worded (and solid!) document being returned to you with a stamp of "I don't get it, so not approved."

It is worth your time to make sure that everyone who will be approving the document has seen the movie, book, or [insert shortcut here] you wish to use to illustrate the one-liner before sending out a formal document. Not everyone is a history buff, not everyone working on a comic-book-based game has ever even read comics, and so on and so forth. Such is the nature of the industry. In order to make your job as painless as possible, it is in your best interest to communicate the gist of your intent to people before you send out formal documentation.

Finally, once you finish your documents (or even while you're still working on them), something that is always connected with mixed feelings and emotions starts: the iteration process. Much work in the game industry is done via iterations, and many of them happen during the concept phase. Later, in Chapter 9, "Troubleshooting," processes and techniques for the rewriting and revision of material will be discussed. But one important lesson needs to be shared now . . .

The Writing Feedback Process (Kill Your Darlings)

There is a well-known saying among writers in general: "Kill your darlings." In the game industry, this can take a whole new meaning, ranging from "kill that bark," to "kill that questline," to "kill that character" (and not in a fun, in-game, break the players' hearts, *mwahahah* kind of way).

Often the decision to change or entirely remove a narrative element will not be your own—it will be driven by the requirements of other departments, by core leads,[9] or by the fact that it is often simpler to change the writing than to change fundamental gameplay, animation, or programming elements. Sometimes a mission will be playable and in-game, and upon review, the team will agree that it's not working. The writer's job will be either to go back to the drawing board (as will everyone else from gameplay, to level design, to level art) or to attempt to salvage the mission in a way which requires the least work possible from other departments while creating a unique headache for the narrative/writing team.

Remember Chapter 1, when we said iterating will be your best friend? You'll iterate in this phase as much as any other. No plan ever survives the field of combat, and no story ever survives exposure to production intact. Having a backup plan (or several) is never a bad idea. And writing is often the simplest thing to change of all the elements of a game's production.

Conclusion

Regardless of which one-liner style you pick or how many iterations you have to go through, by the end of this critical first phase of development, you should have a clear idea of the heart of your project and how to communicate it. You will know about the important game-design concepts you'll need to consider, as well as how to develop one sentence into a document, which is the pitch you and your team create to hopefully inspire many, especially those who make the decision. In the end, you'll find yourself on to the next step: the production, which will be covered over the course of the following chapters. Each chapter will focus on one specific topic.

Exercises

From this point on, try picking your own idea for an original game story, and use these exercises to help you develop it. Wherever the exercises use a template, you can find the template on the book's website, https://routledgetextbooks.com/textbooks/9781138787087/.

Again, all of the samples only show a possible solution and what may be expected as a solution. They do not reflect perfect answers, but rather give you ideas for completing the exercises. They should help you to find your own style and approach as well as give you an insight into the diverse nature of the game industry.

Exercise 2.1
Write three one-liner descriptions and one-liner comparisons for your favorite games. Also, write the one-liner description and one-liner comparisons for your current story project.

Exercise 2.2
Use the one-page design or one of the other alternative pitching techniques to develop a JRPG[10] with a female protagonist that deals with the topic of emotion and reality.

Exercise 2.3
Write a one-page narrative pitch for the game project you picked.

Samples

Sample 2.1: *One-Liner Descriptions*

An ordinary technician battles trans-dimensional monsters after an accident at a secret research facility.

—Half-Life

An ordinary man travels to an epic, fantastic, medieval world and becomes their symbol of virtue and righteousness.

—Ultima series

Be a god-like mayor and manage the city of your dreams.

—SimCity

A young girl battles her low self-esteem and her emotions, while traveling into her enemies' dreams to save the world.

—Fictional JRPG

Comparisons

An FPS with a physicist who has to save earth from an alien invasion starting in a secret research facility.

—Half-Life

An RPG with an ordinary man who travels to a medieval fantasy world to defeat evil and become their avatar of the virtues.

—Ultima series

A city-building simulation with a modern building style where players become mayors and have to manage and build a city, keeping their people safe and happy.

—SimCity

A Japanese-style RPG similar to *Final Fantasy*, with an emotionally scarred heroine who must journey into the dreams of her enemies in a modern-day fantasy world.

—Fictional JRPG

Sample 2.2: *The Dream Catcher*

Overleaf is a possible solution using the one-page design

The Dream Catcher

date
SAMPLE FOR THE NARRATIVE DESIGN TOOLBOX

Genre
JRPG

Platforms
Windows PC, Playstation 4 and XBox One

Setting
The game takes place in a stylized, manga-like modern Asian setting, mixed with Tim Burton-style fantasy elements when showing the dream world.

One-Line Description
A young girl fights with her self-esteem and her emotions, while traveling into her enemies' dreams to save her world.

One-Line Comparison
A Japanese-style RPG similar to Final Fantasy, with an emotionally scarred heroine who must journey into the dreams of her enemies in a modern-day fantasy world

Story

Kiyoko, a 17-year-old student from Okinawa, moved recently with her parents to Kyoto. Not used to the high-paced, fashion-oriented city life, she struggles to find friends and a social life in her new home. Often she escapes to Umekoji Park, to be on her own and live in her books and daydreams. Life was so different back in Okinawa and her problems just got worse when she met Akemi, the most popular boy in school.

But as the game begins, Kiyoko learns that her daydreams can have teeth, as she and Akemi become trapped inside an elaborate revenge fantasy Kiyoko has concocted against Akemi's vicious girlfriend. Now trapped in the dream world, Kiyoko will have to find Akemi and escape the fantasy she herself has created. And their problems don't end once they're back in school. The dreams follow them, their emotions taking form to haunt their waking hours, until Kiyoko starts to wonder if she'll ever be able to escape.

Example of Gameplay

The player as Kiyoko is in the school yard as she runs into Akemi, who waves at her and asks her over for a chat. During the conversation he asks if she's seen his girlfriend Hitomi, who's been missing since yesterday. While they talk the player can see in the background that a shadow, Kiyoko's personified jealousy, passes by, carrying someone in a bag. With the "X-Button" the player can interrupt the conversation and start hunting the shadow to its hideout. If she decides not to interrupt the conversation, she will have to find more clues before finding the shadow and having the chance to defeat her own jealousy in a turn-based boss fight. During the fight all skills are based on emotions instead of a magic system. The player for example can "cast Delight" if an enemy hits her with an "Anger spell". All in all the mechanics and visuals of this project are built around the themes of emotions, dreams and consequences.

Gameplay in short
- Final Fantasy-like turn-based combat system
- Exploration of both known and unfamiliar worlds that change with the choices of the player
- Random events during the story make every playthrough unique
- Dialogues with multiple options allow players to influence the outcome of dialogue
- Quicktime events during dialogues allow "spontaneous" actions

Gameplay Innovations / KSPs
- A world that shows how dreams and reality blend
- Decisions have visual consequences
- Multiple endings
- Emotion-based combat system
- Multiple ways to solve tasks

Target Audience
Teenage girls ages 14 to 20, with an interest in anime/manga.

Sample 2.3: *Smarts Empire*

Disclaimer: The following narrative pitch was developed for a Christian game project and includes biblical topics. Dealing with these topics can be difficult and may offend some readers, so please feel free to skip this example if you need to. The example is included not only to show an example for a narrative pitch but also to illustrate a possible way to pitch a story on a difficult topic. Today, many games make use of symbols and topics based in a religious context, and it is a challenge to work with them in the right way so that people do not feel offended. An example for a game series that deals with Western historical and religious topics is the *Assassin's Creed* franchise, and you may have noticed the disclaimer they show at the start of the game.

One-Line Description

The player will dive into the world of the Smarts, a world full of stories and adventures. It's a world new and old at the same time, and only together can players achieve their goals and solve the mysteries around the ancient book.

Fluff Text

Find those *hopes* . . . They can't possibly be right . . . There is no one truth! Truth, what's it anyway?

—Emperor Hulianos

Setting

Smarts Empire is set in a low-fantasy world which reflects the real world but places the player in the shoes of very little creatures to change the point of view. The background of these creatures is based on the real-world Roman Empire around the year AD 110. Many things portray the real-world history in this fantasy world in a way that is suitable for children. The world is inhabited by Smarts, small humanoid ants, and all kinds of animals and insects which fit size-wise in this world. The plants and trees have the same size as in the real world. The main conflict of the world is between the Smarts and the Hopes, a subgroup of the Smarts who started to believe in a new worldview. It is a conflict between the old ways and the new way. It's a conflict about what one believes and what truth may really mean.

The Smarts

The Smarts are humanoid, ant-like beings that have two legs and four arms. They dress up like humans and live in houses made out of mushrooms, branches, tree holes, and plants. Many centuries ago, they started to gather in small communities, the villages. The villages grew bigger and, at some point, became cities. With ever more Smarts living together, the old tribe-like organization didn't work any longer, and so they decided 300 years ago to form the mighty empire of the Smarts.

An emperor, together with a consul of wise Smarts, reigns over all the Smarts.

The Hopes

The Hopes are a small group of Smarts who have adopted a new worldview, which is strange for most of the Smarts. It is, to a certain degree, so new that some see it as an insult. In their new way of living, they share a message of hope and love, a message that speaks about a great sacrifice made for them, one they never could have made. It was made for them, so that they are free and can live in the original, intended way.

Story Integration

The story is told via a multilayered narrative model. Each interactive inhabitant of this world will have its own little storyline which is part of either a bigger regional or a world plot. The narrative content is delivered to the players via short quest texts, which are enriched by short emotes from the NPCs to make them more lifelike.

From the gameplay side, the story is told through quests tasks that suit the narrative. For example, if a character loses a specific item, then a "collect" task can be used to have the players look for this item.

Another way to communicate the story is through events, which are only present for a certain time frame within the game. These events can recur but don't have to. During the events, the game world is altered visually and acoustically according to the told story. Also, NPCs can offer specific quests and questlines, which are only available during this specific event.

Conclusion

All in all, the *Smarts Empire* narrative will enrich the game as it connects the mechanics with the stylized content, allowing players to learn about and experience historical events and developments, in connection to their importance to modern-day free speech and diversity of worldviews.

Notes

1 System designer: A subgroup of game designers often just referred to as "game designer." Responsible for the rules and mechanics of a game.
2 Producer: A project manager overseeing the business part of the development process. Responsible for the project's schedule and available resources.
3 Player vs. player: A game activity where at least two players compete against each other within the set of game rules.
4 First-person shooter: A genre where the player sees the game world through a first-person perspective and where the core mechanics are built upon weapon usage.

5 *Portal*, 2007, Valve Corporation.

6 *BioShock*, 2007, 2K Games.

7 See Stone Librande's GDC 2010 presentation, "One-Page Designs," last modified April 2, 2010, http://stonetronix.com/gdc-2010/OnePageDesigns.ppt.

8 KSP: Key selling point. A business term used to describe which features let your product stand out in comparison to similar ones.

9 Core leads: Directors and leads of various disciplines within the project. People like the technical director, lead game designer, art director, producer, etc.

10 Japanese roleplaying game: a specific style and subgenre of roleplaying games.

Worldbuilding

Worldbuilding is a term often associated with science fiction and fantasy settings, where writers literally must decide the history and geography of entirely fictional worlds. But in a broader sense, all writers must engage in worldbuilding, detailing the unique setting where their story takes place. Story centric or light on story, games of all genres take place in a world, including action-adventure games, FPSs, RPGs, RTSs,[1] text-based adventures, mobile games, indie games, platformers, hidden-object games, social games, and VR games. Along with creating settings and determining the world's scope, a narrative designer's worldbuilding influences art design and sound design by suggesting what the game should look and sound like.

IN THIS CHAPTER, YOU WILL LEARN TO . . .

- Approach worldbuilding from a macro or micro level.
- Use research and personal experience to inspire your worldbuilding and make the world feel authentic.

DOI: 10.1201/9781003369332-3

- Design realistic worlds in fantastic and science-fictional settings.
- Use world archetypes as the foundation for your world's design.
- Identify the worldbuilding details you need to share with your team versus what players need to know.
- Give players knowledge of the world and ways to experience it through means other than dialogue and story progression.
- Develop worlds for licensed intellectual property.

Macro- vs. Micro-Level Worldbuilding: Where to Begin?

"Macro level" and "micro level" are terms often used in regard to worldbuilding. Specifically, they refer to your starting point, whether you're designing a realistic world or a fantastical one. That starting point could be a licensed property (covered at the end of this chapter) or an original intellectual property (IP). The **macro** level is a top-down approach. You work with broad concepts and ideas and apply them to the world. These might be a shared history between cultures, the scale of the world (including the sizes of cities and towns, and the distances between them), or the world's genesis. The **micro-**level approach starts small and expands out. An event like a coronation or election or a city central to the game's story can influence the beginnings of your world's design.

You can use either approach, but one may make more sense than the other. The game's genre, major gameplay features, the type of narrative (linear or branching), and the type of player-character may all factor into your decision. If the game is an open world that encourages players to explore and discover, you might start on the macro level and think about

Screenshot from *Drakensang: The Dark Eye* (Prototype). Protected by United States and international copyright law. © Bigpoint.

how big the world should be (its scope) and what kinds of locations would be in it. If the game's protagonist is a fixed character with a well-defined history and backstory, you might start with that character's place of origin. (For more on fixed characters, please see Chapter 4, "Characters.") In order to determine which process to adopt, it's good to ask yourself what immediately stands out about the project's gameplay and story:

- If your game uses combat, are fighting techniques based upon magic systems, technologies, or martial arts? What are the origins of these fighting systems?
- What is the game's main story? Where does the conflict begin, and who is involved?
- Is there a major event that happens before the game's story begins? What effect has this event had on the world?
- Does the story focus on a character or group of characters? Where do these characters come from, and what is unique about their culture and history?
- Can players pick a character class? How many character classes are in the game, and what are their homelands and cultures like?

Before you begin, brainstorming questions like these can give you a better idea of whether you'll want to start on the macro or micro level. You'll find that you'll end up with answers that can direct your research. Once you know the approach you'll take, doing some research can make your worldbuilding more authentic and credible.

Worldbuilding, Research, and Inspiration

Research gets a bad reputation sometimes. Some find it too intimidating, or they see it as something academics do—when creating a world, the imagination's all that's necessary. Why would facts matter? But research should be a part of every narrative designer's toolset. It provides a starting point. There are circumstances throughout history that might be similar to what's going on in your game's world. If you base elements of your world on real-life counterparts, you know the scenarios, conflicts, characters, and settings are plausible because their inspirations are plausible. Research is fundamental in developing worlds based upon real-life counterparts. But it's also important in creating more fantastic settings. Just the act of reading about past cultures and historical events—where they happened, and who was involved—can give you ideas for your worldbuilding.

One reason research may seem intimidating is because you might not know where to begin. There are many avenues you could take, but would they be fruitful? Whether your worldbuilding's on a macro or micro level, there are six simple questions you can keep in mind. They're great for identifying initial research topics. They'll give you points to consider when analyzing a source to see if it has information relevant to your project. They'll generate a series of more focused questions, giving you more direction in your research. And they're questions everyone is already familiar with:

- Who?
- What?

- When?
- Where?
- Why?
- How?

In looking at these questions to formulate research topics, think about what you're planning for your world and its characters. In a hypothetical scenario, a world features a natural disaster that cuts off people in a large city from the rest of civilization (macro-level worldbuilding). The population forms dangerous factions in order to survive. Here are some questions regarding the conflict:

- **What** kind of natural disasters could create this scenario?
- **Where** (geographically) could such a scenario happen?
- **When** in history has a similar scenario occurred?
- **How** did people survive?
- **Who** survived?
- **Why** did dangerous groups form?

Research develops big concepts, but it also revises and finetunes ideas and details. Team Bondi knew they wanted to set *L.A. Noire* in 1947. This was the year of the unsolved Black Dahlia case, which has an analogous storyline in the game. Since the case went unsolved, this gave Team Bondi creative license to put their own spin on what might have happened. With the year determined, they looked at newspapers from every day in 1947 and made observations about what was appearing on the front pages. There were brutal images of murder scenes, which were common for that time.[2] Since people were often exposed to these images, they weren't shocked or disgusted by them. This discovery set the tone for the game's violence and the NPCs' responses (or lack thereof) to the violent displays at crime scenes. Instead of looking away, NPCs are curious as they flock to the crime scenes. This may not seem like a big detail, but the NPCs' responses reinforce how commonplace these murders had become.

Creating Analogues from Research and Personal Experiences

As mentioned above, *L.A. Noire* uses the Black Dahlia case as inspiration for a storyline and its corresponding cases. Analogues can be developed from research you uncover. They aren't exact copies, but they're allusions to their counterparts. Analogues can be used for any aspect of worldbuilding, from government systems, settings, world inhabitants, to specific characters. It doesn't matter if the game takes place in a more realistic setting or a fantastic one. Creating analogues based on real-world counterparts makes them more believable. They take details from something that actually exists, so it's not hard for players consciously or unconsciously to acknowledge their plausibility.

Some analogues in games:

- **Characters**: Alan Wake is a best-selling horror writer like Stephen King, and he'd fit right into a Stephen King novel.
- **Settings**: *Deadly Premonition*'s Greenvale is patterned after real small towns in the Pacific Northwest and the fictional town of Twin Peaks.
- **Philosophies**: In *BioShock*, Rapture's worldview is based on Objectivism.
- **Time periods**: Games in the *Assassin's Creed* franchise take place during Ptolemaic Egypt, Classical Greece, the Viking expansion, the Italian Renaissance, the American Revolutionary War, and the French Revolution.

Research isn't the only tool for creating analogues. Your own personal experience and the experiences of your team members are excellent sources of inspiration. Creators often use their personal experience in other media. Ridley Scott's memories of Hong Kong shaped San Angeles's atmosphere in *Blade Runner*, and the character of Edward Scissorhands is based on how director Tim Burton felt growing up. Aspects of characters, locations and worlds, and storylines can all be based upon your personal experiences or personal experiences of your team members. Try a brainstorming session where you and your team focus on generating personal details you might add to the game.

Worldbuilding inspired by personal experience is just as believable as worldbuilding based on larger-scale historical counterparts. Many films you've watched and fiction and comics you've read have been based on personal experiences. No matter your background or where in the world you grew up, gamers can relate to aspects of the life you've lived. The reason for this is that the personal is universal. If your parents divorced when you were younger, for example, you might use the experience of having to get acclimatized to new cities after traveling back and forth. That disorienting feeling of moving from place to place might inform the transitory atmosphere of the cities in your game. Players who have traveled constantly and anyone who has moved a lot—not just players who were shuttled back and forth between visits with divorced parents—can relate to the disorienting nature of these cities. Anybody can engage emotionally with personal experiences because they've been through similar experiences or felt similar emotions. Everyone is an expert on what happens to them, so elements inspired by personal experience are authentic and believable—they're based on actual events or observations. While these experiences are unique, they can be appreciated by a diverse group of players.

Developing Direct Representations

While analogues are fictionalized, direct representations are more true to life. Some games (or parts of games) are set in real cities, and their

**Grounding Your
Science Fiction
Worldbuilding in
Reality
Research**

While you may have
more creative freedom
to determine how
magic and technology
work in fantasy-based
settings, the key word
for any hard science
fiction IP is **research**.
There is a plethora of
current-day scientific
research and theory
which can easily be
used as a starting
point for any future
miracle of science
such an IP would need.
These resources are
readily available on
the Internet, though
cross-referencing
and fact-checking
should always be
a rule. While there
is good information
to be found on the
Internet, there is also
(understatement) a lot
of inaccurate data.

Some of the resources
you can use are as
follows:

• Science posting
  boards and forums.

• Mailing lists.

• Science news and
  journals.

• YouTube videos.

• Professional blogs.

missions or stories may be based upon actual events. The recreations
of these cities, missions, and stories need to be factually accurate.
Authenticity is more important than creative license because the
game is looking to recreate historical events, use historical figures as
characters, or create scaled-down facsimiles of real places from the
past or present. Direct representations may require a great deal more
research than analogues.

While *L.A. Noire's* story and missions are based on analogous
real-world cases, Team Bondi wanted Los Angeles's representation
to be as accurate as possible. The team spent months researching
everything from architecture, to clothing, to local flora. Some research
destinations included vintage clothing stores to determine not only
the way people dressed but also their builds and statures; UCLA's
Spence Air Photos Collection to survey aerial photos of LA; and the
Huntington Library to analyze the city's commercial and residential
zones from the 1930s.[3]

The Need for Authenticity

Direct representations need to be authentic, and so do analogues.
Both need to be plausible. This means that players need to be able to
identify something that rings true in both. If you want to realistically
represent Costa Rica, you don't want to write a mission where the
player-character must find a member of the Costa Rican army, because
the country abolished its military. A character class based upon the
Inuit and living in an Arctic region would find using fire-based magic
difficult. Any inaccurate detail, whether widely recognizable or not,
can take players out of a game.

It's unlikely every aspect of your research will end up making an
impact on the game, but you want to cover as many areas as you need.
If you have a team, you can assign who'll be researching what topics.
Nonwriters and designers should also be involved in research. For
example, several artists might study Costa Rica's architecture, while
several others collect information on the country's fauna. Research
might be more difficult if you're the only one doing it, so it's important
to know exactly what topics you need to cover. Whether you're going
solo or with a team, come up with your topics and areas of research
before you get started. It'll be harder to complete your necessary
research if you're constantly adding topics, especially if you're faced
with deadlines. Of course, your initial research can lead to new, more
focused subjects to review. Move from more general topics to more
specific ones as soon as you can; put your energy where it needs to be.

Bring Something New to the World

Games tend to take place in a few archetypal worlds: urban sprawls,
medieval European-esque societies, dystopian futures, zombie

apocalypses, etc. When worlds become familiar, this means players are more likely to find the game predictable. Certain types of characters have the same types of storylines in these worlds. Familiar social dynamics and scenarios play out between these characters, and players can figure out conflict developments and choices they'll have to make. Just a few details inspired by your research can give your players new experiences in these worlds. While the direct representations and analogues are believable, they will be unfamiliar and unusual elements in your worldbuilding. Players will be more engaged by these settings, characters, and storylines simply because they're different.

Building Realistic and Fantastical Worlds for RPGs

Roleplaying games traditionally involve a vast realm to explore. While it's possible to make a smaller-scope RPG that focuses on other parts of the genre (like stats, character sheets, and inventory), while staying in a very small space (say, a *Hunger Games*-style arena), you'll have an easier time in the marketplace if your RPG has a large explorable world to back up your story.

Realistic Worlds

Designing a game set in the real world offers both freedom and baggage for a narrative designer. A modern-day military or spy story is far easier for new players to understand than something that starts with a five-page history of the Skraelingborn before the opening scene. In a realistic story, language is easy—the characters speak and use slang that is much the same as the players', or at least dialogue that players have heard in a hundred TV shows.

Settings, likewise, use the names of real countries and cities that players know—Russia, North Korea, Paris, London—and designers inherit a huge bank of existing associations and images that evoke those places. Saying that the orc hordes of Verxmerplank have torn down the Tower of Rovengraad means nothing to players, but tell them "Terrorists have set a bomb to take down the Eiffel Tower," and both your setting and motivation are immediately clear.

However, there are risks involved with setting fictional stories in the real world. Some of your player base might be in Moscow, and they'll know immediately if you skimped on the research—or take offense if you make their countrymen the player's enemies. Narrative designers who write realistic games should do extensive research. In the age of the Internet, you must assume any factual errors will be found and posted within hours of your game's release. More importantly, as the writer on a game, you should be careful not to accidentally (or intentionally) demonize an entire nation or ethnicity for the

- Library books (university libraries are a gold mine).

- Science fiction novels (know your genre).

- And more. Look for more ways. There's always more.

Research is key in establishing the science for a hard sci-fi IP. Founding your science in what already exists can lend an air of believability to even far-fetched science and aids in suspension of disbelief on the part of your players.

Know the rules of the science worldbuilding for your IP (hard science as in *Mass Effect*, or more science-as-magic as in *Star Wars*), and stick to it. Don't be afraid to explain your science, but be aware—the more in-depth you go in the details, the more thorough your knowledge and consistency will have to be.

Consultants

A lot of people who work in science fields will actually be very enthusiastic about talking science and, more so, talking science for a game. If you're approaching someone by cold call or email, make certain you are respectful of their time and engagements. Keep your email or call short and to the point. Thank them for their time. And if they don't answer or decline, thank them again for their time.

Should they agree to assist, or if you are fortunate enough to know people who happen to work in the fields you wish to research for your IP, treat them with the utmost respect and consideration. They will be a gold mine of information. Having someone who can fact-check the science you've created for your IP, particularly when it's a hard-science IP, is invaluable.

A few other important rules to keep in mind:

- Make sure your company's legal department and your project management are comfortable with you discussing NDA[4]-worthy material with someone who is not contracted.

- Procure and get an NDA signed if Legal requires it.

convenience of your plot. If the game is about Islamic terrorism, consider having a Middle Eastern character who is a strong ally or love interest for the player-character as well.

Since RPGs as a genre originated with *Dungeons & Dragons*, there is always a tendency to follow the "all dwarves are like this" model. But while the "tell me everything about your race" dialogues are tiresome even in fantasy, in realistic settings, they cross the line into offensive, when writers assume that they can define entire real-world racial, religious, or ethnic groups by a few stereotypical sentences. If you ever find yourself writing a line like "We Africans love music . . .," consider whether you really feel able to write a character who can speak as the voice of an entire continent's worth of cultures and individuals.

Fantastical Worlds

If the RPG you're writing is science fiction or fantasy, you're faced with the less touchy, but more enormous, task of creating an entire game world from scratch. In this case, there are two temptations inexperienced narrative designers often fall prey to.

The first is not creating a sufficiently detailed history. These are the fantasy worlds where all of the races are obviously ported directly from Tolkien/*D&D*—elves love trees, dwarves use axes, and orcs are evil, end of story. It is immediately clear upon talking to the characters that they have no idea what their own history is and no life outside their role in the plot. There used to be a tabletop RPG (now long out of print) which had a playable race described as "no one knows what gender they are under their robes" (which begs the player reaction of "I lift up my robe and look.").

Some writers may even be unaware that these "fantasy archetypes" originated in very specific works—generally *The Lord of the Rings* and *Dungeons & Dragons*—so, before beginning any fantasy writing, it is wise to examine your assumptions and even Google some of the fantasy races you're using, to learn where ideas about those races originated. And, of course, if you're making up names for gods or cities or characters, it's always wise to Google the names you're using before you get too attached to them—you may not intend to plagiarize, but calling your original fantasy world "The Forgotten Realms" can still get you into trouble.

When creating a fantastical world, it's all right to use shorthand by making some of the races or situations familiar, because that helps players to overcome their fear of the new and stay long enough to get invested in your game. New IPs are always risky investments for a game company, since players are much more likely to buy sequels to things they already know and love. A wise use of tropes and genre conventions can help launch a new property by convincing gamers that they're not buying some total unknown; they're just buying "*D&D*,

but in a world where everyone hates mages and elves" (the *Dragon Age* franchise). There was a point in the development of *Mass Effect* when Asari were just "sexy blue girls" in the *Star Trek* tradition, but the inclusion of a detailed culture and memorable characters has turned them into an iconic science fiction alien in their own right.

However, say you do take the time to create a detailed world with a history dating back five thousand years and the names of every bow-wielding, stereotype-defying dwarven queen going back to the original matriarch. That level of detail is great, because by the time you've figured it all out, you are deeply invested in your world. But once you've put that much work into something, it's very, very hard to accept that no one else needs to know it.

This is what's behind the epidemic of game characters who want to quote entire *Encyclopedia Britannica* articles about the history of their race every time they say hello. And assuming every player wants to learn everything about your world is the quickest way to ensure they don't listen to your dialogue at all.

This may be a result of the genre's historical ties to tabletop RPGs. In a tabletop game, the only way to keep a game line alive is to put out sourcebooks, which are generally filled with precisely the fictional equivalent of *Encyclopedia Britannica*, hundreds of pages of nothing but backstory, descriptions of cities, and ecology of monsters. But this is a feature that is unique to tabletop RPGs, which are an extremely small market. And even within that small market, this information is generally marketed to only one sixth of the audience—the GM,[5] not the players.

There is rarely an equivalent in books and movies. (Things like *The Silmarillion* and other "World of . . ." books are specialty volumes, marketed to hardcore fans; they are not necessary to appreciate or even love the main story.) Instead, the history that comes up in dialogue is what is relevant to the story.

Create a world that is rich in detail and history, and draw on real cultures and lesser-known events in history, since reality is often stranger than fiction,[6] but then ask yourself which parts players need to know *right then* to be able to accomplish their goals. If they don't need to know it, save it. If your game does well, all that information will be mined again for the sequel.

- Ensure that your contact is provided appropriate payment; this can range from thanks in the game's credits, to a copy of the game, to actual remuneration.

- If your contacts are helping for free, ensure you never abuse their helpfulness; courtesy goes a long way, and proper appreciation should always be the rule.

- If you are a junior, you may not be the one to talk to the consultants; this does not mean you won't be asked to provide a list of questions, or that you should not talk to whomever is in charge of talking to the consultant to pass along your questions.

Worldbuilding and Level Design

As a narrative designer, the work you do on worldbuilding becomes an important foundation for the entire content design team on your project. The level designer will mine your backstory to find narratively appropriate content to put in the game, and artists need to know what to model.

Level design is the gatekeeper between your world of imagination and the practical concerns of implementing the project and creating a physical world from it. Often, there are limitations due to art or gameplay that your world vision will have to change to accommodate. For example, level designers will tell you that all floors have to have a certain minimum width, and this will rule out narrow paths into a dark underground. Another important element for level designers to consider is where light sources will be placed to guide players through areas. A dark alley without any light may sound cool, but it will quickly leave players without any clue where to go.

Besides those gameplay aspects, level designers will also be the ones who need to implement most of the content, and they are usually very well aware of any technical limitations. Maybe the engine your project is using is only capable of rendering objects close to player-characters, or the scripting language cannot trigger animations in NPCs, or quests cannot branch. Whatever the limitations on your particular game, until you get the sign-off from the designers, artists, and programmers who will be creating your world, the worldbuilding phase of your design isn't over. If you can't build it, the world will never exist.

Here are a few questions that can help when designing your world while keeping level design in mind:

- How do the players know where to go?

  ○ A tall tower or big capital can be a clue to the player to go to a certain place, for example.

- What are the highlights, landmarks in this region?

  ○ Scenic waterfalls, small villages, tall towers, castles, huge mountains, and so on help to identify certain regions in your world and help the player to find those places if requested. Does the content require any new mechanics that haven't been used so far?

  ○ As an example, imagine your region is on top of a huge mountain, and there is no path to walk to this place. This would require a mechanic to fly or teleport there. If your game doesn't support reaching the location yet, it's something that needs to be designed and developed, if you want to include this concept. Can the scene be built with limited assets? Which assets can I reuse?

  ○ You have only three kinds of rocks, and you want to build a rock desert, for example. Can it be done with the available assets, or do you need to design new ones? If you decide to design new ones, can they be used in other places within the game world?

- Do I have a list of the important elements of the world? Are they visual?

  ○ Know what is and isn't important to your world. Also, whenever possible, try to use visual storytelling. That's what level designers and environment artists excel in.

- What characteristics define your world? What are its dos and don'ts?

  ○ For example, the people of your world believe it brings bad luck to have a graveyard in a settlement. All the graveyards are outside of the city for this reason.

- Who lives in this world and why? What are their daily problems, besides what's happening in your storyline?

  ○ In a believable world, no one exists just for a hero to pass by and knock on the door. The cultures of your world need a normal life. This normal life defines how they build cities, how they do their jobs, and how they shape the world. The level designers need this information to create believable designs and layouts.

DIFFERENT WORLD ARCHETYPES

Sometimes it's helpful to start with an archetype when creating a new world. This archetype defines the fundamental, general world conflict. Here are a few suggestions. This list only mentions some common archetypes and is not complete, but it should be helpful when you start your next world, and even when you figure out your own archetypes.

War-Torn World

The creatures of this particular world make up two or more factions that are almost always in constant conflict.

Example: *Warhammer 40K* universe. The universe of *Warhammer 40K* is all about war and constant conflict, which is reflected by the franchise's logline: "In the grim darkness of the far future there is only war." All the background lore is designed to reflect this premise of conflict and constant state of war.

Besieged World

This is a world that is attacked by an outside force or beings from another world, dimension, etc.

Example: Thedas (world of *Dragon Age*). Life in Thedas is threatened by the Blight. The Blight is formed by demonic creatures with the goal to conquer and destroy the world. These creatures and their threat "besiege" the world of Thedas.

Fallen (Dystopia) World

All hope is lost. Everything has ended with the worst possible outcome. Suffering and war are more or less the usual in such worlds.

Example: The original *Warhammer Fantasy* setting. Similar to the *Warhammer 40K* franchise, the first fantasy version of this universe was also painted by war. It was a very hopeless and dark fantasy in which life has barely any meaning, and everything is about a constant struggle against despair. *Warhammer Fantasy* and *Warhammer 40K* are both fallen and war-torn worlds. While *Warhammer 40K* is a little stronger on the war-torn side, *Warhammer Fantasy* is stronger on the dystopian side.

Perfect (Utopia) World

This is the opposite of the fallen world. In a perfect world, everything has ended with the best possible outcome, and everything is perfect. For good storytelling, something in these perfect worlds must create a conflict. Otherwise, there won't be any story.

Example: The Founders' territory in the air city of Columbia (*BioShock Infinite*). Columbia is supposedly an ideal, peaceful world, but soon the players learn that something is wrong under the surface, something brought into this world by its imperfect founders.

Awakening (Newborn) World

This is a world that has just seen its creation. It is young and has almost no history. It still has to show what kind of world it will become. Everything is possible.

Example: In *Spore*, players grow a new species into a microscopic being, which is a part of a new world, the planet it inhabits. That creature will evolve into a complex being that will eventually master space travel. Player decisions help to determine how the creature becomes a dominant force in its world.

Changing World

This is a world awaiting a major change. Forces within or from outside the world have created a conflict so strong that the world will never be the same again. The moment the change is decided is when the players/audience enter the scene.

Example: Middle-earth at the time of *The Lord of the Rings*. Middle-earth in the Third Age is on the brink of change. The elves are leaving, and humankind needs to take responsibility for the world. Part of the global conflict in *The Lord of the Rings* is whether humankind will step into this role or leave the world to those who want to destroy it.

Ending (Dying) World

This may sound similar to the fallen world, but it isn't. A dying world is simply a world which is very old, has a lot of history, and will cease to exist in the near future. Heroes may be able to save the world's inhabitants, but no matter what they try, they may not be able to rescue the world or delay its destruction.

Example: The Kingdom of Zeal in *Chrono Trigger* is prominent during the Ice Age, and it is a place of great technology and magic. The queen of Zeal and her subordinates try to obtain power from an alien by summoning it. They're unable to control the alien, and Zeal is destroyed, sinking into the sea.

Newly Discovered World

One or more races have discovered a world for the first time. Conflicts involving the unknown begin to arise.

Example: The influence of the human scientist on Adelpha in *Outcast*. Adelpha is a world that is developing and has its own culture separate from those of humans. Within the story of *Outcast*, players try to defeat a tyrant after learning that it was their influence that brought this tyrant to power.

Destroyed World

A world which has been destroyed beyond recognition or completely annihilated. Putting the pieces back together and/or learning how to move on are the fundamental ideas of this archetype.

Example: New Vegas or Washington, DC in the *Fallout* franchise. Both cities represent a world after an all-out nuclear war and what it left behind. Life recovers and moves on, but the world is often a dead desert, and ruins cover the landscape, signs of a glorious past.

The Worldbuilding "Iceberg"

How much do players need to know about the world? How much does everyone else on your development team need to know? Please take a short break and think about these two questions. What were your answers?

Maybe you came up with the same picture: the iceberg of worldbuilding.

An iceberg has a part that can be clearly spotted when encountering it from a ship, and a part that can't be seen. The same is true of worldbuilding or lore, which is the collection of all material that describes and defines your world and its history. Only a small portion of your worldbuilding work will ever be visible to players. The majority of the material you'll design and write will be hidden. But why?

The famous fantasy world of Middle-earth, mentioned earlier, answers this question. Did you know that Tolkien designed several different languages, continents, kingdoms, and cultures that never made it into one of his books? He designed all this material not because it was used directly by the reader but because it helped him to flesh out and understand the world of his story better. A language, for example, always reflects the culture of the ones who invented it. The Elvish languages are soft, elegant, and rather proud, while the language the dwarves speak is practical, short, and hard.

The iceberg of worldbuilding. Picture created by Tobias Heussner.

So Tolkien created detailed background material to better understand his world, and while such detailed worldbuilding is helpful to the author, it can be even more helpful for other team members. Originally, Tolkien wanted to create worlds for his languages and to give Great Britain its own great mythological stories. One aspect of language creation is that one needs to know the culture of the people who use the language. For this reason, if someone wants to create a language, the culture this language came from has to be defined. A culture requires a world that defines it. Tolkien used this simplified process. To create his languages, he had to define cultures and the world for these cultures. All this secondary material, including the languages, inspired many other authors to write stories that play in Middle-earth. With the help of his original material, the content could be kept relatively consistent. The same is true for the world a narrative designer builds for a game development team.

Your worldbuilding can inspire others to expand and build your world in ways you never could imagine. That is the reason why narrative designers have to work on the whole iceberg and also help other team members to see below the water's surface. For an artist, it can be extremely beneficial to understand the culture of a specific character before starting to work on a first sketch. Imagine you design a nation of Amazons, and you only tell your artist to sketch the leader. Without any cultural information, your artist will most likely draw you a stereotyped version of an Amazon, and depending on the artist's own imagination, it can be very unfitting. Providing your team member, the artist, with more information on the character, culture, and environment of the area in which the character lives will make it a lot more likely that you only have to go through small iterations. This saves a lot of frustration on both sides—yours and the artist's. Just imagine how wrong the sketch would be if the Amazons of your game world were actually dwarves. The team requires detailed backgrounds, and your team needs to know as much as possible about the world. But what about the players? How much do players need to know?

In regard to the Amazons, do players need to read a text about the climate, vegetation, or environment? No, because they will see it in the form of the level design and art design right on their screens. Do they need to know anything about the former leader of the Amazons or the personal backstory of the current leader? Not unless it is needed for gameplay or to understand the story or plotline. Do players need to know what the Amazons do at night even if it will always be day in your game? No, because this information would be irrelevant to them. Still, your development team needs this information because it influences how artists and designers will design the villages and environment of this culture.

So, in general, players need to know things that directly affect them and their story experience. Any kind of backstory can be placed as

lore books or optional dialogues in the world, but this should not
be part of the main story experience. Roughly 10 percent of the
writing and design content during your worldbuilding process will be
immediately relevant to players. The rest will be relevant for your team
and potential transmedia projects. Through transmedia, you can tell
multiple stories in one world across different types of media, including
games, film, comics/manga, prose fiction, and animation. These
projects are excellent ways to deepen the world experience for your
most devoted fans.

Ways to Experience the World: Spreading Around the 10 Percent

The 10 percent of the iceberg players experience doesn't have to
be limited to the story and the world's inhabitants. There are plenty
of opportunities to spread lore throughout the world. Some lore
you'll incorporate into the story, plot development, and character
development. The rest can be fun information devoted fans and
players can discover while exploring the game. You can design how
players will encounter lore in the game in ways that make the world
more believable. While a priestess shouldn't spout off all of the
ways her order is forbidden to use certain magic, it makes sense that
she'd keep books or parchment scrolls on the subject in her library
and on her desk. Players who like to look around the environment
can read up on the history of her religion and how the forbidden
laws came to be.

How Players Can Experience Your World

Environmental Narrative

The way the world looks and sounds can say a lot about its past and
present. Players might come across bombed-out buildings in a city that
was never rebuilt, telling the story of a people who were defeated and
unable to rise up again. Surviving NPCs that once lived there might
be spread across the region. In ambient dialogue, they share traumatic
memories of the war. (Environmental narrative is discussed at length in
Chapter 6, "Implementation and Production.")

Dialogue

NPCs, or even the player-character, might mention lore tidbits in
conversation. "I lost her during the palsy epidemic", suggests a major
event in the world's history, while "Trust those mercs with your life?
Damn fool . . ." says something about the way one character class
views another.

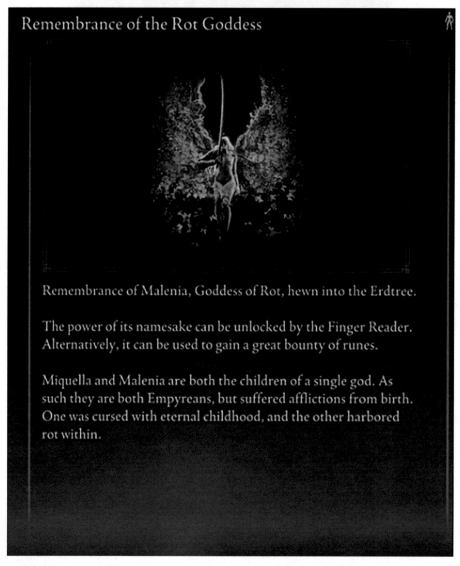

Remembrance of the Rot Goddess

Remembrance of Malenia, Goddess of Rot, hewn into the Erdtree.

The power of its namesake can be unlocked by the Finger Reader. Alternatively, it can be used to gain a great bounty of runes.

Miquella and Malenia are both the children of a single god. As such they are both Empyreans, but suffered afflictions from birth. One was cursed with eternal childhood, and the other harbored rot within.

Malenia's flavor text explains a little about her parentage, sibling, and physical being. Asmongold Clips, "Asmongold reads all bosses [sic] flavor text in Elden Ring," April 2, 2022, YouTube video, 3:17. www.youtube.com/watch?v=TwZ0gbiHysg. © FromSoftware Inc., BNE Entertainment, Namco Bandai Games America Inc.

Journal Entries, Books, and Codices

These give players opportunities to read up on just about any subject: geography, culture, history, mythology, art, personal experiences, etc. Information from codices can be added to journal entries, books, diaries, etc., scattered throughout the world. In more modern settings, this information might be found in emails, in texts, and other digital formats. *Life Is Strange* uses texts, emails, and physical journal entries to explore relationships Max has with other characters (texts), illustrate how NPCs interact with each other and hint about their relationships (emails), and detail Max's inner world and how she processes the events of the story and her feelings about other characters (journal entries).

Flavor Text

Items and abilities need descriptions explaining how they can be used in gameplay, what skills are needed to use them, how much damage they inflict, how much health they replenish, etc. When those functional definitions are given a fictional spin, it is known as "flavor text," which turns dry descriptions into entertaining nuggets of world lore. Text might include who made the item (and the item maker's fate), how a culture or race values an item, or a (very) brief story about the item's exploits. After players defeat bosses in *Elden Ring* and loot their weapons and equipment, they can read in those item descriptions histories of the bosses, including their relationships with other characters players have or will encounter and their involvement in backstories that have shaped current conflicts. Flavor text is also an excellent way to add story to mobile games that aren't story-centric, such as the card game genre in which players collect cards of weapons, creatures, heroes with short bios, etc.

DLC and Transmedia

Sometimes there's more to explore in the world than one game can allow. Downloadable content (DLC) offers players new game experiences after the initial game has been released. DLC can launch fascinating side characters and antagonists, situate action in a new location, or provide playable stories of events only hinted at in the original game's main storylines. DLC gives you the freedom to return to a world and expose players to more of your worldbuilding.

Transmedia is similar to worldbuilding, but it's not limited to games. Aspects of the world can be experienced in *all* media—fiction, comics/ manga, film, animation, and games. The *Star Trek* and *Star Wars* franchises have extensive transmedia and are able to tell many stories in their highly developed universes.

Once you've finished building a world, you have all sorts of options as to how you'll introduce it to players, from the story and the objects they'll encounter in the game, to DLC and transmedia produced after the game's release.

Working on a Licensed IP

Much has been explained in this chapter about creating narrative and writing for an original IP. Creating such games provides incredibly exciting challenges, most notably at the beginning, when it comes to narrowing down your focus in order to create a world in a consistent and structured way. However, **Licensed IPs** (games based on an existing media property, such as a movie, TV show, or novel) should never be underestimated as a source of creative innovation and learning opportunities. Not only does working in a licensed game or sequel to an existing game provide its own interesting set of challenges and advantages, but these are the games you are most likely to encounter as a junior writer entering the AAA field. The fact is, working on already existing IPs is a wonderful way to start out on your first project in the game industry—it provides you with a safe environment to start learning about production processes and narrative design, and allows for a golden opportunity to acquire knowledge which will serve you for the rest of your career in the industry.

The most important thing when starting to work on an established IP is to respect the existing content and lore.

Know the Tip of the Iceberg

While this may seem obvious, it bears stating nonetheless: the first step to working on a licensed IP rests in knowing and understanding the existing lore. What is often shown to players (the tip of the iceberg) is easy to approach simply from playing the game and doing thorough research online via wikis and discussions with other players. This is something any narrative designer should do when applying for a position on an existing project. Even experienced writers sometimes neglect to show an understanding of the game they are interviewing to work on. And with the heavy competition for writing positions in the industry, every advantage you can show when starting out can be the foot in the door you need. Knowing the worldbuilding and IP you are hoping to work on should be the first advantage you aim for when applying for a specific position.

Learn Everything You Can about the Rest of the Iceberg

Once you've been hired for a project, the first thing you should focus on as part of the narrative team is the rest of the iceberg: that is, everything which was created internally as a means of providing a consistent worldbuilding structure but which is often not released or openly discussed in game. Sometimes, there will be a wealth of material available via internal documentation or wikis. Making sure that information is up to date should be your first step before immersing yourself in the content which will provide the framework you will rely on thereafter. Once that is done, you'll move on to the next step.

Figure Out Everything That's Missing from the Iceberg

Then comes the critical step—grasping what remains undefined within the context of the existing material, which is where you'll be stepping in should the lore need expansion as a result of the work you and your team are doing. Knowing where and how you can contribute to the existing lore in order to expand the narrative design of the IP in a consistent way is an essential part of working on any IP.

In short:

- **Tip of the iceberg**: Know the existing worldbuilding and lore as they are exposed to the public.
- **Rest of the iceberg**: Understand how the lore works, inside and out, from an insider's perspective.
- **The new stuff**: Know what areas of the lore remain undefined or can be expanded for your own purposes, while making sure to respect what is already part of the IP.

A Note on Retroactive Continuity Decisions (Retcons)

Sometimes you need to change existing lore for reasons which are valid and important to the healthy expansion of the IP. A decision to retcon existing lore (i.e., change lore while accommodating existing published material, so you can pretend the change was planned from the beginning) should never be done without due consideration and with every pro and con properly weighed. Including—there's no way around this one—fan engagement and potential reaction to the retcon.

Internal Wikis

Keeping careful track of the details of your work will be, if you are extremely lucky, a specialized individual's purpose in life at your company. This kind of internal specialist, however, is rare. Most times, the task of keeping track of All The Details™ that were, are, or will be in the game will come down to the narrative team.

Note: Knowing All The Details™ often is a way to make yourself invaluable to your team, across all disciplines. When even quality assurance is checking with you on this or that detail, you know you're doing something right.

Fans Will Know

As engaged as you are with the work you are doing on your licensed IP, keep in mind that the fans are likely even more engaged than you are and will remember every single detail contained in a game. While the conclusions they draw may not always be the correct ones, it is important to keep in mind that if you put something in the game, they will find it, no matter how deeply you bury it. Be smart and leave as few traces "behind the scenes" as possible.

Cameos and Fan Appreciation

Judiciously applied, cameos and fan-appreciation type content can be the ultimate reward for fans and developers alike. Be warned, however, that one must always be wary of how often such things are inserted into the content, obviously or not.

Conclusion

Every world has unique characteristics. As a narrative designer, you will influence how your players experience and enjoy them. That means how you approach worldbuilding will be important, and you might need to do extensive research to make the game's world more believable. Your ability to take inspirations from realistic places and diverse cultures and mix them with your own imagination can create worlds that players will find new and unexpected.

As you're designing your world, game designers, level designers, sound designers, and artists will need to understand what you're planning. There'll be a lot of important information to communicate. While the team has to have a much deeper foundational knowledge of the worldbuilding, players only need a small percentage of the details to feel the world is alive. *How* players experience that information will be up to you and the team. Will players uncover history through lore in codices? Will they get revelations about cultures through dialogue? Whether the setting is high fantasy with dark magic, a sweeping space opera, or a suburban Connecticut retirement community featuring love and loss, consider what you need to include in the world, and design what players will encounter as they interact with it.

Interview with Chris Avellone (while at Obsidian Entertainment, Now Freelancer)

How Do You Approach the Development of a New Story World?

Start with the knowns: game target platform (affects visual fidelity, level construction, controller options, and interface constraints in how the player interacts with the world), the budget (both personnel and cash-wise—how much of a world can you build?), system pillars (what do you do in the world?), the player's movement set (whether or not a player can jump or fly makes a big difference), camera angle (how does the player see the world?), and the core gameplay experience (fantasy RPG with leveling and dungeon exploration for three base classes: rogue, mage, fighter).

None of these may be especially sexy to consider, but all are important. You need to understand the computer or console on which the world's going to live, what the physics are for that world (on console especially), and how the player will interact with those physics—seeing the world from an isometric experience vs. first person makes a huge difference in vistas and level design, and world design needs to complement those limitations.

Once those are established/known, you can have more fun, and that usually begins on my end with what tone the world will have, who the principal adversaries and heroes are, what each of them wants, and the new mechanics and interactions you're bringing to the table. Using *New Vegas* DLCs as an example, we did survival horror with exploration/navigation challenges, crazy 1950s science with home-base-mechanics focus, a more linear-driven end chapter that provided an expanded arsenal of some of the best weapons and armor sets in the game (including companion upgrades), and provided a conclusion to the DLC limited series.

Do You Prefer the Macro-Level or Micro-Level Approach? Why?

Both have their uses, and there are times when it pays to choose one over the other depending on the goals. For example, early on in narrative design/world design, it pays to hit the bigger beats of the story and the world and get down the major pillars that make up the world (or at times, agree that you're **not** going to explain them but establish some rules for them). Once you've decided that, boil it down into a single pitch sentence (or single concept piece) that sums up the world, like "*BioShock* with dinosaurs." If more often than not, people (hopefully your boss, your coworkers, and your Kickstarter backers—or publishers or someone with financing money) go, "That sounds cool," then it's time to start drilling down. The trick is knowing when to stop—sometimes too much detail, too many constraints, and overexplaining something that works better as an abstract (midichlorians and the Force) can hurt a world more than help it. Giving designers freedom to do level and system design can achieve stronger results if the lore is designed to allow for that freedom, or if you tweak it to allow for a cool gameplay experience.

What Advice Would You Give to a New Narrative Designer When it Comes to Maintaining a Game World?

Think about the player's environment first—what do they see? Why would it be cool to explore at a glance? Then construct history and lore around creating those cool adventure spaces that people are instinctively drawn to. If they want to explore a series of barge-like wooden island platforms floating on a quicksand sea, build a culture and history around that. If they want to explore a modern city consumed by a vegetation apocalypse, build the lore around that. The goal is creating interesting gameplay spaces and vistas, interesting foes and challenges, and focusing on the fun of the world, not being a slave to its history and concepts.

Next—be sure to create a story and concept doc as you write. Set up conventions and standards as they are decided, especially if more writers are expected to join the project. Maps. Definitions. Spelling conventions. A grammar and style guide. And when a decision is exposed to the player, make a record of it and ensure consistency.

Someone needs to take care of the world and be its shepherd. It doesn't have to be the lead designer or project director. Appoint someone to carry the torch for the game world and the story if need be, and assist them in fleshing out the world. One of the creakiest things about a new game world can happen when there's no creative lead to monitor it, and the world ends up with holes and contradictions that arise from not fully understanding the world you're writing for.

What Are Your Top Three Resources When Researching for a New Game World?

Traveling to a similar location in the world (example: for *Wasteland 2*, I went to some of the locations in *Wasteland 1* and drove across sections of the Southwest), reading novels, comics, and watching shows in the same genre tied to the premise of design locations (for example, I read/watched *Food of the Gods* and the many variations of *Day of the Triffids* for the Ag Center in *WL2*), and lastly, Google searches and *Wikipedia* as a starting point to build upon. I keep an inspiration art folder of NPC portraits, quest ideas, and random design ideas that I accumulate from various media, and I draw upon those as well when designing characters, quests, and locales.

What Is Your Favorite Fictional World? Why?

That's a tough question. If I had to choose, it'd be *Warhammer Fantasy*—they hit all the right notes when it comes to adventure and conflict, and you feel like you're in the trenches, and you are all that stands between Chaos and the end of the world. But I have plenty of favorites beyond this: Iain Banks's Culture books, GURPS Supers International Super Teams, the *Wasteland* universe, the *Fallout* universe, *D&D*'s Planescape, *Snow Crash*, Sanderson's *Mistborn*, Glen Cook's *The Black Company*, and (probably on most everyone's list) *Game of Thrones*.

Exercises

Now it's time for you to start designing the world for your game. In the worldbuilding exercises, you'll identify some topics for research and create a document detailing the major features of your world.

Exercise 3.1

For the game you're designing, determine if you'll need to take a macro- or micro-level approach to your worldbuilding. Then come up with some topics you'll need to research.

Exercise 3.2

Once you've conducted a little research, develop a World Overview Document based on the following template and sample provided.

World Overview Template

Setting
Technology/Magic
World-Altering Events
Cultures/Character Classes
Major Landmarks/Locations
Summary of Conflict in the World

Sample

Sample 3.1

World Overview

Setting

The game takes place in a low-fantasy world with the sensibilities of a fairy tale. The entire story is set in Leneda, a country in the Eastern Hemisphere on the planet Vidon. The time is the late 900s, analogous to the Industrial Revolution in the early 1800s.

Most of Leneda's population lives in the central region and in the western mountains. The royal government, simply referred to as "The Crown," is situated in the central region in Leneda's second-largest city. The largest also has the largest university.

Leneda is ethnically diverse, due to scholars from all over the world settling in its educational centers throughout the centuries. Ethnic Lenedans are similar in complexion to Greeks, the people of Asia Minor, and those from northern Africa. Most ethnic Lenedans live in the west and central regions. Many Eastern Lenedans are analogous to Germanic peoples. Their ancestors settled along the coast, tamed the marshes, and established farms.

At the beginning of the game, all of Leneda is on edge as it anticipates the Dance of the Ghost Berries. It's a time of hope, deep disappointment, and peril. Too few Lenedans will benefit from the ghost berries, while the rest of the country will commit or be subjected to desperate acts to get their hands on them.

Magic and Astronomy

Leneda is most known for its astronomers. Astronomy in Leneda is a study of the stars, but it's an act of divination as much as it is a scientific discipline. Astronomers can determine years of famine or abundance, deaths and births of great or terrible leaders, natural disasters, and spiritual blessings—all from reading the disappearances or reappearances of constellations and certain stars.

Astronomy is revered. Astronomers' foreknowledge has prepared Leneda against invading countries and devastating natural disasters. It's possible the country would have fallen centuries ago without the art of astronomy.

World-Altering Events

Dance of the Ghost Berries

Ghost berries get their name from "vanishing without a trace," just as a spirit will appear and disappear out of the corner of one's eye. When eaten, these berries instantly heal any afflictions or diseases. The berries appear in a field somewhere in Leneda once every year. They last from dawn until nightfall. If they aren't picked before then, they lose their corporeal form. It's as if they never existed.

Astronomers can determine where and when ghost berries will appear by reading the stars. Because of the berries' curative properties, many Lenedans are desperate to find them. Those who search for them have different motivations for doing so. They may eat the berries for themselves or give them to sick loved ones and family members. Others hoard the berries and sell them at exorbitant prices.

The farther from the field one lives, the less likely she or he will get to the field in time and claim some of the berries. For this reason, Lenedan roads become dangerous places during the Dance of the Ghost Berries. Travelers returning home with berries are robbed, beaten, and worse.

Greed's Fever

Before the game begins, the contagious Greed's Fever has visited Eastern Leneda for five years straight. It's named for its need to return again and again, never seeming to be satisfied with the devastation it causes. For wealthier cities with resources, herbalists treat the sick, and they recover. For someone in a rural town, the prospects for survival are next to nil. Several towns have died off over the past five years.

Cultures

Eastern Leneda

The people of Eastern Leneda are mostly farmers and fisherman. They're considered to be the backbone of Leneda; their hard work keeps most of the country fed. While their work might be appreciated, their lives are undervalued. Most Eastern Lenedans are peasants.

Few Eastern Lenedans have the opportunity to pursue astronomy. It requires not only a gift for the art but also an apprenticeship under a master or mistress. Most simply don't have the time for proper training. Astronomers from the region are seen as truly gifted.

The Sky People

The Sky People get their name from living in the Sunhigh Mountains in the west. Many storied astronomers have come from the region. Lenedans believe it's because the Sky People live so close to the stars and can read their secrets clearly.

The Crown has always given financial support to the institutions in the region, making it one of the most important cultural centers in the country. Sky astronomers, herbalists, philosophers, teachers, and artists go on to wield great influence on the rest of Leneda and the world.

Major Landmarks/Locations

Daymede

Daymede is a tiny, struggling town in Eastern Leneda. It's Collen's home. Daymede has been struck by Greed's Fever every year for five years. As a result, there are few left. The town is in even more dire financial circumstances, as the farmers are dying off.

Daymede gets its name because it's one of the first towns the sunlight touches each day.

Creek Grin

Creek Grin is one of the smaller cities in the Sunhigh Mountains and is Nima's home. It's known more for its herbalists than its astronomers. A hospital for patients with debilitating injuries is situated here. These injuries are incurable, so herbalists try to minimize their patients' suffering as much as they can.

Creek Grin gets its name from the creek of the same name. Where the creek deposits into the Slewbank River, it looks like a wide smile with toothy rocks.

Summary of Conflict in the World

Both Collen and Nima are astronomers. Collen wishes to divine the location of the Dance of the Ghost Berries so he can bring the much-needed cure back to Daymede and save the sick the next time the fever visits.

Nima's daughter is one of the injured in Creek Grin's hospital. Nima desires to find the field of ghost berries and bring the cure back to Creek Grin, not just for her daughter but for all of the patients.

A few days before the Dance of the Ghost Berries begins, both Collen and Nima realize they are many miles from where the field will appear. They will have to travel the dangerous roads to the dance and hope all of the berries haven't been picked. When they arrive, they may find themselves fighting over the few that are left and doing whatever they must to get them.

Since players will choose to play as either Collen or Nima, players will begin the game in Daymede or Creek Grin.

The worldbuilding for this game follows a micro-level approach, using as inspirations the annual Dance of the Ghost Berries event and the two player-characters' circumstances and motivations for finding the ghost berries.

Notes

1 Real-time strategy: A genre where the player has to make decisions in real time and not in turns.
2 Keith Stuart, "*L.A. Noire*: The Interview," *The Guardian*, May 11, 2011, accessed February 8, 2013, www.theguardian.com/technology/gamesblog/2011/may/11/la-noire-exclusive-interview.
3 Charlotte Stoudt, "How the *L.A. Noire* Makers Re-Created the City of 1947," *The Los Angeles Times*, April 24, 2011, accessed February 8, 2013, www.latimes.com/entertainment/news/la-ca-noir-city-20110424,0,2500813.story.
4 Non-disclosure agreement: A legal contract between two parties, which regulates the kind of information these parties can share with third parties and what information cannot be shared.
5 Game master: The person who leads the storytelling in a traditional roleplaying game.
6 George R. R. Martin based the "Red Wedding" in *Game of Thrones* on the Black Dinner and Glencoe massacre in Scottish history. See James Hibberd, "'Game of Thrones' Author George R. R. Martin: Why He Wrote the Red Wedding—Exclusive," *Entertainment Weekly*, June 2, 2013, accessed March 29, 2014, http://insidetv.ew.com/2013/06/02/game-of-thrones-author-george-r-r-martin-why-he-wrote-the-red-wedding/2/.

PLEASED

NEUTRAL

PROUD

PENSIVE

AMUSED

HAPPY

Characters

Creating compelling characters is common to all types of writing. In games, players need great characters to interact with, whether those characters are player-characters or non-player characters. Some techniques for writing characters apply to all types of media. These include using common character archetypes, character diversity, giving characters flaws to keep them interesting, avoiding or subverting tropes, and making villains believable and relatable. However, you'll discover that some character-design choices are particular to games.

IN THIS CHAPTER, YOU WILL LEARN TO . . .

- Identify and choose the right type of player-character for your game.
- Use player-characters and NPCs to keep the player emotionally invested in the story and world.
- Work with the development team to help bring characters to life.
- Develop characters who are emotionally complex.
- Create diverse characters that are nuanced.
- Subvert tropes as a tool of character creation and development.

In some ways, writing characters for games is similar to writing characters for other media. You'll determine their backstories and histories. Working with artists and animators, you'll give them appearances and behaviors. But these characters fill roles that

DOI: 10.1201/9781003369332-4

are unique to games. Before creating characters, it's important to understand different types of game characters, how a game's genre and story will determine the kinds of characters you'll write, and how players will relate to them.

Types of Player-Characters

Unlike in a movie or novel, a game's protagonist doesn't simply exist—he or she must be inhabited by the player. The most important characters in games are the player-characters. They are the representation of the player in the world. Players will see the world through the eyes of player-characters, experiencing challenges, obstacles, and adventures. In short, they are the main characters of the story because they are the players. Generally, there are four different types of player-characters: the **cipher**, the **fixed character**, the **customizable character**, and the **fixed background, customizable character**. How much of a mark the player makes on the character is the number one question for designing your protagonist.

Cipher

Ciphers have no discernible personality and are "blank slates." They're windows into the world for players to feel as if they're playing themselves. For this reason, ciphers aren't given their own desires or sense of agency (the character's ability to make decisions and act out her or his desires and motives). Unlike completely customizable characters, ciphers usually have a name and appearance which makes them part of their world, implying a backstory the players can fill in with their own imaginations.

Famous example: The *Half Life* franchise's Gordon Freeman is a name attached to a vessel through which players play themselves. Freeman is partly a defined character because his occupation and look are known. However, he is in large part undefined. Players know very little about his background and motivations. Thus, players bring him to life by filling in those gaps with their own imaginations.

The Fixed Character

From a writing perspective, the fixed character is the easiest, but it's also the most work-intensive when it comes to character design. Fixed characters are defined by the development team, and players have no (or very few) options to change them. The clear benefit is that, as a narrative designer, you have full control over all decisions regarding these characters: the way they behave in certain situations and how their personalities develop. Their personalities, backstories, and abilities are fixed, and players only control their moment-to-moment actions. On the other hand, for this character type, you have to convince your players to get into specific roles and identify with these characters and their choices. All the power you have with fixed characters means you have to define them well—there will be no other way for players to fill in the blanks.

Famous examples: Edward Kenway (*Assassin's Creed IV: Black Flag*), Mario (*Super Mario Bros.*), Sonic (*Sonic the Hedgehog*), Link (*The Legend of Zelda*), and many more. Nearly all games based on existing intellectual properties (movies, comics, etc.) with existing characters will use this type. Nancy Drew, Indiana Jones, Harry Potter, and Batman cannot be changed by a player's decisions. These are characters with detailed histories and stories that already exist in popular culture (and in copyrighted material!).

The Customizable Character

At the other end of the spectrum is the customizable character. Here the developer knows barely anything about these characters, as players build and define the character during a character-creation process. In games with this type of player-character, players determine their character's stats, gender, and race, as in a tabletop RPG. As a writer, you may still have some influence on the choices you give players; ultimately, however, you don't have any control over the story's protagonist. Customizable characters give players a lot of freedom, but they also require a solid world and very well-developed NPCs to give players material to define who they are. Giving them the choice to design their characters and then forcing players into a certain behavior pattern is normally a very bad call. For example, if players want to use stealth and nonlethal means of progressing through missions, you don't want to put them in situations where they have to kill enemies. Forcing players into these behavior patterns makes it extremely hard for your players to identify with their characters.

Customizable characters are often used in MMOs, sims, and RPGs like *World of Warcraft*, the *Animal Crossing* franchise, and the *Fallout* franchise. The gameplay is designed in such a way that players explore the world and who they are. Everywhere in the game, they have chances to make choices that matter and feel natural for their characters.

Fixed Background, Customizable Characters

Finally, this last type is a mixture between the fixed character and the customizable character. Some RPGs provide a character with a name and loosely defined background but otherwise allow the player free reign. Characters who have some fixed features and some player-defined features allow writers the freedom to define some content in order to help develop the story around the player-character. However, this is at the expense of allowing the player total freedom to define who player-characters are. It's hard to say how much content you should define and how much you should leave open. This depends highly on each story and game.

Some factors you can keep in mind: Does the story depend on a strong protagonist? Does the story depend on the character having a certain background, development, culture, etc.? And do the other characters in the story require the player-character to behave a certain way towards them? The stronger the dependency is, the more you need to design, because you have less freedom to give your players.

In general, it is a good idea to define as little as necessary to bring your story to life and make it an engaging and immersive experience. If this means players can only alter their character's appearance, that's fine. If it means your players can choose between different backgrounds, and later this choice will be reflected in the game—great.

Here is a short example:

> Character John is the protagonist of your murder-mystery story. The player should be able to define John, but as part of the story, John must have a friend who is part of an underworld organization. When John finds out, the friend turns against him, but ultimately can't bring himself to kill John. When the friend is later murdered for the mercy he showed, John is motivated to avenge him.

John is a typical fixed-background, customizable character, in which the player has the freedom to design his look and some of his background. However, the story requires some elements to be predefined. Therefore, while they have different appearances, every John ever created by players will have a friend who is part of the underworld organization.

Famous examples: Commander Shepard and the player-character from *Dragon Age: Origins*. In both examples, the characters have a defined background, and the stories give motivations for their actions. However, players can define the protagonists' looks and the future of these characters by making choices during gameplay. Each player's Commander Shepard is in a way unique—based on the same background but with an individual look and individual experiences.

Writing Interesting NPCs

Writing NPCs that fulfill the purpose required of them in the game is just as important as setting up a proper player-character. As is the case with creating player-characters, narrative designers must keep in mind their game's genre and what will be required of the NPC throughout the game in order to maintain consistency and/or solid character-centric story arcs.

NPCs can be introduced purely as tools to reflect the player-character, and with no other purpose beyond that. Keep in mind that while this is often used in games, it can also result in a lack of engagement on the part of the players.

When opportunity allows, you will want your NPCs to be something more. That is when your NPCs become full-fledged characters with lives of their own, as opposed to them being used only as tools for the main character to progress through the game, without any agency or interests to flesh them out. The work that will be put into creating such NPCs increases accordingly and should be something that the entire team has committed to in terms of project scope.

Bringing Player-Characters and NPCs to Life

When you're ready to design characters, you'll need to provide the team with important information in character profiles. (Please see the character-design sample at the end of the chapter.) As the narrative designer, you need to explain characters' personalities, motivations, histories, affiliations, relationships to other characters, and appearances (including details like race and ethnicity, height, weight, age, hair color, eye color, etc., and providing artist references). This information helps team members get a sense of who characters are and how their personalities and outlooks affect their body language, the way they move, and even what they might wear.

Many departments will be essential in bringing both player-characters and NPCs to life:

- **Narrative design and writing**: Provide the character profile and the psychology of the character.
- **Concept art**: Provides the visuals for the character and works with narrative in order to establish visual signifiers that will stand out and be particular to the character.
- **Character modeling**: Creates the model for the character, taking cues from concept art and narrative.
- **Animation**: Creates tailored animations, sometimes specific to that character, which can be a reflection of character psychology.
- **Cinematics**: Uses the work of all these departments to bring the story to life, using those characters while placing them in the appropriate setting.

As a narrative designer, you will be called to work in concert with all of these departments, from the beginning of character concept, all the way to the creation of the scenes and locations. The better you communicate with them, the more attention will be brought to the character design, which will allow for a visual representation consistent with the narrative intent.

Note that it is just as important to make yourself available to these other fields of expertise as it is to acknowledge that they are the experts in their own domain. You work with your colleagues on bringing your character to life, but each department will have input that is particular to its field. Knowing to adjust to technical or budget constraints is always a must.

THE HR MANAGER

Name: Ms. Melendez

Title: HR manager at Fat Chicken Meat Company™

Age: Early 50s

Ethnicity/Race: Latina

Complexion: Medium to dark

Height: 5 ft 4 in

Weight: 140 lb

Eyes: Brown

Hair: Black, thick, chin length to shoulder length, "corporate"

Personality and Demeanor: Ms. Melendez is no-nonsense and type A. She remains unfazed by the good times and the rough times. She's unmoved by tears, whining, and/or excuses. Dedicated and loyal, Ms. Melendez gives both her underlings and her bosses the news they need to hear without puffing them up or patting them on the head. If she cracks a smile, the Apocalypse might be upon us. The only way to tell her mood is to pay attention to the amount of arch in her eyebrows.

Appearance: She wears a company shirt with the Fat Chicken logo, a gold chain necklace, and belted business slacks.

Motto: "That's the Fat Chicken way!"

Bio: Ms. Melendez has been in Fat Chicken's head HR offices for over thirty years. In that time, she's become well acquainted with Fat Chicken's procedures and advancements in factory farming. She developed Fat Chicken's training manual and relishes working with new employees to indoctrinate them in The Fat Chicken Way™. She is fluent in corporate speak.

Emotional States: Amused, annoyed, pleased, proud.

THE PROTESTER

Name: Barry "Gravy" Graveson

Title: Chief Guy, Motivator Guru, and PR Dude of Watchful Well-Being Watch

Age: Late 20s, early 30s

Ethnicity/Race: Caucasian

Complexion: Fair

Height: 5 ft 10 in

Weight: 220 lb

Eyes: Green

Hair: Light brown, long dreads with dread accessories (beads and rings)

Personality and Demeanor: Gravy has a laidback fire in his belly. He's a talkative guy and aims to be persuasive. He never tries to *push* anybody to believe what he does. Nope. If he's not a nice guy, who would want to follow a jerk? Gravy always tries to come across as supportive, to both his fellow protesters and the individuals he's trying to bring to his side. He can be ruthless, though— *non-aggressively ruthless*, of course—when it supports his cause. Gravy can be an emotional guy. He can get flustered, and he doesn't mind sharing his joy.

Appearance: He carries a "Watch the food, dude!" sign with him to protests. He wears colorful and big, breezy shirts (protesting is sweaty work) and comfortable jeans. He wears a disguise when he needs to.

Motto: "Watch the food, dude!"

Bio: Fed up with the USDA, the FDA, and the growing health and environmental concerns caused by factory farms, Gravy started the Watchful Well-Being Watch (he's still working on the name). WWW seeks to educate consumers by organizing protests and end factory-farming practices through targeted drone strikes. Gravy's always looking for sympathetic employees to help sabotage factory farms from the inside.

Emotional States: Flustered, happy, joyful, pensive.

Artist renderings of *Fat Chicken's* characters based on bios and physical descriptions.
© Relevant Games LLC.

Supporting the Player's Ego

While characters might have complex personalities, unique looks, and intriguing story arcs, they won't be successful as player-characters or NPCs if they don't keep players invested in the world and story. Since the player is the protagonist, writers must surround that protagonist with characters who enhance the player's self-worth, rather than deflate it. These characters must keep the player involved and feeling important, but not *overly* important so that the world no longer seems believable.

For the villain and supporting cast, the biggest consideration that affects games, but not other fiction, is the player's ego. Game characters have the power to emotionally involve players in ways no other medium can. While watching Batman in a movie, you may feel empathy for him and suffer when he suffers. However, you may not feel personally insulted that it happened. When Catwoman shows him up, you may not be so angry that you leave the theater. But *playing* as Batman, you're responsible for his successes and failures. If the Joker gets the better of Batman, it means he's gotten the better of *you*.

Players can have a range of emotions due to their experiences with other characters, from fist-pumping joy to quitting the game in a rage. Writing characters that can support players' egos while entertaining and still challenging them creates some unique problems. These are some questions narrative designers should ask themselves:

- How do you make your end villain threatening enough that the player is motivated to defeat him/her, while allowing the player constant victories against the forces of that same villain throughout the plot?
- How do you characterize a villain when the player can't meet him/her face-to-face without expecting to win the final showdown then and there?
- Is it ever acceptable to use the old "Haha, I'm only a hologram" or "I disappear in a cloud of smoke" trick in order to build up the conflict with the protagonist, even though players hate it?
- How do you sow dramatic suspicion and mistrust between a player and the supporting cast when players expect the right and ability to kill any character any time they dislike them?
- How do you make players care for characters? In a movie, when the audience sees Batman's parents getting killed, they all understand why he's motivated to avenge them because they're somewhat familiar with Batman's history. But in a game, seeing their "parents" die may not be impactful, especially if they've only just met those characters.
- How much sucking up is too much? Is there a limit to the amount of "Oh, thank you, great hero" and "You're the most important person in the galaxy" that players want to hear, or is that number infinite? (Hint: It is.)

Writing Your Game Characters

The type of player-character will determine many of the writing challenges you face. Writing a fixed character like Batman is not far different than writing the same character in a film because you control every word he says. No one expects the chance to have their Batman side with the Joker and rule Gotham City as dictator. But in RPGs with a customizable character, players may want just that. Players get extremely possessive of "their" character, objecting to dialogue they feel is out of character, or to times when the plot pushes them into a particular attitude or a decision.

This can be tricky for developers since the protagonist is the first point of entry into a game. How do you make a character who believably grew up in a fantasy world, when that character can't say anything the player doesn't already know? Chapter 7, "Dialogue," will talk more about how to use dialogue to let players define their characters. In the meantime, there are two very important questions to answer before starting to write a game with a customizable protagonist: What does the protagonist know, and why is the protagonist so ignorant?

What does the protagonist know? Any time the character knows something players don't, it causes a disconnect, a sense that the character isn't really "theirs." For this reason, if it's crucial that the protagonist already knows, say, that Elven necromancers live on the blood of freshly killed hummingbirds, you have a window of maybe forty-five minutes at the beginning of the game in which they must announce that information. If you wait until the player feels bonded with the player-character, you've lost your chance for the player-character to know any world-specific information.

Why is the protagonist so ignorant? Conversely, if you're playing someone who's grown up in the world of the game, it can be just as jarring if they constantly ask things like "What religion am I?" and "Tell me about my own race." There are a few different ways to address this: giving the protagonist amnesia, making her or him an outsider, or carefully writing the ignorant protagonist:

- **The protagonist has amnesia**. This overused technique is the most popular because it answers all questions with a single stroke. The character doesn't have any background or history, so players are free to make their own. While this trope is often met with eye rolls, it rarely seems to actually stop people from playing. This strategy generally works best if the player-character's background and reason for amnesia are important, and uncovering them is a major part of the story.
- **The protagonist is an outsider**. This is almost as quick a fix as amnesia if you go far enough. The modern-day American teleported through time or space literally allows the player to start from square one, sharing all (presumed) values and experiences with the player and none with the other characters in the world. All questions are

Motivation

In noninteractive media, the protagonist's motivation, otherwise known as "what the character wants," is what drives the story forward. Most of the time, good stories provide the protagonist with both an external and an internal want. Harry Potter externally wants to defeat Voldemort, but his internal motivation is to preserve the family he has found among wizards. "Harry Potter: The Story of a Boy With No Friends Who Defeats an Evil Wizard" would not have become nearly the phenomenon it did. Ideally, as in this example, both the protagonist's external and internal wants are resolved (satisfactorily or tragically) in the climax of the story.

For game characters, where the player controls the protagonist, this often means the story provides only an external motivation ("defeat the enemy"). However, in cases where a character has at least some defined backstory, it can be worthwhile to

fair game, as is a comfortably casual dialogue style. If going less outside than that—like a character from a different nation in a fantasy world—writers get less leeway. The player-character can still ask a lot of basic questions, but the writer must consider what someone from that nation of origin would know about the land they're in, as well as what their own customs are.

- **The writer is really careful**. This is obviously the hardest because there's no trick to it. But it is possible to get basic information across to players, despite their characters already knowing it, by having players ask questions about recent changes in the world. The NPC can then answer by explaining through implication both the change and how things used to be. For example, if the player needs to learn what the religion is in your fantasy world, and your game opens with a battle scene, you can try something like the following:

Player: How has this war affected the priesthood?
NPC: Well, you know the temple officially supports the rightful king, but there's a schism among the priests. Some still think the king is descended from the gods. But others despise him because he won't make human sacrifices. You'll find them on both sides of the battle.

This exchange tells the player that there are multiple gods, a priesthood, a divine king, and human sacrifice, all while plausibly being something that one person living in this world might tell another.

As you are working on the game's story, keep in mind the relationship players will have with the player-character (an extension of themselves) and the NPCs they will encounter. How much control will players want to have, and how much control will they *actually* have? What interactions might make the NPCs (and the world, by extension) less believable, pulling players out of the experience? As the narrative designer, identify these particular challenges and plan out ways to keep players engaged in the world.

Characterization and Character Development

Whether working on defined player-characters, semi-defined player-characters, or NPCs of any kind, it's crucial for narrative designers to consider how to flesh them out so they're real and interesting people. Contradicting traits and abilities are very powerful tools to create compelling characters. This tool will help create better characters and, ultimately, better, more vivid worlds and enthralling stories.

When you look at others around you, when you look at yourself, you can recognize conflicts every minute of your life. Everyone is far from being perfect and struggles with weaknesses, whereas they succeed with certain strengths. Everyone has them, hates them, or loves them, but this battle is part of what makes everyone unique human beings, unique characters. Understanding this is something that can help you create better characters.

This conflict—internal conflict—serves as inspiration for a method called "Merits and Flaws." (This terminology is inspired by the system of Merits and Flaws in White Wolf's influential tabletop gaming Storyteller System, which allows players to select helpful or harmful traits to flesh out their characters beyond bare statistics.)

Traits are identifying characteristics and habits. Abilities are the qualities of being able to perform something, whether physical, moral, intellectual, conventional, or legal. **Merits** are defined as benefits, as something which gives people superiority in a certain field. **Flaws** are weaknesses or undesirable characteristics. You may already see and feel the conflict between these two attributes. That's what you want for your characters too: conflict. You can take a step back, look at yourself, and see how you, and all human beings, work according to this very principle of inner conflict.

Back in 1962, Katharine Cook Briggs and her daughter, Isabel Briggs Myers, published a book on their research about psychological types, which had first been defined by Carl Gustav Jung in 1921. They define sixteen types and the so-called MBTI (Myers-Briggs Type Indicator). While the accuracy and value of these character types in real human beings has been the subject of fierce debate, they are still a valuable tool for writers and designers as they provide a detailed and effective shorthand for creating and defining characters. When looking closer at these types, you'll again find the principle of strengths and weaknesses, or merits and flaws. Within MBTI, a character has a specific type, not a collection of traits. This is caused by the presumption that people do prefer certain ways of thinking or acting but are still able to vary them. Even so, everyone can act in different ways. Every one of us does have a dominant function and an inferior one, according to the MBTI. This conflict will be a part of everyone their entire lives since it's so important to the human psychology.[1]

Another equally useful and even older theory is the four temperaments theory. This theory was first formalized by Hippocrates and, in essence, can be found in many modern theories. Even so, it is usually not named or referenced. The basic idea of this theory is that there are four temperaments: sanguine, choleric, melancholic, and phlegmatic. Everyone has a blend of two of these temperaments that best describes their personalities. Each of these temperaments defines a set of strengths and weaknesses in certain situations. For example, a sanguine is a highly extroverted person with a short attention span, while a melancholic person is more introverted and tends to plan out things. This theory, due to its nature, gives a good set of tools to define strengths and weaknesses for characters in a similar way as the MBTI does.[2]

consider adding an internal motivation as a counterpoint. In *Star Wars: Knights of the Old Republic*, the external motivation of "find the pieces of the Star Map" dovetails memorably with the internal motivation of "remember who I really am" in a way that makes the game's climax far more exciting and impactful than the external story alone.

To create great characters, enrich them with internal conflict. To achieve this, use merits and flaws that are applied to their traits and abilities. This battle isn't invented for the sake of storytelling; it is the battle within everyone.

Now here's a possible workflow which is useful for creating characters with internal conflict. This workflow was designed to be fast and simple because narrative designers usually don't have the time to write backstories or use the "Frankenstein Method"[3] on all of their characters. All characters should have at least some details, some conflict, even if they are just minor sidekicks. Characters are the meat of the story, so you should respect every little piece. Respecting them means respecting their stories. Only a story that is told with respect is a good one. So, look at the steps needed to nest conflict into your characters:

1   Before defining anything else about a specific character, define her/his purpose or function within the story. Functions can be "protagonist," "major sidekick," "friend," "villain," "minor sidekick," and so on.
2   Decide if you want to use traits or abilities as vehicles. You can mix them, but for a first iteration, choose one. Contrast one trait with another trait, and an ability with another ability. Mixing them at this stage would be confusing, like trying to blend oil and water into one uniform liquid. Say your character is "honest" (trait), and you contrast it with the ability "perfect killer." It would be better to say he is "honest" (trait) and "cold-blooded" (trait). Now, both attributes can be valued against each other. They both belong to the same super-set of definitions.
3   Define exactly one adjective for your character, an adjective like "trustworthy" or "cruel."
4   Now pick a type from the MBTI and/or a temperament blend from the four temperaments theory for your character. Assigning a specific type to a character can be really helpful in picking better-fitting traits or abilities. It can also overcome writer's block. Ensure that you can roughly explain the theory behind the type indicator you picked.
5   Now select a governing trait or governing ability, depending on the vehicle you have chosen. This is the trait or ability that drives your characters and makes them act the way they do. A governing trait or ability can be anything you can imagine. As stated before, it could be helpful to look at your type indicator to find a suitable one. Sample governing traits can be "obsessed with power," "cares for those less fortunate," or "worried what people think of her."
6   This is the last mandatory step but also the trickiest one. Pick a suitable conflicting trait or ability, something that is almost the complete opposite of your governing trait or ability. The stronger the conflict is at this stage, the better the internal conflict will

be for your story. Here are two samples for the abovementioned governing traits: "Little self-respect" or "vulnerable." You may notice the conflict already, and that's what you should feel when defining your characters as well. Imagine a villain who's cruel, obsessed with power, but also very self-conscious, and you'll see how this inner conflict makes him or her more interesting.

This is the complete, short workflow, but you can enrich your characters even more by picking secondary traits and abilities, other expressions of personality you may know, like love languages[4] and Type A and Type B,[5] or adding details from other characterization processes, such as the "Frankenstein Method." Hopefully, this workflow proves useful for you as you find your own ways to use and improve it.

Creating Diverse Characters

Building characters around their inner conflicts and personality traits is only one aspect of designing great characters. Players also appreciate experiencing characters that come from backgrounds or cultures that reflect their own (or that introduce them to *new* backgrounds and cultures), and they're becoming more vocal in saying they want more diverse character representations. So far, in games with non-customizable player-characters, the player-characters are predominantly heterosexual, white males. There's greater diversity among NPCs. But characters that are female, of color, gay, and/or transgender are sometimes problematic because they present hurtful stereotypes, they lack agency, and they aren't as complex. These portrayals of minority and disenfranchised groups are in *all* media, not just games. "Traditional" heroes, characters that are heterosexual and male, can be negatively stereotyped too. While this section focuses on designing more realistic and nuanced characters that are minorities, these techniques can be used to create *any* character. Diverse and well-written characters will not only give many players the characters they've desired, but they will also provide players chances to experience storylines and worlds from new perspectives.

Many creators—including those from minority and disenfranchised groups—have a fear of "doing it wrong" when it comes to designing or writing characters from backgrounds different than their own. What if these characters are hurtful? What if some find these character portrayals offensive, despite all of the work trying to guard against this? The fear of failure might be present, but writers can push past this. "Doing it wrong" is an excellent opportunity to learn from mistakes and get feedback. Plus, applying good character design and changing thinking about creating characters that are minorities will

Environmental Narrative as a Tool for Character Insight

Rather than resort to heavy-handed exposition to provide information on a character, an area or room can be tailored in such a way that players are allowed to explore and absorb who the character is. Adam Jensen's apartment is an example of the melding of narrative design and environmental design serving to highlight character history and psychology, which the player can explore in *Deus Ex: Human Revolution*. The setup in the apartment gives broad-stroke insights into Jensen's current mental state (bare essentials, hobbies, etc.), while the bathroom in particular provides specific detail as to Jensen's integration process, pertaining to his augmentations. He is conflicted, to say the least.

Near the beginning of the game, Jensen returns home after sustaining life-threatening injuries during an explosion. His employer saves him and "augments" his body with cybernetic modifications. The player enters Jensen's apartment, and there's a barely settled-in feeling, with boxes still strewn about the apartment, not yet unpacked. His personal effects, such as pictures and a baseball bat, also have not been unpacked, although the player can find a baseball on Jensen's desk. Get-well cards in the bedroom on the dresser speak to his near death and time recuperating. There are many drugs in the bathroom (and a box on the bedroom dresser), which one can assume are a consequence of Jensen's augmentation process. On his coffee table is an e-book on building water clocks and the parts to build one, suggesting a fascination with assembling parts, as Jensen has been reassembled. Items such as the repeated writing exercises and the punched, broken mirror (along with the note indicating it's not the first time it's been broken) are clear indications that Jensen has had to get used to his augments and

TABLE 4.1 Common Stereotypes

Characters	Stereotypes
Female	Beauty/appearance obsessed, seeking a man's affection, nurturing/supportive, less athletically gifted than men
Of Color	"Exotic," "bangas and hos," physical or intellectual prowess attributed to race, magical/spiritual
Gay	Flamboyant, effeminate, "bitchy," fashion/youth obsessed
Trans	Prostitutes, mentally unstable, victimized, simply cross-dressers/transvestites

make the process easier, less stressful, and as enjoyable as developing any character.

When these characters lack nuance, why have they failed? Table 4.1 lists characters that are minorities or disenfranchised and some common ways they're stereotyped.

It's often easy to see that characters with stereotypes can be badly designed and offensive. But here's the problem: Stereotypes can "slip under the radar." Exposure to these media representations is so prevalent that sometimes the very groups being stereotyped don't even realize it. (When you read "gang banger" or "terrorist," who immediately comes to mind?) And because there are some truths to stereotypes, you may not notice that a character is flat and without nuance. Here are some ways these stereotypes are applied:

Female

Characters may be defined by their femininity. Even with strong women, the focus can be on their sexuality. They may have "the most common super power,"[6] breasts that mesmerize men. Or they're masters of seduction, subtly or not so subtly relying upon their beauty and sexiness to accomplish their goals. On the opposite end of the spectrum, they might be "cute" or "girly," and this is their main personality trait. They might be in a relationship or seeking a relationship with male characters. In supporting roles, they might be secretly in love or have a crush on the player-character. If there's more than one female in a party or in a group of supporting characters, they're in competition for the male lead's attention and affection. Even a female villain may be secretly in love with the player-character or have some history with him where they were romantically linked.

Example: Before her redesign in *Tomb Raider* (2013), Lara Croft's "most common super power" has been a focus of her character, despite her prowess in archeology and success as an adventurer.

Of Color

Characters of color can have racialized roles, which are based on racial or ethnic stereotypes. Characters from the Middle East are brown terrorists. African Americans, Asians, or Latinos are "bangas and hos," gang bangers and prostitutes. They might be "exotic" because of their culture or beauty. A character that is a Black male may have imposing physical strength or serve as a tank. If characters are of East Asian descent, there's a strong possibility they've mastered a martial art, or they're nerdy, smart, and good with technology.

They tend to be in supporting roles where they're "magical"—their wisdom or spiritual outlook is based upon their culture, and they're present to be a guide on a white character's journey. As the "best friend" or "guru," they do everything to benefit the player-character, who is most likely white. In these instances, they don't have agency, and they don't act upon their own motives or desires. This makes them at the service of the story and other characters, not active participants in storylines with the ability to make choices and affect the plot.

Example: Playing the "magical" role in *Cognition: An Erica Reed Thriller*, Rose helps two white main characters discover and control their psychic abilities and serves as a sympathetic ear to a third. The game does introduce Rose's history in a storyline, but her presence in the game is to aid the white protagonist and main antagonist on their journeys.

Gay or Bisexual

Characters that are gay or bisexual can also be relegated to "best friend" status. They're supportive of the player-character, whether these player-characters are male or female. They're snarky or bitchy with witty one-liners and quick quips. They tend to be of thin builds. They dress in flamboyant, "girly" clothes in loud colors.

Like characters that are female, they might be secretly or not so secretly in love with the player-character. In a lot of media, a gay character that is spurned by a heterosexual male might suddenly become "psycho" and plot and act out revenge. This is also true of a lesbian who turns on a main character that is female. Or the character's unrequited love might be used to garner sympathy. While other characters and players know their endless support and friendship is based upon their romantic love, their friends remain oblivious.

Examples: Thomas in *Deadly Premonition* is effeminate and cross-dresses in secret. He has an unrequited love for George, one of the game's villains. George uses Thomas to help carry out his elaborate murders. By the end of the game, Thomas is insane, with little of his original personality remaining. Seiko in the *Corpse Party* franchise has an unrequited love for Naomi, who, based on the particular game, may or may not realize her best friend has romantic feelings for her.

hasn't had an easy—or happy—time of it.

All of these things are there to allow the player the choice to learn more about Jensen's life during the time between the explosion in the introduction and when the game resumes. They aren't forced, but neither are they so subtle that they are easy to miss.

The player-character's apartment is a picture of his recent circumstances (almost being killed, which led to his augmentation), his current circumstances (still trying to get used to his new body), his current state of mind (his inability to get unpacked and "settled in"), and his inner turmoil (anger over being so radically altered).

More ways environmental narrative can be used to communicate information to players about the world, story, and characters will be explored in Chapter 6, "Implementation and Production."

Trans

Depictions of characters that are trans may portray them as simply "men in dresses" without recognizing the complexity of their identities. (Characters that are trans women also outnumber characters that are trans men.) She might be "fooling" a man, and there's a grand "reveal" that she's a "dude in a dress," if other characters don't know she's trans. Trans characters may be made the butt of jokes because of their appearance. Their treatment may be used to make them more sympathetic. Like characters that are gay, they may have an unrequited love. If spurned, they turn "psycho." Or they may simply be "psycho" to begin with. This is connected with the transphobic belief that they're somehow delinquent or mentally unstable.

Example: *Grand Theft Auto V*'s characters who are trans women are used as jokes. They're prostitutes with hypermasculine appearances, even though they're dressed as women and wearing makeup. Michael, a main character, says that they "[a]lmost fooled me."

Characterizations Based on Wholes, Not Parts

Characterizations lack nuance when they are based solely upon a stereotype or archetype. (This is absolutely true of characters that are white, male, and heterosexual as well.) This isn't usually done with malice. There's a need for authenticity, but the focus is on the characters' gender, sexual orientation, or race and ethnicity. Their personalities, and maybe even their physical appearances, are based upon these. But personalities are never based solely upon race and ethnicity, sexual orientation, or gender. These may inform someone's personality and identity, but they aren't the *only* factors. As narrative designers, your character design can't end with assigning characters' race, gender, or sexual orientation. They must be three-dimensional human beings whose gender, race, and sexuality are just part of the overall picture.

To create more well-rounded characters, don't put a label on them. In other words, it's not a "female character," but a "character that is female." The character isn't a "Vietnamese character," but a "character that is Vietnamese." If you focus on one aspect of the character, you can start looking at generalizations. An inquiry such as "What are Vietnamese people like?" might lead you to stereotypes about the Vietnamese. Focus on characterization first, and not sexual orientation, gender, or race and ethnicity. In this way, the characterization becomes the template to build upon, not one part of the character's makeup or identity.

Also, research how media portrays and stereotypes minorities and disenfranchised groups. You'll get a sense of how they've been portrayed throughout history and discover the origins of stereotypes.

It's easier to avoid or subvert stereotypes when you can recognize them and understand why groups find them offensive.

Well-Rounded and Diverse Characters

People's identities and personalities are complex. They're informed by personal experiences, cultural backgrounds, and talents, among many other things. Sexual orientation, gender identity, and race and ethnicity are only some of these determining factors. When you contemplate what makes you, you'll start mentally listing many things that have shaped who you are. When designing characters, think about what makes them who they are and all the possible experiences that have gotten them from their past to their present. Players may never know all of these details, but they will help you consider the following:

- How characters view the world and themselves.
- What their motivations and desires are.
- How they fulfill these motivations and desires.
- How characters carry themselves (attitudes and demeanors).
- How they talk.
- What their interests are.
- How they dress.
- And many other specific details . . .

When you're creating characters, no matter their sexual orientation, gender, or race and ethnicity, here are a few things to keep in mind:

- Spiritual beliefs.
- Gender identity.
- Social status.
- Philosophical leanings.
- Political leanings.
- Relationships with parents.
- Relationships with siblings.
- Relationships with other family members.
- Work experience.
- Experiences in childhood.
- Education, etc.

This list isn't exhaustive, but it will help you design complex inner conflicts for your characters. It's also a good starting place for identifying what's important to them and how this shapes their desires and goals. What will they fight for? What *won't* they fight for? Have their political leanings informed what they believe is worth dying for, even if that means risking their lives for an antagonist? These are the types of questions that will help characters grow beyond simple labels.

Tropes: When to Use Them— Stereotypes: How to Avoid Them

You can also use labels to your advantage. While labeling a character with a stereotype leads to flat, uninteresting, and potentially offensive characters, labeling a character with a trope is a good way to introduce him or her to players.

The difference between tropes and stereotypes is important:

> **Trope**: A known concept which is usually popular enough or such a deep part of cultural knowledge that you can expect your audience to know it.
>
> **Stereotype**: A cliché using a single concept to provide superficial character development—and nothing more.

This difference between a trope and a stereotype is in how you use it. Tropes are easily used, narrative-shorthand elements which are part of the culture, or of the knowledge base of the intended audience for the game. They can be used to introduce a character and set expectations that the player can quickly and easily recognize and react to. Tropes can—and, in fact, should—be used, while keeping in mind that tropes become stereotypes when that is *all* the character is about. The ever-popular space marine in games is disciplined and an excellent fighter. This trope is based upon real-life marines. However, disciplined, killing-machine space marines become stereotypical when all the characters express are toughness, discipline, and lethal fighting skills. They don't reveal their inner worlds, desires, motivations, or any sense that there's a realistic personality behind the soldiers aiming those humongous laser rifles.

A basic truth is that, depending on the game you are making, sometimes a stereotype may be all that you need or have time to introduce. Ideally, you'll have the leeway to create characters with depth. Either way, working within the framework of the type of game you're making and the focus (or lack thereof) being devoted to the character development and narrative will determine how, and if, you make use of tropes or stereotypes, or avoid both in order to simply present a complex, multilayered character. Keep in mind that even if you are resorting to stereotypes or tropes that aren't explored all that much, you can still make it fun if you do it right.

It is infinitely more rewarding for both writer and player to use a trope merely in order to speed up the introduction of a multilayered character with emotional depth, rather than letting the character remain a one-note stereotype. Subverting a trope can be a fun process when not abused.

Subverting Tropes

When you introduce a character using a common trope as shorthand, and then turn it on its head to introduce a different—and unexpected—

arc in that character's development or a plot twist for the story, it's called "subverting" the trope.

Keep in mind that while subverting a trope is a good shorthand for character introduction, it shouldn't be misused—or used gratuitously. If you have the space and time to introduce a character properly, then the focus should be on that, rather than risk turning your trope subversion into a gimmick, particularly when overused.

You'll still need to understand why some tropes are negative when you subvert them. Again, researching media portrayals of certain groups and understanding the *history* of those portrayals will give you insight into why particular tropes, archetypes, and stereotypes are deemed problematic or even traumatic. But it will also give you insight into how to subvert them and challenge views on particular groups, whether those views are widely accepted and "under the radar" or only accepted by a few.

The Walking Dead's Lee Everett is a character that challenges portrayals of African American men in media. He begins the game in the back of a cop car, immediately labeling him as a Black man in trouble with the law. However, since Lee is the player-character, it's not long before players must save him from danger, getting them to care about him. Players discover that Lee is a history professor, a profession most characters don't have, whether they're African American or not. His physicality isn't stereotyped; he's of average build. As players decide what choices Lee will make, they empathize with his willingness to do anything to survive. Most importantly, Lee develops a father–daughter bond with Clementine. She's not his biological child, but he dedicates his life to her survival. After his introduction as a criminal, Lee develops into a fully realized character with very specific desires, motivations, and goals that players of all backgrounds can appreciate. Some players so empathize with him that they can try to protect Lee when his criminal past is brought up.

There are two keys to subversion: There must be a strong understanding of the subverted trope, and the characters must be believable. As is the case with all well-written characters, players need insights into their inner worlds, what's important to them, and why they choose to respond to external conflicts the way they do.

Working with Diversity Consultants and Sensitivity Readers

Even if you're careful to avoid stereotypes, your characters may still come across as inauthentic in some ways. Over the past few years, games have featured greater representation, including more player-characters from marginalized groups and cultural representations of these groups in stories and worlds. If you're tasked with writing characters from backgrounds outside of your experience, consider hiring diversity consultants or sensitivity readers. (Even writers who belong to a marginalized group will need feedback on characters of different backgrounds they don't belong to!) The diversity consultant is from a similar background as the marginalized group(s) in the game. Diversity consultants will point out problematic and inauthentic representations and give feedback to help you write more believable characters.

Working with diversity consultants is becoming a more common (and much-needed) industry practice. Notably, DONTNOD's *Tell Me Why* featured a trans man as a protagonist, a couple of queer secondary characters, Indigenous characters, and depictions of Tlingit culture. GLAAD (Gay and Lesbian Alliance Against Defamation) and Huna Heritage Foundation consulted on the project.[78]

(If you're responsible for hiring team members, consider hiring writers and narrative designers from the marginalized groups represented in your game. Also, a lot of diversity consultants are gifted storytellers in their own right, and developers can overlook the fact that these individuals can be contributing on projects as writers or narrative designers.)

Conclusion

As narrative designers, you have both traditional character-creation techniques and the uniqueness of the player's interaction with both the game's player-character/protagonist and NPCs to design compelling characters. Because players will experience the game through the player-character, this gives you an opportunity to make players feel more a part of the world, the story, and the choices they may have to make. This is true for any type of player-character, whether it's fixed, customizable, customizable with a fixed background, or a cipher. Keep in mind that your NPCs should be well developed too. Inhabit your world with characters who are from diverse backgrounds and who have clearly expressed personalities, desires, and motivations. This will give players new experiences through enjoyable perspectives.

Interview with Rhianna Pratchett (Freelance Writer)

What Would You Say Is the Biggest Challenge When Working with an Existing IP?

The biggest challenge is the fact that you'll be working for a license holder who will usually have very specific views on how the IP is dealt with. This can be a lot more than just the storyline for the game, but also how the characters are portrayed, right down to how they speak and dress. There are already a lot of barriers and restrictions imposed on writing for games, merely by the nature of the medium, but working on an existing IP often increases them.

How Did You Approach Your Research for Lara Croft?

I spent a long time talking to Crystal Dynamics about their vision for the project and how they wanted to portray Lara's character and state of mind. I definitely had my own ideas about wanting to tone down the previous rich-girl/trust-fund babe angle, and make her a little more self-reliant, independent, and vulnerable. Thankfully, these ideas gelled with where Crystal wanted to go with the character. I also drew a lot upon some of my female friendships when helping craft Lara's interactions with her best friend Sam. Basically, I focused on creating a human being whom I hoped would resonate with other human beings.

What Was the Biggest Challenge?

As with many games, the biggest challenge was to try to get the narrative and gameplay to align and support each other, rather than be at odds. That can be a particularly difficult thing to balance because you're trying to juggle the needs of the story and characters with the needs of the gameplay and the needs of the player to have a fun experience. It certainly helped to keep the player without a weapon for the first section of the game, which increased the sense of vulnerability and fear that the character was feeling. After that, we let Lara have a bow (since she studied archery at school and university), and it was quite a while before she actually got a gun for the first time.

What Is Your Favorite Part When Working with Existing IPs?

It's finding a little bit of space to do something surprising or unusual with a character or world that maybe players haven't seen before. With *Tomb Raider* it was showing the more human and vulnerable side of Lara, and allowing her to do things like show fear or react realistically to loss and emotional pain. That's fairly common in other entertainment forms, but not quite so much in games.

What Advice Would You Give to Novice Narrative Designers?

Hone your writing skills, play lots of games (and look at the different ways narrative is being used), and network at industry conferences and events. Try to design a few small games using things like RPG Maker, Unity, or Twine, and gradually build up your skills. There are also some great books out there on narrative in games, and useful resources like the IGDA Game Writing SIG (www.igda.org/writing or www.gamewriting. org), which is populated by games writers from all across the industry.

Notes

1 A good starting point to learn about MBTI is the *Wikipedia* entry, accessed May 12, 2014, http://en.wikipedia.org/wiki/Myers-Briggs_Type_Indicator.

2 For more on a four-temperaments primer, see the *Wikipedia* entry, accessed May 12, 2014, http://en.wikipedia.org/wiki/Four_temperaments. A good book on this specific theory is Tim LaHaye, *Why You Act the Way You Do* (Carol Stream, IL: Tyndale House Publishers, 1998).

3 Frankenstein Method: An informal process writers use, taking elements from the lives of people they're acquainted with to create a character, as Mary Shelley's Dr. Frankenstein made his monster from pieces of individuals he sewed together.

4 A good source for the topic of love languages is Gary Chapman's book, *The Five Love Languages: How to Express Heartfelt Commitment to Your Mate.*

5 Type A and Type B contrast the "workaholic" with the laidback creative. See "Type A and Type B Personality Theory," *Wikipedia*, accessed May 12, 2014, http://en.wikipedia.org/wiki/Type_A_and_Type_B_personality_theory.

6 "Most Common Super Power," *TV Tropes*, accessed February 9, 2014, http://tvtropes.org/pmwiki/pmwiki.php/Main/MostCommonSuperPower.

7 Aimee Hart, "Tell Me Why, Tyler Ronan and DONTNOD's Strides Towards Complexity and Authenticity in Their Characters," *Gayming*, January 31, 2020, https://gaymingmag.com/2020/01/tell-me-why-tyler-ronan-and-dontnods-strides-towards-complexity-and-authenticity-in-their-characters/.

8 "Bringing Delos Crossing to Life Through Tlingit Design," *Tell Me Why Game*, accessed July 31, 2022, www.tellmewhygame.com/bringing-delos-crossing-to-life-through-tlingit-design/.

Exercise

Exercise 4.1

Use the following character-design template and sample character bio to help create three major characters from your hypothetical game. The information will be used by game designers, game writers, character artists, and animators.

Character-Design Template

Name:

Gender:

Age:

Height/Build:

Race/Ethnicity:

Complexion/Skin Color:

Hair/Hairstyle:

Eye Color:

Real-Life or Fictional Inspiration:

Appearance (how personality is expressed through appearance, demeanor, posture, clothes):

Personality:

Governing Trait:

Conflicting Trait:

Secondary Traits:

Breaking Point:

Extroverted or Introverted:

Strongest Dream:

Strongest Fear:

What Makes Them Laugh:

What Makes Them Cry:

Dark Secret:

Religious/Spiritual Beliefs:

Attitude toward Government:

Attitude toward Law:

Attitude toward Cultural Norms:

Belongs to Subculture(s):

Education:

Economic Status:

Current Job/Career:

Love Life:

Family:

Behavior toward Strangers:

Favorite Food:

Favorite Drink:

Favorite Clothing:

Bio (background/history, defining moments/experiences that have shaped who they are, current status):

Story/Plot Involvement:

Character Development:

Character Growth:

Relationships with Other Characters:

If characters are customizable, like players choosing their physical characteristics, personality traits, and/or backgrounds, you can indicate this in the bio, for example:

Name: Casey (default)
Gender: Determinant

"Default" and "determinant" signal that players can choose their character's name and gender. Studios may use other terminology like "varies," "player determinant," or "player choice." If there are several backgrounds, personalities, or other characteristics for the player to choose, list these in the bio and clearly describe each.

Samples

Sample 4.1

The following is a highly detailed bio using all of the Character-Design Template. Your game's bios may not need this much information.

Name: Ada Méndez Ochoa

Gender: Female

Age: 37

Height/Build: 5 ft 1 in; slight and fine boned

Race/Ethnicity: Colombian (Amerindian and European descent)

Complexion/Skin Color: Medium gold

Hair/Hairstyle: Brown; near shoulder length and feathered

Eye Color: Light brown

Real-Life or Fictional Inspiration: N/A

Appearance: Ada wears unassuming clothes in muted colors. She wears simple shirts and jeans to remain in the background and keep from drawing attention to herself. The only part of her attire that stands out is a glass pendant she made. It's in the shape and color of a red blood cell.

In public, Ada makes sure to blend in at all times. She's never too friendly, never too assertive, or never too mean—she doesn't engage in behavior that will get her remembered. To be "normal" is to be invisible.

Among her colleagues and the few friends she has, she exudes a quiet, yet intimidating, presence. This makes her appear much taller. She's kind, but she doesn't let anyone take advantage of her. People are often taken aback by how direct she is when she gives advice . . . or a warning.

Personality: She's laid-back, but she can be assertive. Ada is keenly observant. She's happy to fade into the background and not be the center of attention; this lets her observe without distractions.

Governing Trait: Great empathy

Conflicting Trait: Calculating

Secondary Traits: Loyal, patient

Breaking Point: Ada might act against all of her ethics and morals if she's betrayed again. There are few people she can trust; she knows her loved ones might be harmed if people understand who she really is. She'll do anything to stop those who might try to put her loved ones in jeopardy before they can do so.

Extroverted or Introverted: Introverted, but has an ease in conversing with people

Strongest Dream: Creating a sculpture that encapsulates the beauty of all the patterns she's ever witnessed

Strongest Fear: To be exposed

What Makes Her Laugh: Small furry rodents

What Makes Her Cry: Not being able to get involved in situations she knows will lead to severe consequences; involvement could mean exposing her work

Dark Secret: Sometimes enjoys living vicariously through others' negative emotions/experiences

Religious/Spiritual Beliefs: Grew up Roman Catholic but finds organized Christianity drained of spirituality

Attitude toward Government: Finds it a flawed institution created by flawed individuals; more often than not, it fails those who need it most. But she pretends to respect governmental institutions.

Attitude toward Law: Finds the law necessary to keep people in line. She knows how destructive people would be if they didn't fear it.

Attitude toward Cultural Norms: Resents how she would be treated should anyone find out about her ability, but following cultural norms keeps her "invisible"

Belongs to Subculture(s): N/A

Affiliations: Cage Crimson

Education: Master of Fine Arts in Studio Arts

Economic Status: Middle class

Current Job/Career: Tracker

Love Life: Has no time for relationships, and her work may endanger potential partners

Family: Both parents live in Aracataca, Colombia; her brother lives in Cincinnati, OH. She hasn't seen them in over ten years.

Behavior toward Strangers: Always friendly because she never knows when she can use this to her advantage

Favorite Food: Mussels in spicy red sauce

Favorite Drink: Guava bubble tea

Favorite Clothing: A steel blue slouchy tank top

Bio: Ada Méndez Ochoa was born in Aracataca, Colombia, in 1986. She's the older of two children; her brother Aurelio is three years younger. Her mother, Gloria, is a teacher, and her father, Ernesto, an accountant. Ada takes after both parents. Seeing the positive influence Gloria had on children in her neighborhood gave Ada a desire to teach. Ernesto spent many hours working in his office in solitude. Ada can't recall a time when a situation seemed to shake him. She is convinced the time Ernesto spent alone, away from everyone's problems and conflicts, helped him to stay centered.

Ada discovered her unique tracking ability at the age of 7. She was awakened by a crash near her brother's room. While she snuck towards his room, she stepped in the glass he'd dropped. She turned on the light to find her own bloody footprints. She wasn't shocked to find she'd been cut. She was amazed by the patterns of the footprints that emerged from the blood. Since then, she's recognized prints everywhere—fingerprints, footprints, handprints, tongue prints. Ada remembers the swirls, the bumps, the grooves, and can find anyone by tracking their unique patterns.

She started recording her memories of patterns in drawings but never explained their inspirations to anyone. Her parents encouraged her artistic side, and she excelled in painting and glass sculpture. For graduate school, Ada attended the University of Iowa on a scholarship. She met David Macmillan, the other half of Cage Crimson, during her second year. She was leaving a diner when a tongue print on a spoon fascinated her. She walked by the table to get a better glimpse of it before stepping outside. David followed her and asked if she saw something someone left behind on the table—something very few could see. Before Ada could question him, David told her he could see auras. She finally knew someone who could view the world as she did; he became her closest friend. Ada ended her college years taking a job as a high school art teacher.

Ada and David started Cage Crimson in 2013, and Ada left her teaching job behind. David informed her of two young children who had disappeared. The police had given up, and their parents had hired David to find them. After Ada helped him find the kidnapped children abandoned and near death in the Mojave Desert, she knew it would be selfish if she didn't use her ability to save and protect the defenseless. But her jobs with David have introduced her to danger she couldn't have foreseen. Sometimes she has to earn the trust of devious people, getting them to share their secrets. Once they've learned of her manipulations, some have threatened her family.

Ada now lives in the background as much as she can. Staying "invisible," she moves from city to city, from job to job. She stays out of touch with her family to protect them. David remains her closest friend and the person she trusts more than anyone.

Story/Plot Involvement: As the player-character, Ada is the protagonist and involved in the major storyline and all side missions.

Character Development: A keen observer, Ada trusts what she sees. She's confident in her ability to interpret human behaviors because she understands people's motives and the emotions driving them. However, when she's blindsided by David's betrayal, she'll be faced with her own weaknesses. She'll be left confused as to why she didn't see what he was planning or why she couldn't stop him. She had needed to trust David because he's the only person who understood her. At the same time, he's the only person Ada has ever given the *chance* to understand her. In pursuit of David, Ada will learn to overcome her fear of being exposed as she opens up to and depends upon other characters.

Relationships with Other Characters:

David: David has been Ada's most intimate friend. He encouraged her to use her abilities as a tracker and founded Cage Crimson with her. When he betrays her, she can't understand how he could take hostages for money. She feels personally responsible for his actions and is determined to find him and bring the hostages to safety. This search leads her to rely upon others. David knows her strengths and weaknesses as a tracker.

Chloe and Jack: Ada crosses paths with them when they're hired to track David. Because they're young trackers and still trying to master stealth, Ada mentors them. Ada has to open up to them as she shares what she's learned about human behavior through observation and tries to understand how she was fooled by David. In working with them, she's forced to no longer remain closed off.

Sample 4.2

The following is a short bio for a customizable character. While it contains some information from the Character-Design Template, it has many fewer sections. The formatting is also different from other bios in the chapter. You can be flexible with format, structure, and presentation, as long as they effectively communicate your concepts!

Player-character: Paranormal Investigator

Age: 39

Name: Player Determinant

Default: Timothy Braun

Gender: Player Determinant

Default: Male

Ethnicity/Race: Player Determinant

Default: Australian (White)

Height: Player Determinant

Default: 5'9"

Weight: Player Determinant

Default: 178 lbs

Eyes: Player Determinant

Default: Grey

Hair/Hairstyle: Player Determinant

Default: Thick and sandy blond; strands of hair tend to hang in his left eye

Occupation: Paranormal investigator running a one-person detective agency

Bio: Ghosts figured out early on that they could talk to Timothy, the only living person they could find who could see and understand them. For someone who talks to people who have died in a number of horrible ways, Timothy is cheerful and fun to be around. Life is, indeed, way too short, and he wants everyone to have a good time while they still draw breath, even if they're assisting him in uncovering the tragic mysteries of the dead. Being everyone's cheerleader and tackling the supernatural are quite the exhausting tasks, however. A day's work saps him of his strength. He doesn't have time for hobbies or to spend time after work with friends. As soon as he hits his apartment, it's a quick dinner, a shower, and then bed.

Background: The player will choose one of three backgrounds. Each background will unlock certain dialogues, dialogue options, and quests specific to the background.

Visionary Child:

At the age of 5, Timothy began having visions of ghosts, which he eagerly shared with his parents. Frightened by their son's abilities, Timothy's mother and father tried to convince him that what he was seeing was merely the result of an active imagination. But what Timothy saw and heard were all too real—ghosts speaking to him who were so three-dimensional he was baffled he felt nothing as he reached for them. After he helped his grandmother find her long-lost brother's resting place, his parents understood that these strange abilities could somehow be useful to those in need. By the time he was a teenager, strangers from near and far sought his help to discover how their loved ones died. And ghosts themselves sought him to assist them in unfinished business.

Reality Show Star:

As a gifted medium, Timothy was cast in *Spirit Speak*. Part of a three-person team, he traveled the world visiting legendary haunted locations. His cohosts faked their gifts, but Timothy, being the real thing, always made contact with spirits and revealed the secrets of centuries-old mysteries. He became a celebrity, which embarrassed him because he was just doing his job. When *Spirit Speak* was canceled, Timothy opened his own detective agency. He never lacks work, as everyone (including ghosts) wants the famous paranormal investigator to take their case.

Family Business:

Timothy was born into a family of mediums. As a young child, he attended séances led by his grandparents. Sometimes those sessions ended in happy tears, and sometimes they ended in mourning, but Timothy learned to respect the work and the profound meaning it had for those looking for answers. At 12, Timothy's grandparents let him reach out to the dead during a séance for the first time. He spoke with Emma, a girl his age who had drowned while vacationing with her parents. Her parents blamed themselves for her death, but Emma never did. Timothy and Emma remained friends for years after, until Emma finally felt the pull to cross over. He still misses his friend.

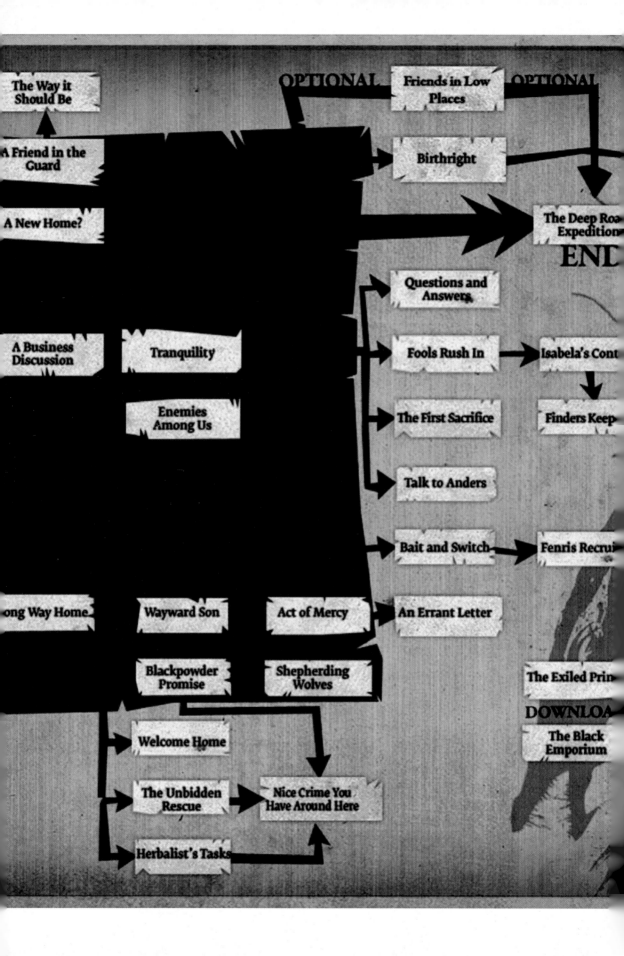

The Way it Should Be

A Friend in the Guard

A New Home?

A Business Discussion

Tranquility

Enemies Among Us

ong Way Home

Wayward Son

Act of Mercy

An Errant Letter

Blackpowder Promise

Shepherding Wolves

Welcome Home

The Unbidden Rescue

Nice Crime You Have Around Here

Herbalist's Tasks

OPTIONAL

Friends in Low Places

OPTIONAL

Birthright

The Deep Roa Expedition

END

Questions and Answers

Fools Rush In

Isabela's Cont

The First Sacrifice

Finders Keep

Talk to Anders

Bait and Switch

Fenris Recrui

The Exiled Prin

DOWNLOA

The Black Emporium

CHAPTER 5

Story

Story in games can take many shapes, from the nonexistent (*Pong*), to the straightforward (many movie-to-game adaptations), to the epically sprawling narrative (like *Final Fantasy VI*). While the nature of the story you work on will vary from company to company, and project to project, the one thing even the simplest video game stories have in common is that they are, by definition, interactive. It is that interactivity which sets games apart from traditional media and which will be your greatest frustration, challenge, and, ultimately, your best inspiration as a narrative designer.

When creating an interactive game, the goal is generally (with rare, usually artistic exceptions) to make the player feel in control of the experience. Players should feel as if their actions drive the story and be convinced that the story would not have happened—or would have turned out catastrophically different—if they hadn't been there. And for much of the history of video games, this need was used to justify a lack of narrative. Since a "story" was assumed to be something "told" to the player, it was seen as an enemy of interactivity. Fortunately, two things have happened to change this. First, many players have made it clear that they want an engaging story in their games and that they don't mind giving up *some* freedom of interaction to ensure that

DOI: 10.1201/9781003369332-5

everything they do is meaningful. And second, game writers have developed a more sophisticated toolbox for interweaving story and gameplay.

In this chapter, that toolbox is opened to give you a thorough grounding in how to structure and write a game story in a way that maintains and supports player agency.

IN THIS CHAPTER, YOU WILL LEARN TO . . .

- Keep player agency at the forefront of your story experience.
- Choose between linear, branching, and open narratives.
- Plan your game story's genre, length, villain, and tone.
- Break your narrative into tasks, missions, and quests that are integrated with gameplay.
- Manage complexity within branching and open narratives.
- Create the documentation needed to bring a game story to life.

Player Agency

"Agency" is the term used to describe players' beliefs that their choices and actions are what drive the events of the story. On the simplest level, this means that when players succeed in a task, the next plot point should narratively come about *because* of their previous success. So, if players in a military shooter have taken out a terrorist cell, it gives them a sense of agency if the next mission is to deal with the parent terrorist group kidnapping civilians in retaliation. Whereas if the next mission were to do an unrelated drug bust, there would be much less of a sense that the player's actions were driving the story.

The more complex the narrative in your game, the more player choices you need to honor to give them that sense of agency. In a game like *Mass Effect*, player agency requires designers to consider all of the past decisions a player has made in gameplay and dialogue before writing each new line.

A failure to provide a convincing sense of agency is frequently a reason that game scenes (or entire games) fall flat. When planning a game story, narrative designers should be sure to consider at each stage whether they have maximized the player's agency, or whether they can take steps (make the player come up with the great idea instead of the NPC, put cutscenes that reward players' actions instead of interrupting them) to improve it.

EXERCISE

Think about memorable game scenes that you've loved or hated. Then examine how powerful each moment in those scenes made you feel. Chances are your favorite scenes kept your character at the forefront and made you feel important and influential, while your most hated scenes upstaged or invalidated your character in some way. Briefly rewrite/design your most hated scene to give the player greater agency.

So, What Exactly Is a Game Story?

"Game story" is nowhere near as precise a term as "movie script," with story-light titles like *Mario Kart* falling into the same broad category as two-million-word epics like *Star Wars: The Old Republic*. Add to that the rapidly changing market for games (when the first edition of this book came out, consoles were the dominant platform, and mobile visual novels had not yet exploded in popularity) and it becomes difficult for any book to give a comprehensive overview of how to create game narrative.

However, even with the constant changes to what platforms and genres are popular, it remains possible to divide game narratives into three broad categories, each with their own writing requirements. These are **linear narratives**, **branching narratives**, and **open narratives**. The type of narrative structure a project requires is often determined before writers even come on the project. Many studios have a particular style of game they specialize in, while other studios make games with every type of narrative, basing their decision of which type to use on other factors, such as the game's length, genre, and anticipated audience.

Since linear stories have the most in common with traditional media, the majority of this chapter will be spent on branching and open formats, as these provide the most challenge for a writer from a non-games background. If you're working on your own project, read on to learn the strengths and challenges of each structure type.

Linear Narratives

A linear game means a game in which every player experiences the same events in the same order every time the game is played. Note that this does not mean the same thing as "straightforward." *BioShock Infinite*'s story is linear, in that the vast majority of it is seen by every player on every playthrough, but contains enough plot twists to make your head spin.

Think of a linear narrative as following this structure:

While linearity may, at first glance, seem to work against interactivity, many games tell quite effective stories using a linear structure. Many movie-to-game adaptations follow the same linear story as the movie, only in an interactive format. And games like *Uncharted*, which try to mimic the emotional arc of an action movie, also use a relatively linear story structure to achieve that feel.

However, even the most narratively linear game story is still not the same as a movie. The narrative designer must still deal with the question of how the story and gameplay intersect and how the player is kept at the forefront of the action.

When designing a linear game narrative, narrative designers should consider the following:

How Will Story Be Presented in My Game?

Linear stories rarely use interactive dialogue, as they have no way to respect player dialogue choices. This means that story in a linear game is usually conveyed by a combination of cutscenes (see Chapter 8, "Cutscenes and Cinematics") and environmental narrative (using level design, supporting characters, and ambient dialogue). For smaller-scale games, other tools may take the place of full cinematic cutscenes: animatics (comic book panels or static images appearing in sequence) or still images with text or narration can be the equivalent of cutscenes in lower-budget games.

Narrative designers must also consider how dialogue is communicated in their game (see Chapter 7, "Dialogue"). A fully voiced, AAA-game title can deliver a lot of narrative punch from ambient barks shouted between characters as they fight, climb, run, or parkour their way through the world. But for a title without VO,[1] where dialogue must be read, it can be problematic to communicate any dialogue at all during sections of active gameplay. In this case, narrative designers must rely on telling most of their story during the breaks between gameplay tasks.

How Can I Maintain Player Agency in a Linear Narrative?

If the narrative is linear, then what the player does can't matter, right? Any narrative designer who answers "yes" to that question does not pass Go or collect her $200.

Whether or not players can *actually* have any effect on the narrative, it's important that they *feel* like they're in the driver's seat. In a linear game, this often means that the player is doing a series of pass/fail missions, in which a pass lets them survive to reach the next mission, and a failure is a "Game Over" screen. However, game designers have numerous ways to disguise this structure, including modifying the pass/fail into a fail/good/better/ best system—in which successful players have degrees of success that can affect things, such as how many enemies appear in the next mission and how well armed they are. Designers might also mix up traditional missions the player takes with more narrative-driven reactive moments in which the player is put on the defensive, as things happen to their character that they don't initiate.

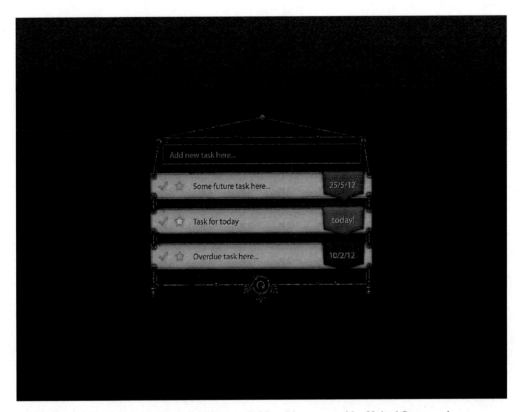

Task list app. This image was made by Mateusz Pohl and is protected by United States and international copyright law. © Mateusz Pohl.

TASKS AND MISSIONS AND QUESTS, OH MY

Different genres of games call the tasks players must accomplish by different names. For purposes of this book, "task," "mission," and "quest" are used in the following fashion:

Task: The generic term for any goal a player needs to accomplish through gameplay. Both missions and quests are tasks, but they may involve more than one task to complete.

Mission: A task or group of tasks composing a single part of a **linear story**, the equivalent of a chapter in a book. Missions are therefore always played in the same order and can build upon each other, with Mission 1 leading into Mission 2.

Quest: A task or group of tasks composing a single, self-contained storyline that may be a part of, or alongside, a larger plot in a **nonlinear story**. Closer to a short story from a themed anthology than a chapter in a single narrative, quests can be played in varying orders and do not have to affect each other or build on each other (though narrative designers can restrict some quests to being played in sequence).

Do I Need a Theme?

"Theme" may sound very academic or esoteric for a video game, but more and more projects are realizing that if you begin with a theme, you end with a product that is more unified and effective than a game that lacks one. All stories leave the reader/viewer/player with an implicit message, intended or not. The majority of games made with no specific theme in mind end up with a theme of "good will conquer evil against all odds." Games in which you are not playing the "good guy" tend to have a theme of "do whatever it takes to get ahead." This can apply equally well

Regardless of the structure used, a key job of the narrative designer is to ensure that the flow of missions builds directly on the player's accomplishments in the previous mission to create the illusion that it is the player's actions that drive the story forward.

What Is My Story?

This is at once the simplest and most complex part of the job. It's simple because no one would be reading this book if they didn't already have a million story ideas floating around in their heads. But getting down all of the details of what happens when, who finds out from whom, and what villain you fight where can be the work of months, if not years, of painstaking iteration. Chapter 2 already discussed how to handle the broad strokes of outlining the story for a game. But when it comes time to actually write detailed mission plans, be sure to consider:

- **Genre.** A good game story will contain a mix of elements that conform to players' genre expectations, plus a few surprising twists that subvert them.
- **Villain.** Most action-driven games need a concrete villain, ideally one with enough henchmen that the player can mow down a few thousand over the course of the game without actually damaging the villain's plans.
- **Length.** Decide with your team what length of game you're looking for, then look at similar games and chart how many cutscenes, levels, and plot twists they managed to effectively fit into that length.
- **Tone.** A humorous action-adventure title will have a lot more off-the-wall situations and more back-and-forth banter than a serious

military simulation. But even within something like a military-shooter title, there can be significant variations in tone, depending on whether the team wants to emphasize the horrors of war, or to draw the game's realism from the gallows humor of actual military units, such as in the HBO miniseries *Generation Kill*.

In general, a linear narrative is always a good start when designing a new story for a new product, even if you decide to change it later to a branching or open narrative. You can see the linear structure as your core story concept. Having this core storyline developed helps you decide whether a more complex structure, such as branching narrative, would make sense. If a more complex structure doesn't improve your story a lot and isn't required by your company's culture/intended audience, it can be much simpler to stick with a linear structure and enrich it with complex elements, rather than risk the scope creep of a more complex structure.

Branching Narratives

The majority of RPGs and adventure games pride themselves on being nonlinear. Yet many games in these same genres also boast of being "story driven." Which is a bit of a contradiction if you think about it, since a truly nonlinear experience would let players perform the gameplay in any order and result in a story that was muddled at best.

Instead, most of the famous story-driven, nonlinear games, such as BioWare's, Telltale's, or Supermassive's products, are what are called "branching narratives." The player makes choices that affect individual sections of plot and gameplay. So, for example, if player A chooses to support the rebels, she might experience a quest to rescue a rebel prisoner from inside an imperial base, while if player B supports the empire instead, he might have a quest to stop the rebels from freeing the important prisoner he's escorting. However, both plots come back together again at pinch points to ensure that the player stays along the path of the overall story in which the rebels and empire must ultimately come together to defeat the rising demon hordes.

to *Grand Theft Auto* or *Kim Kardashian: Hollywood*.

If you want your game to address a theme outside of these, it is wise to consider that theme early on in development. For example, in *Dragon Age II*, the theme of "freedom vs. security" drove the majority of design decisions. Most quests were structured in some way around a choice between the freedom of some or the safety of many. Having this theme in place made it easy for the development team to coordinate a large writing team under tight deadlines without endless iteration.

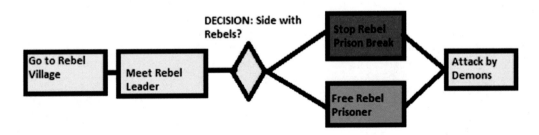

This means narrative designers for RPGs or branching adventure games must consider both the narrative throughline of any individual quest or quest chain, plus how those quests come together into a coherent storyline across the entire game.

You can visualize a branching narrative as having this structure:

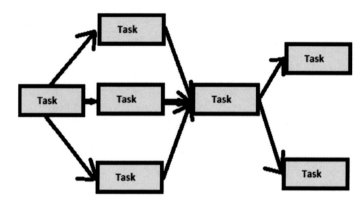

In most RPGs, branching is handled by having numerous quests—up to hundreds of individual quests in a lengthy game—of which the vast majority are optional for the player to complete. Players find these "side quests" by exploring the world and talking to minor characters, and it is of no concern whether they ever even learn of this content's existence. The string of *non-optional* quests which the player *must* complete in order to advance to the next point in the plot is known as the critical path, or "critpath."

You can visualize this kind of larger branching narrative as having a structure more like this, in which the unconnected tasks are side quests, and the connected ones are the critical path:

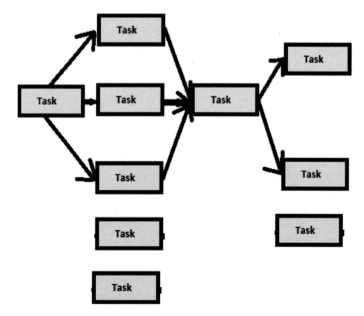

Branching Games and Player Agency

Branching narratives are all about giving the player choices. And to respect the player's sense of agency, that means the game's design must honor those choices. It is only when the consequences of a choice are seen in-game that the choice becomes meaningful, whether the impact is purely on the narrative, on the game mechanics, or both.

Meaningful Choices

The range of choices goes from small (which ammo to equip, which companion to bring on a mission, etc.) to incredibly big (whether to save an entire planet or not, choosing which companion will live or sacrifice their life for the greater good). These consequences should always be visible to the player. Sometimes, they should be long-lasting, though some of their aspects will remain invisible unless players do several playthroughs of a game to explore all the alternatives. *The Quarry*'s prologue, as an example of both smaller and more consequential choices, introduces players to both types in its tutorial. After Max crashes the car, Laura can go deeper into the woods without him or get him to help her into a clearing. If Laura leaves him at the car, Max will later see the ghost she encounters in the woods. Max seeing the same ghost is a creepy moment, but it doesn't affect the branching storyline. Later, however, Travis, a cop, confronts Laura and Max. Laura can either be honest or dishonest with him. One consequence of this choice resurfaces toward the end of the game in Chapter 7. Travis will be more likely to trust Laura or not, depending on whether the player chose to be honest or dishonest.

More relevant to you as a narrative designer are important consequences that can seriously impact the development side, particularly when the narrative acquires a permanent branching path, as in *The Quarry* example. This means more budget and work from several departments across an entire game, and potentially game sequels.

When offering players a large choice that will increase the scope for you and the team, you get the most bang for your buck by ensuring:

- The choice is telegraphed clearly during the buildup, so players are excited to make the choice.
- Players have some idea what the consequences of their decision will be before they make it.
- Ramifications from the decision are seen both immediately (within the next thirty minutes after making the choice) and at the end of the game. These are the two times in which your callbacks will have the most emotional resonance.

A classic example of a meaningful choice with a profound impact is found within *Mass Effect*, during the "Assault on Virmire" storyline. Two critical areas of the final map require that two of your squadmates

Retconning

"Retcon" is short for "retroactive continuity," or the process of making a change to a game's world or story in a way that strives to be true to what's already published about that game. For example, if you're writing a fantasy game in which it's stated that all dragons are extinct and then, in the sequel, the designers decide to include a dragon boss fight, writers can add to the lore that a small group of dragon worshippers have been secretly breeding dragons underground for thousands of years. This "retconning" allows the design team to use dragons without actually contradicting previously published materials.

Whenever a decision to retcon narrative is implemented in a project, one of the biggest concerns is whether this will affect player agency by interfering with a player's previous decisions or impressions of the world. Be aware that if you affect too many player decisions while retconning material, you will anger your players and fan base.

go out and ensure that a nuke successfully detonates. And you only have time to save one. Both argue that the other should be your choice, and the one you choose to save is furious with you for letting the other die. Consider that you may have been romancing one of the two . . . and for most of the audience, there is an emotional impact, with long-term consequences that range across the rest of the trilogy for the player (only one character to interact with) and the developers (two story paths and characters to account for, not just in narrative but also in game design, animation, cinematic scenes, etc.).

Moral Agency

Whenever a player makes a decision in a game that can be framed as "right and wrong" or "good and evil," this is moral agency. Offering this kind of decision is one of the most complicated things you can deal with as a narrative designer, as including consequences for these choices must reinforce *why that player made that decision.*

This is mind reading more than science, and you will never get it right for everyone, but when offering moral choices, narrative designers should try to step into the shoes of the player (and character!) making the decision and thinking about why they would pick every option. So, if offering the ubiquitous "kill or spare the bad guy" decision, think about why someone would choose to spare him: Does he beg for his life? Talk about his family? Promise to reform?

But also make sure an opposing character voices a good reason to kill him: This guy is a known liar. He's a murderer, and he'll be sure to kill again. Killing him will win you the favor of the king.

Never, ever, assume a player will make the moral choice in a game. And never assume that your moral choice is someone else's moral choice.

Moral Choices and Gameplay

Be careful not to tie your moral agency choices into gameplay so deeply that choices which don't follow the "proper" or "good" moral path become so punitive that the game is no longer appealing to the player. If you intend to add moral agency to your game, with gameplay consequences such as gained abilities/powers, etc., then you must be sure to balance the game appropriately, not only for "light " and "dark" choices but also for players that choose a more neutral path.

And be careful to check all the ramifications of any gameplay consequences! While having gameplay changes is a good way to make players care about narrative decisions (even the least story-driven players will care about whether they get the ring of ultimate evil power), be aware that this can backfire. Sometimes, by tying a game system to a narrative decision, designers can boot even involved players out of the narrative. In *Dragon Age II*, while the story made very clear at the end that one of the party members was a villain whom the majority of players would likely have killed, many players reluctantly kept the character alive because he was their party's best healer, and his gameplay value trumped their engagement in the story.

Designing Quests

A quest is a single, relatively linear section of story within a larger game, in which all of the player's actions serve a specific goal. When the goal changes, you've started a new quest. Depending on the game, however, the distance to that goalpost can vary considerably. In *Dragon Age: Origins*, "Get the dwarves to ally with you" is considered a single quest—"A Paragon of Her Kind"—despite being a 70,000-word+ section of the game, with eight or more levels, and at least four individual dungeons. A different game might have considered each stage of that story to be its own quest—"Meet the Candidates for Dwarven King," "Prove Your Loyalty to One Candidate"—and the overall dwarven story arc to be a questline.

So, the first thing narrative designers must decide is how many steps make a quest. This can be as short as one—every time the player completes a step, it ends that quest and begins the next quest in the chain—or as long as "A Paragon of Her Kind." This decision will be influenced by the overall game plan. A very large quest makes more sense as a piece of the critpath backbone, while four or five steps tend to max out the complexity for a side quest.

The basic structure for an RPG quest is as follows:

1   Players meet NPC with problem. Players are asked or take it upon themselves to get involved.
2   Players go to a place, or series of places, where they find clues or talk to characters to learn the reasons for the problem.
3a Players solve the problem.
    or
3b Players must decide whether the problem should be solved.

QUEST STRUCTURE EXAMPLE: JENNIFER

When I was evaluating writing candidates at BioWare, I used to give the following template for our quest structure: "A man asks you to rescue his wife, who was kidnapped by a wizard. You fight your way to the wizard's tower, only to learn that the wife went with the wizard of her own accord, because her husband was abusive. The wizard asks you to kill the husband instead. You have the choice to fulfill the original quest, or confront the abusive husband." Breaking this down, this means a structure of:

1. **Quest-giving conversation**: Goal and promised reward are established.
2. **Fighting**: Getting to the goal involves a lot of gameplay but few story moments.
3. **Twist**: Arriving at the goal undermines your original reason to be there.

Story

4. **New goal**: New goal and reward are made as a counteroffer. If the new goal is more desirable, the reward is lower; if the new goal is less desirable (the wizard *did* kidnap the girl and now wants you to kill the husband as part of a dark ritual), the reward is higher.
5. **Decision**: Which goal will the player complete?
6a. **Complete the original goal**: Usually this involves a final fight with the twist NPC.
6b. **Complete the new goal**: Usually this involves returning to and fighting the original quest-giver.
7a. **Quest turn-in**: Return to quest-giver and accept reward.
7b. **Twist turn-in**: Return to twist quest-giver and accept reward.

Writing candidates then wrote their own original story that contained these same steps, using the template as an example. For instance, if working in the *Star Wars* universe, a candidate might design a story about a Sith apprentice who is commanded to destroy a settlement on a small planet. When she arrives, she learns that she was kidnapped from this settlement as a child and raised as a Sith. She must then decide whether to destroy the settlement and receive the reward from her master, as promised, or turn her back on Sith teachings and fight her master to save the settlement. While very different than the "wizard and lovers" story above, it follows all the same plot steps.

Note that the story in the template relies heavily on gender stereotypes. These clichés make it a useful shorthand to demonstrate a plot style, but they wouldn't impress anyone as a final product. Flipping the genders or otherwise using this structure without relying on stereotypes is a good step toward a strong, finished sample.

Designing the Critpath

Large RPGs with lots of quests often require more than a single writer. However, this can make it difficult to keep the critpath coherent. If you're ever fortunate enough to be on a multiwriter team for a large RPG, here are some suggestions:

- Work out the information flow early and check back in on it often. If the central storyline is a mystery ("Who killed the king and started the war?"), then figure out early how many red herrings and clues you'll need before you learn the answer, and what players do once they know. Pick one or two large reveals for each critical-path quest, and build the quest around that reveal. Otherwise, you tend to end up with great individual quests, in which the critical-path information feels unrelated, or worse—skippable.
- Make the critical path simple, so the parts can all function separately. One of the reasons RPG storylines often revolve around an "ancient evil rising" is that it's a very straightforward way to link a bunch of otherwise unconnected large quests. Whether you're gathering allies for the big ending battle, or taking out *X* number of lieutenants of the bad guy, each subsection can remain distinct and link back to the main plot only at the end. A mystery is far harder to coordinate in a large game, since each plot (and thus each writer) is very dependent on knowing exactly what has come before.

- Make the goal worthwhile, concrete, and easy to remember. A concrete goal (defeat the evil king) is much easier and more motivating for players than a more abstract one (become popular enough to get elected). Which doesn't mean that a more philosophical and abstract game couldn't work, only that it will succeed with a smaller audience and should be budgeted appropriately.

- Keep the critical path alive. It's easy in an RPG lasting sixty hours or more to lose the thread of the critical path. Players play for a few hours at a stretch and care much more about the problem of the moment than what they were told at the beginning of the game (which they might have started months ago). Before signing off on a quest, it's important to look at how to tie it to the main plot. Working on that kidnapped wife plot? Consider having the husband be a soldier of the evil king. Writing a side quest about rescuing a girl's cat? Maybe the cat is in a cave full of orcs, and you can find their notes about troop movements. Every chance you get, remind players what the stakes are for their success. Player agency is as important across the entire flow of the game as it is during any individual questline. And the best way to make players feel like what they're doing is important is to design plots where it's true.

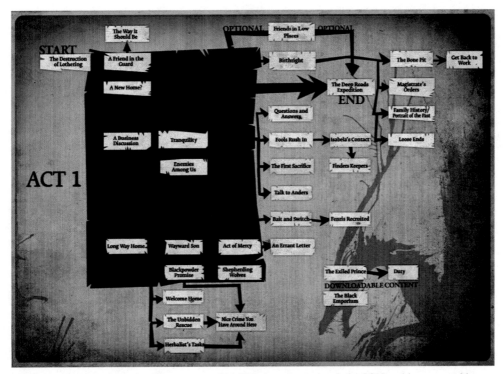

IGN's unofficial *Dragon Age II* strategy guide. This image was made by IGN and is protected by United States and international copyright law. © IGN.

For example, in *Dragon Age II*, the critical path can be represented by just a few large events: (1) The player escapes Ferelden and must reach refuge in Kirkwall. (2) The player must find a way to join an expedition into the Deep Roads to make his/her fortune. (3) The player, now an influential citizen, must find a way to deal with an attack by the Qunari Arishok; and (4) the tensions between mages and Templars come to a head, with Anders blowing up a chantry to bring about an open war. The player must defeat Meredith, who has been given terrible powers by an ancient artifact.

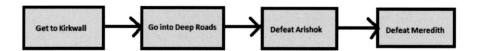

But in each of those spaces represented by the arrows above, many other quests and questlines can be played. Some of these relate to the critical path and are required to progress in the storyline, such as quests showing the growing war between Templars and mages. Others are unrelated and optional but tell their own story, such as the player seeking to control a profitable mine that turns out to be a breeding ground for dragons.

And while those steps in the critical path appear linear when written that way, in the game, they contain many branching moments, such as the choice of whether to defeat the Arishok in battle or in a duel, or to buy peace at the cost of a friend's life.

The Problem of Railroading

Forcing the player into a narrative choice which is inconsistent with the player's own choices during the narrative beforehand, or forcing a gameplay situation despite anything the player may have access to in terms of skill set or available mechanics (i.e., the villain uses poison gas to knock out the player-character and drag her back to his lair despite the fact that she used a spell that makes her invulnerable to poison) is known as railroading.

The desire to impose authorial vision in a nonlinear narrative, the need to control the critpath narrative after previous choices, or last-minute changes can all account for forced-narrative points in a storyline. They are normal in the industry, where budget does impact how much actual narrative choice can be offered to the player without development costs mushrooming. Regardless of how much player agency you want to offer, the fact remains that you are creating one game, not three, and the player agency you can offer in a branching narrative is tightly controlled, with all possible consequences and options managed at all times.

When badly managed—that is, when the process becomes so transparent or badly executed that the player notices it and feels hampered or angry because of it—this becomes railroading. If it happens too often, you risk the player stopping the game.

It is critically important to be aware of the throttle points in one's narrative, the moments when the branches come back together at a single point, and to understand how one reaches those points both from the narrative-design perspective and the player's perspective (which can be two vastly different things). Otherwise, you risk the player feeling railroaded. (See "Wireframing" below for information on how to represent and keep track of throttle points.).

Note that using the exact same structure for all your meaningful choices—or always the same type of meaningful choices—can also be seen as railroading. A static (or outright boring) structure will certainly work against players becoming involved in the narrative and tend to point them instead to games like "Drink every time I have to choose whether to kill or spare the bandit!"

Branching narratives can become highly complex, and they, as well as open narratives (below), can easily explode their budgets. You should not attempt a branching or open design without understanding that, while branching narratives are a great storytelling tool, they are also an expensive one. Before choosing this structure, keep in mind that you may have to write, at the very least, twice as much as you would have in a single linear narrative, that you have to plan very carefully to avoid broken paths, and that you need a lot of resources to produce all the required content (and even more resources to test every possible variant of it!). In the end, your story must be worth the money it costs to be produced.

LETTING THE PLAYER DISCOVER THE STORY: *RETURN OF THE OBRA DINN*

Set aboard a ghost ship in 1807, indie puzzle game *Return of the Obra Dinn*'s story is nonlinear within a chapter structure. Each chapter represents a specific event or chain of events that led to the deaths or escapes of the crew and passengers aboard the Obra Dinn. Players do not experience the chapters in order. As they explore the ship and move from location to location, they might discover who died and how in Chapter 3, and then learn who died and how in Chapter 1. Using a magic pocket watch, the player-character can see the last memory before someone died when interacting with a body they find. This means the player-character sees and hears an event from multiple points of view. Additionally, the player-character has a manifest of the ship's crew and passengers, which lists every person who was on the ship, and several sketches of all crew and passengers' likenesses. The player must put faces to names, and among the clues listed in the manifest are the passengers' and crews' ethnicities and jobs aboard the ship.

How they deduce the information they see and hear is individual to every player. The game informs players how difficult it is to identify people on a scale of 1 to 3, with 1 being the easiest. However, the player who can easily identify a crewman rated as one of the most difficult might recognize the pattern of his tattoos in a sketch of one of the groups of crewmen. When looking at the manifest, they will notice the ethnicity of a singular crewman who tends to have tattoos like this. They can identify that crewman early in the game by simply looking at his sketch and the manifest and never witnessing him in any of the scenes. For players who don't have knowledge about that type of tattoo, it might take them very late into the game, after they've reviewed scenes from multiple angles and points of view and eliminate crewmen who can't be this man, before positively identifying him.

The design of the gameplay allows players to experience events in different orders, and they can view an event any number of times to review clues and try to piece together information they may have missed or not understood at earlier points during their playthrough.

Many aspects of *Obra Dinn's* narrative design facilitate the gameplay, create the world of the doomed ship, and/or deliver clues:

- **Mechanics:** Pointing and clicking on interactables in the environment reveals individuals in illustrations associated with those objects.
- **UI:** Illustrations, fonts, and pages are in the style of art and typefaces of the early 19th century. Clicking on names and sketches help to identify passengers and crew.
- **Sound design:** Ambient sounds illustrate how people died, set the mood in scenes, and suggest the nature of creatures.
- **Worldbuilding:** Crew members of the same ethnicities bunk together, and crew members with the same jobs on the ship stay grouped together.
- **Environmental narrative:** The environment reveals how crew members lived and slept below deck and how they're grouped together. It also reveals subtle things like the trajectory of bullets and whom they're striking.
- **Cutscenes:** Simple cutscenes with voiced dialogue and sound effects deliver death scenarios, accompanied by the text of the dialogue on a dark screen.
- **Dialogue:** Dialogue gives information about the crew members through revelations about their names and languages they speak.

Narrative design and game design working in concert can structure the story and facilitate players' agency in how they determine the way in which the story unfolds. Specific mechanics, like interacting with objects in the world or the UI, can trigger what the player unlocks or experiences next.

Open Narratives

Sandbox games like *Grand Theft Auto* and many MMOs use a structure that is even more open than a branching RPG, trying for a true nonlinear experience, in which players can choose their own order to complete any content.

You can visualize their structure as:

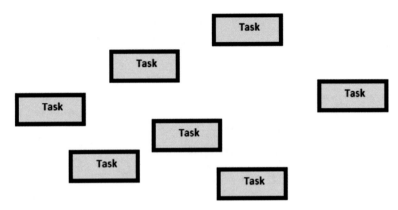

Which players can experience as this:

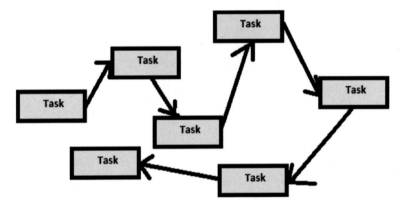

Or this:

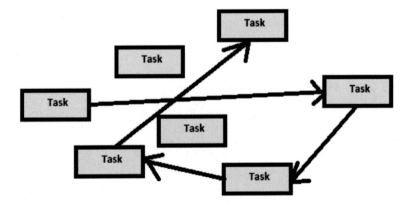

Or even this:

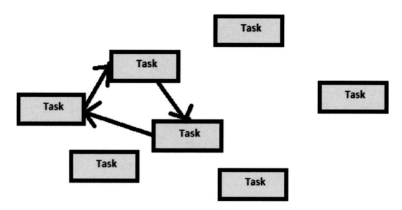

Such an open structure can be a challenge for writers and designers, since a true story can never really be nonlinear. Why? Because a story is a directed or ordered sequence of events experienced by one or more characters. A story always has a beginning, middle, and end. This order technically forbids nonlinearity. So, how do narrative designers still create a sense of nonlinearity in their games?

A good nonlinear narrative follows no predefined sequence of events. Instead, it is built out of small story blocks that can be triggered once a precondition is met. As a narrative designer, you cannot predict which path a player will take, and all story blocks need to be designed in such a way that they work in an almost free order. Players can choose whatever they want to experience and will create their own story based on their choices. The only real block to stop them from playing everything is character-level requirements, in which designers block players from accessing certain content until their character reaches a specific level (for example, in *Star Wars: The Old Republic*, the player is blocked from all content off of their starting planet until they reach Level 10). Using these requirements to contain the narrative allows narrative designers to structure the overall story experience and thus tell a bigger story within a set of freely picked story pieces.

In a structure like this, designers can still offer choices to players, but the knowledge that the plot can be played in any order makes players (and your superiors!) much more forgiving if those choices aren't honored. Many open-narrative games even allow player actions to completely derail the intended story, for example, by allowing players to kill a major villain before the story expects. The narrative may suffer, but open-world players often prefer gameplay to story and are willing to pay the price of a disjointed narrative for the reward of having total freedom.

If working on such a game, be prepared to include numerous alternative paths to get characters to the ending points you want.

For example, in a side quest involving the Thieves' Guild of a major city, make sure that there are several different characters in the world who can play the part of the "Master Thief" you need to begin that story arc.

If the project you're on is using an open story structure, it is worth it to ask yourself and your team: "How much freedom do the players need to define themselves in the world and find their role and story?" In general, open narratives are the narratives with the most expensive and content-intensive structure because everything you plan has to make sense in multiple ways and scenarios, and you may have to produce even the same content multiple times with slightly different outcomes or starting conditions. Open narratives are also usually the narratives that are hardest to communicate and document because of their many possible outcomes. Keeping this in mind can help you understand why this type is suitable or not for a certain project.

Multilevel Storytelling

Multilevel storytelling allows narrative designers to mix the advantages of linear storytelling with the freedom of nonlinear storytelling by letting designers decide how much freedom they want to allow at any given moment.

The Essential Two Stories

Multilevel storytelling is based on the idea that interactive stories always consist of at least two stories. The first is the player story: what the player experiences through his or her actions and imagination. The second story is the world story: everything created by the designers to support the player's experience, including the environment, enemies, plot, and dialogue.

When multilevel storytelling is done well, players experience these two types of stories as a single narrative, in which their actions drive what happens. But without the work the narrative designers put in to create the invisible golden thread that leads them through the world in a logical way, the player's personal story ends up muddled and unsatisfying. By putting the player's possible actions and story events into context ahead of time, the narrative designer allows players to have the best possible player story for themselves.

A good example of multilevel storytelling is *World of Warcraft*. Here, the players' characters take part in individual storylines based on the faction they belong to. This choice of faction, plus the choice of which quests to play, forms their player story, the story of their personal experience in the game. While much of this content may be unrelated from one quest to the next, in the players' minds, they become linked into a larger narrative because of the order they choose to play the quests. In this way, every player-character in *World of Warcraft* is unique and has a unique story to tell.

On the other hand, the game features a huge world story, the "lore" behind the game. Players interact with this story through quests and NPCs, but the setup, events, and outcome of the story are determined by the developers. For example, players can experience, as part of the world story, the fall of the Lich King or the defeat of Deathwing. Players have no influence on whether these events happen or not. They might experience part of the outcome directly through gameplay, but in the game world's history, it doesn't matter if an individual player's hero took part in the events or not. The world story delivers the context for the players' stories, but then it moves on with or without them. At the end of each large world storyline, it is clear that what the player has seen is only part of an even bigger, not-yet-concluded story arc.

MMOs often make use of multilevel world stories because you can have little stories for every interactive character in your world, and all these little stories together tell the story of that region. The sum of many-region stories leads to the overarching world storyline.

Narrative designers don't have a lot of control over the player story, but by the way you structure the events of the world story, you can direct their choices and make them feel natural. If you're really successful with your structure, then you can make the players hate the main villain, which will help determine the choice that they will make. So, the goal of the different layers in the world story is to evoke emotions which will lead players to make the choices you want them to make.

One possible way to connect players emotionally with your stories is to design them in such a way that the players can relate to the obstacles and experiences of the protagonist.

A game doesn't have to be an MMO to be effective at multilevel storytelling. Memorable indie games with small budgets and teams place players in worlds where what they choose to do (or not do) has monumental effects on the story and world. In *Undertale*, the player-character is a child, Frisk, who has fallen into a cavern and into the world of monsters. On one hand, Frisk is looking to get home to the world of humans. On the other hand, however, the player's decisions through Frisk can greatly alter the underground world in which they're trapped and affect all the monsters who live there.

On the surface, *Undertale* is not unlike traditional RPGs as it progresses through a mostly linear story. Frisk faces NPCs and bosses in battle, and they can befriend NPCs traveling through each area. However, it subverts the genre by tracking the NPCs the player kills, with the monsters becoming more hostile and fearful of Frisk the more frequently they die. This means the player experiences a very different story depending on whether or not they let monsters live. Players have named two of the story's routes "Genocide Route" (all monsters die) and "True Pacifist Route" (all monsters live) to reflect how the player's decisions alter the world, the monsters' perceptions of Frisk, and Frisk themself. The story of the True Pacifist Route is of Frisk befriending the monsters and helping them to return to the surface. In the Genocide Route, NPCs that Frisk would normally interact with at certain locations flee. The player never sees Alphys, a major character, as she abandons her lab. Frisk eventually leaves entire areas devoid of any life.

In both instances, the player's story is to get Frisk back to the surface. Depending on how they treat monsters, they will have friends or enemies in that quest. The world's story is how Frisk literally changes the world of these monsters, for good or ill.

No matter the genre, you can design an emotionally engaging story for the player and reflect how their gameplay styles and decisions affect the wider world of the game.

Plot Design: Epic or Relatable?

Players may enjoy superhero stories, but they can't really relate to them. Why? Well, just ask yourself how many worlds you've saved today, or this week, or this year, or in your life. Most likely none, and you most likely never will. But can you relate to things like fighting for a relationship? Or saving a friend? Or finding the love of your life? Yes, because many have done those things. You might say that game players want to be heroes, want to get away from their normal lives. This is true, but having a hero who starts out with a relatable, human motivation makes it much easier for players to identify with the protagonist. Peter Parker wants to avenge his uncle and save his love interest and just happens to save much of New York City along the way. Batman also acts initially out of revenge. Frodo saves the Shire for Sam. He isn't struggling out of some abstract concern for the good of the world. He also saves the rest of Middle-earth, but what's important to him is what he does *for Sam*.

Looking at games, you can see the same pattern in *Starcraft II*. Is Jim Raynor interested in saving the world from Arthurus Mengsk, or the Zerg, or worse? No! He fights for Kerrigan, his love, and as he saves her, he "accidentally" saves the world around him.

This principle—giving characters a relatable motivation on top of, or in addition to, a more "epic" one—can make the difference between an afternoon's entertainment and a gaming story players will be telling and treasuring for years. Give players someone to care for, and they will do everything to ensure that character's well-being, even while they accidentally save or destroy the world. The more players can relate to a character's personal story, the more they will experience the entire plot as an engaging and understandable emotional experience.

131

A WORD ON GAME ENDINGS

Endings are hard. This is a truism of any kind of fiction writing, and games are clearly no exception. If anything, games are more difficult, since game endings often need to contain new and challenging gameplay, spectacular cutscenes that can be used in a trailer, and memorable boss fights, in addition to a narratively satisfying conclusion.

This means that, as a narrative designer, you (or even the whole narrative-design team) might not get much say in how your story will end. In many studios, the game ending is decided by the senior leadership of the project or studio, sometimes before anything else in the game has been developed.

With that said, if you are in a position to design your own game ending, keep in mind that it tends to be impossible to design an ending that satisfies all players. The more freedom players have had up to the ending, the more likely they are to lash out at an ending in which all that open-world potential comes crashing down to a single, narrow end point.

What should you do when designing endings, then? First, make them as rewarding as possible, providing victory over enemies, closure for what happens to friends, and legendary loot for everyone. Second, make the journey towards the end exciting and entertaining, so that no matter what players think of the ending, the way leading there is memorable and fun. And keep in mind that even on critically acclaimed, wildly popular games, few players ever make it to the ending. Only 10 percent of people played the final mission in *Red Dead Redemption*, a 12.5-million-units-selling Game of the Year.[2] So, while endings should never be shortchanged, the industry still has a long road to travel to make sure people ever see them at all.

Game Story Documentation

One of the most important aspects of being a narrative designer is communication. Being able to properly document and present the story you are working on to the rest of the team is essential to invest others in your work. Your two main tools for this will be the game bible and wireframing.

The Game Bible

The game bible (also referred to as a universe bible or story bible) is one of the most important documents a development team uses. As a narrative designer, you'll be responsible for overseeing a game bible's production, or you may write it yourself. The bible serves as a reference for the entire team, including level designers, systems designers, artists, sound designers, and game writers. It documents all of a game's worldbuilding and lore, and may include information covering character development, storylines, and missions/quests.

A game bible is important because it serves as a source of inspiration. Artists can visualize world settings and their inhabitants based on descriptions. Level designers get ideas for the world's layout, while systems designers build mechanics based on the rules of technology, magic, and science. Animators sense how objects, characters, and creatures should move, and sound designers get a sense for sound effects as they read location and character/creature information. Game bibles are a necessary tool for making sure that the vision for the game stays consistent across the potentially hundreds of individuals responsible for building it.

Information included in the bible also helps to keep details in the game and transmedia spin-off projects consistent. Without recording this information, in-game content can contradict itself—and players *will* notice. You don't want one character to state at the beginning of the game that a major event happened in 2016, while another character later mentions it happened in 2026. Or it would be difficult explaining why a character's eye color changes from one game to the sequel. With the details needed to bring a world to life, it's impossible for the team to keep track of them all if they're not documented.

You have a lot of flexibility in producing a game bible. It's a living document, meaning you can add to it or remove content. As you and the team make decisions about the game's world or story, things will inevitably change. You may add more content to the bible if you work on a sequel or transmedia project as well.

WORLD ANVIL: A WORLDBUILDING PLATFORM

In recent years, among others, a wiki-like platform called World Anvil (www.worldanvil.com/) was released, aiming mostly at world builders who create worlds for pen & paper (such as *Dungeons & Dragons*) campaigns. For aspiring world builders, it offers a free tier, as well as various paid tiers in case you need more features to flesh out your universe. Its wiki style makes it easy to link articles together and slowly build your world bible.

Sections of the Game Bible

Depending on the specific needs of the game, the bible can be hundreds of pages or very few. If you're working on an RPG, whether it's for consoles or mobile platforms, the bible is likely to have a lot of sections. However, if you're working on a game that's not story driven, there's probably no need to go into the world's history. Here are some sections your game bible might include:

Setting: Describes the overall characteristics of the world, like time period, geography, and world size. Can also cover locations and their importance to the world and story.

Timelines: Presents major events occurring before, during, and after the game's story.

History: Explains why and how major events have shaped the world, its inhabitants, and the story.

Magic/technology/science: Describes the history of magic, technology, and science in the world, how these came to be, who uses them, and whether they're viewed favorably or unfavorably. If cultures have placed limitations on how these can be used, it's important to note this.

Cultures/societies: Explains who makes up the societies in the game, what's important to them, how their governance is structured, and their relationships to other groups. If art, religion, philosophy, and politics influence the story and characters, you will need to discuss them.

Language(s): Gives the history of languages spoken in the world and who speaks them.

Characters: Includes the bios and descriptions of main characters, secondary characters, and minor characters. Information on character development, relationships with other characters, and story involvement may also be provided.

Storylines/arcs/plot development: Outlines the progression of major and minor storylines, major events during arcs, and important plot points. May also list missions/quests and where they fall in the main story and side stories.

Glossary of terms: Lists important vocabulary for constructed languages, especially words characters use frequently. Also defines important concepts and terms used by the world's cultures, like types of magic or religious rituals.

Appendices: Includes supplemental material like a constructed language's usage rules and dictionary, artist references, maps, etc.

Organizing the Game Bible

Since the game bible is a *reference*, it needs to be structured so that anyone can easily find information. A game bible needs a table of contents that breaks down all of its sections with corresponding page numbers. If you break sections into subsections, you should put the subsections into the table of contents too.

Each time the bible is updated, make sure to indicate its new version and the date it was changed on the cover page. A page detailing a history of changes will keep a record of what's been added or removed. This ensures that everyone on the team uses the latest version and understands the reasons for the changes.

Wireframing

In addition to the narrative summaries that will be included in the game bible, most narrative designers will also use wireframing to demonstrate the structure of stories to the development team. A concept originally encountered in web design, but one which is essential to complex stories in gaming, wireframing is the process of structuring the hierarchy of information flow in a flow chart. In narrative, it helps you keep things consistent as you work out the details of your story and allows you to adjust narrative as needed, keeping a steady view on the entirety of the work. What's more, wireframing can be applied to any kind of narrative element, be it high-level story arcs for a whole game, the process of an entire quest, the structure of a dialogue with multiple branching paths, or even balancing narrative elements for the game as a whole.

Also—and most important of all—wireframing is a means of quickly and effectively communicating the structure of the story to any other department on the team, be it for important presentations during a pitch session, or for communicating with other departments when working on a mission or cinematic. This is the shorthand version of your expanded story document that you can be sure everyone will look at and understand at a glance. Wireframes can be as specific ("this dialogue") or as complex ("every narrative aspect of the game laid out on a timeline") as you wish them to be. There are no limits to what they can be applied to.

There are several tools you can use for wireframing:

- Microsoft Visio or Office OneNote (accessible under a corporate or student license)
- Apps such as Miro and Figma.
- Dry-erase whiteboard
- Note cards pinned to a corkboard
- Google or PowerPoint slide decks with linked slides to illustrate choices, branching structure, and overall story flow
- Sticking notes to a wall
- Free programs available online, such as Lovely Charts, Simple Diagrams 2, Google Flowcharts, etc.
- Commercial programs, such as articy:draft, Celtx Game and VR, etc.

While a few tools have been listed above, there are many more available to you. Ultimately, whatever works best for you is the way to go. Being able to walk someone to your working wall or being able to save and share your work in an easily distributable PDF format should be your only true requirement.

Conclusion

As narrative designers, you have different options for how to structure stories. By the kinds of structures you use, you determine how much freedom you want to give players to experience their own stories. Yet a lot of freedom is not always the best option because it takes away the chance for designers to choreograph the most impactful storyline.

When determining story structure, narrative designers should review the principles in this chapter and consider which will be most important to their players—a sense of agency, a sense of freedom, or a strong narrative thread—then pick the structure (branching, open, or linear) which best supports their audience's needs. Once the structure has been determined, narrative designers can follow the advice given to use that structure to its maximum potential!

Interview with Tom Jubert (Games Writer and Narrative Designer)

What Are Some Key Differences between Working with Small Teams vs. Working with Larger Teams When Implementing a Game's Story?

Large teams have producers whose job it is to schedule everything. This often means, among other things, that everything has to be scheduled. In a large team, there is a high chance you will be reliant on other members of that team to realize your narrative ambition. As a rule of thumb, the smaller the team, the bigger your chunk of the responsibility.

I'm sure there are some large teams that act like small ones, and vice versa. But, in general, the bigger a firm is, the more risk-averse they become. You can't run multimillion-dollar projects on a whim. The result is that there are procedures that have to be followed, and everybody's individual input tends to be minimized in the process. Just ask the guy who spent a year of his life modeling guns. This kills your flexibility, which in turn kills creativity. It's a generalization, but I think an accurate one. In turn, if you work in AAA, you're going to have to fight a lot harder for your story.

To Help the Implementation and Production Processes, Have You Ended Up in Other Roles Besides Narrative Designer When Working with Smaller Teams?

I've done lots of playtesting, lots of voice direction, and some ill-advised voice acting in *Penumbra: Overture*. Voice direction makes a lot of sense to me, because I'm terrified of what someone else will make of my writing.

What Do You Find to Be the Most Important Aspect of Communicating Plans for Implementation and Production?

Finding a team that's going in the right direction already! Honestly, if you and the project leads are on the same page, it makes a world of difference. For writers it's difficult to hold the sway internally that a designer does, and your next best bet is having a story champion inside the inner circle. I have worked on projects where I have effectively been assigned to a project by producers and agents, and projects where the team lead has checked out my previous work and explicitly selected me because I'm a good match. Guess which ones work out better?

What Do You Find to Be the Most Difficult Aspect of Communicating Plans for Implementation and Production?

The most difficult thing is probably bringing everyone on side and working towards the narrative goals. It can be hard to communicate the bigger picture from small details, and really you need a whole bunch of faith sometimes from the people who have to implement the work in order to realize it.

All of those cases basically involved me prototyping things under the radar and then presenting them, so the team could get as close to an end-user impression of what I'm trying to do as possible. If you see the story outline before you read the story, that has an effect on how you read it. It might sound better on paper, or it might sound worse. By skipping that step and going straight to production, I was able to show off what I wanted to do in the best possible light and thus win my bosses' genuine support, not just a grudging green light.

For instance, on *The Talos Principle*, I was tasked with producing some kind of interactive dialogue. I wrote out a number of plans for it I thought were interesting, but the team just didn't get it. Then I took one of those plans and actually wrote out a functional interactive dialogue based on it. Suddenly, everyone was on board. As soon as they saw what I could do with these ideas in a day or two, they were excited to see what I could do within a few months.

What Techniques Do You Use for Implementing Story in Games That Aren't Story Centric?

I always use push/pull in my head: Consider what is the minimum narrative content players need to understand what the game is, and push that at them through dialogue, cutscenes, or whatever. Then take all the small, optional details and hide them away in the pull narrative—the text logs, the other mechanics the player has to make an effort to investigate.

Exercises

Exercise 5.1

Using a wireframing tool of your choice, whiteboard the high-level, core-story concept you wish to propose for a game. The high-level narrative should be linear at first blush; choices and different endings can be integrated on the second pass, once a solid narrative structure has been established.

Exercise 5.2

Expand upon your earlier wireframe by picking a plot point from the high-level narrative to make into its own flow chart. Within that flow chart, document at least:

- The player's starting point, coming off where the previous plot point ends.
- Every gameplay mission or critical-path quest.
- Any decision points which lead to branching in the narrative.
- The ending state or states of the plot.
- Any optional side quests available to the player during this plot.

For example, this is the flow chart used in production of the beginning of the post–Season 4 content of *Game of Thrones: Ascent*. All quests are represented, with variants color-coded by the player's House, and the quest type noted in the diagram. (Words are blurred out to avoid spoilers.)

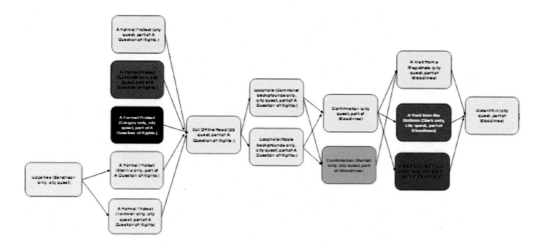

Recommended reading for this exercise:
FILM CRIT HULK's "The Myth of the 3 Act Structure."[3] (Warning: Article contains use of profanity.)

Samples

INTRODUCTION	TARIS	DANTOOINE	TATOOINE	KASHYYYK	MANAAN	EVENT – Caught!	KORRIBAN	EVENT – Crash land!	STAR FORGE	CONCLUSION
Tutorial Intro Escape from ship/space battle	Crash land on Taris (with Carth Onasi) Find Bastila Shan Find way off Taris (steal ship) Learn about your force ability	Go to Jedi Enclave Enter training Local quest: find 1st star map & Star Forge lore/importance Become Padawan -> Acquire main game mission: "Find StarForge"	Vision + clues for location of next star map Obstacle: Sand People Gain access to 2nd Star Map location	Vision + clues for location of next star map Find Wookies + ask help Obstacle: Wookiee Chief + evil corporation Go on trial quest - find 3rd Star Map Help Wookiee NPC	Vision + clues for location of next star map Go to Republic Embassy Get quest to help Republic + find 4th Star Map Minor event: Dark Jedi encounter	Ship is caught by Dark Jedi (Enemy: Malak) Interrogation Engineer prison escape Player character discovers identity Bastila stays behind to cover escape	Vision + clues + Enter Sith Academy to gain access to Star Map fragment Sith politics/culture Win sith prestige contest Find 5th Star Map Defeat Sith students & depart for Star Forge	Crash land on unknown world when trying to reach Star Forge Explore ship graveyard planet Find Temple of Ancients 1st Confrontation: Dark Side Bastila	Lead strike force of Jedi into Star Forge Defeat Dark Jedi Access Star Forge center Final confrontation: Dark Side Bastila Boss fight: Malak using Star Forge power boost	Defeat Malak Escape Star Forge destruction Jedi Knight ceremony

Sample 5.1

Here is an example of a high-level, core-story concept, using the game *Star Wars: Knights of the Old Republic*. As you can see, this example is entirely linear, even though the game in question is one that offers a lot of choices and variations on a granular level of narrative. This is because, while *KOTOR* is a story which allows for player choices with notable impact on narrative, the high-level, core-story concept is what provides a solid template and direction when working on things such as choices, consequences, etc.

Some notes:
- **Each step already takes into account narrative twists**. These will open into gameplay opportunities.
- **Keep things simple**. The plot details don't need to be known at this level, just the general events and what makes the story progress
- **Only key characters are named**. Some may not even have names beyond "henchperson" and "big bad."
- **Note down details if you have them**. Don't integrate them at this stage.
- **If you want multiple endings, keep it to naming the box "Multiple endings here."** Sort it out later when you have a more detailed framework to feed into the crafting of those endings.
- **Note that the creation of a high-level core story isn't always linear itself**. Sometimes you know your ending(s) before the main bulk of the game, and you craft things accordingly.

Sample 5.2: *Quest Outline*

This is an example of a full outline for a quest with a midpoint twist, as described earlier.

Side Quest: Deserving

Ambient Dialogue 1

A young human mage is arguing ambiently with an elven guard in front of a mage college. He wants access to the college's famous library, but the rules are that only elves can study at the college, and the guard dismisses him rudely.

The player can click on the human mage (Galrith) to begin the conversation.

Conversation 1

The player starts the conversation by saying that they couldn't help overhearing the argument with the elven guard. Why is it so important to the mage to get into the college here? Isn't there a human mage college in the next town over?

Galrith confesses that he is interested in more than just the books in the library. He himself is half elven, something that his mother hid from him until quite recently. He modestly admits that he is one of the best students in the human mage college, but says that he has exceeded the limits of what they can teach him. He wants to get inside the elf school in order to prove to them that he should be admitted as a student to their superior college.

Galrith begs the player to help him sneak inside and present himself to the headmaster directly. The player can agree, refuse the quest, or haggle with Galrith for a reward for helping him (Galrith is poor, but offers a nonmonetary reward, like a new spell). Galrith cautions that the player can't attack any of the mages or they'll never let him into the school—they will have to get inside by stealth.

If the player accepts the quest, they go to the Gameplay section below.

Gameplay

The quest has two gameplay stages:

> Stage 1: The player waits until nightfall, then uses stealth gameplay to search for a door that they can pick the lock of and get inside without being seen by regularly patrolling elven guards.
> Stage 2: Once the player is inside the school, Galrith joins them on an escort mission, in which the player and Galrith must both avoid being seen by patrolling elven guards before they reach the headmaster's office.

Ambient Dialogue 2

Once they reach the headmaster's office, the player asks Galrith what his plan is now. Is he just going to wait here until morning? But Galrith doesn't answer; instead, he searches the office wildly for something, muttering to himself about how it "has to be here . . ."

The player can try to initiate conversation, but Galrith is too consumed with his search.

Conversation 2

Suddenly, they are interrupted by the arrival of the headmaster (Waveal), who demands to know what they are doing in his office. Galrith turns on him in a fury, holding up a handful of papers and declaring triumphantly that he finally has the evidence he needs! Waveal is completely taken aback; he has no idea who Galrith is or what he's talking about.

Galrith Hisses at Him, "I'm Your Son!"

The player has a chance to respond to this with shock, blasé indifference, or anger that Galrith lied to them. Over the course of a few questions from both Waveal and the player, the whole story comes out—Waveal had an affair with Galrith's mother twenty years before, something deeply shameful in the proud elven culture. When Galrith was born, Waveal turned his back on his mother. When Galrith's mother came to Waveal to ask for support for the child, he claimed not to know her and had her arrested for trespassing. Galrith has grown up determined to get revenge on the elven father who so cruelly abandoned him.

Waveal is horrified to have his past thrown at him. He says that none of this is true; Galrith's mother is just a madwoman who fixated on him, and her son is obviously just as insane. But Galrith found letters between them that proves there was a relationship. Both mages start to gather magic for a duel of wizards, both turning to the player to ask for their aid in the battle.

- Waveal says that if this comes out, it will ruin his reputation—whatever Galrith is paying the player, Waveal will double it if the player takes his side.
- Galrith can't pay the player anything more—because of Waveal's indifference, he grew up in poverty—but he begs the player to take his side and do the right thing.

Gameplay
The player can pick which side to join in the Wizards' Duel.

Conversation 3
When the duel is over, the player has a brief wrap-up dialogue with whoever they assisted.

IF: Took Galrith's Side	IF: Took Waveal's Side
Galrith thanks the player for their help and says that he is going to bring his mother the letters that prove she was telling the truth all along. He tells the player that they are welcome to take anything they want of his father's; he doesn't want any of it. Players have a choice of whether to convince Galrith to take some of Waveal's money to support his mother, or just take everything for themselves.	Waveal haughtily thanks the player for their assistance, pretending that the player helped because they believed his lie that Galrith and his mother were crazy. The player can either play along politely or remind Waveal that they only helped for a reward. Waveal pays the money and says that he is a powerful man, and he will make sure that the player's name is respected by the elven council.

Notes

1 Voice-over: Auditory narration not accompanied by a visual of the speaker.
2 Blake Snow, "Why Most People Don't Finish Video Games," *CNN Tech*, last modified August 17, 2011, www.cnn.com/2011/TECH/gaming.gadgets/08/17/finishing.videogames.snow/.
3 FILM CRIT HULK, "Hulk's Screenwriting 101 Excerpt: The Myth of 3 Act Structure," *Badass Digest*, last modified December 11, 2013, http://badassdigest.com/2013/12/11/hulksscreenwriting-101-excerpt-the-myth-of-3-act-structure/.

Implementation and Production

This chapter will cover two major areas of game creation which are equally important and interdependent: implementation and production. Previous chapters have introduced early preproduction processes (Chapter 2, "The Concept"), as well as the basic narrative tools needed to build a story (Chapter 3, "Worldbuilding," Chapter 4, "Characters," and Chapter 5, "Story").

Once you've worked out what your story is about, who your characters are, and which world they are moving in, the bulk of the work remains: bringing the game together so that others can actually play and enjoy your story. Some of the narrative tools available to bring your story to life in an actual game will be discussed in this chapter, in the **Implementation** section. Topics such as narrative spaces, graphical perspective, narrative types and an extensive section on environmental narrative (an often undervalued storytelling tool) will be elaborated upon. Information on how to approach **production** while working with a team is the other necessary ingredient for putting together a game— your own implementation work cannot meet with success unless it is properly integrated with the work of everyone else developing your game. Once you've figured out how to embed your narrative in your game, and ensure it works with the genre of game you're creating, communicating your intent and needs to the team is vital.

DOI: 10.1201/9781003369332-6

IN THIS CHAPTER, YOU WILL LEARN . . .

- Implementation:
  - Narrative spaces and how to account for player attention span.
  - Graphical perspective and how it can impact storytelling.
  - Various types of narrative and how they are conveyed as quests.
  - Environmental narrative as a storytelling tool across all narrative tools.
- Production:
  - Narrative design and how the team interacts with other disciplines (upstream and downstream teams).
  - How to work with cinematics.
  - How to work with QA (quality assurance).

Implementation

Any tools the narrative designer can use to eke out a bit more depth to the narrative should be considered, though always without a negative impact on other disciplines. Tools include quest- and mission-based narrative types, environmental narrative, graphical narrative perspectives, and consideration of player attention span. While traditionally it may not be thought that the latter two fall under the umbrella of narrative design, graphical perspective and player attention span should be considered whenever possible.

Creation of a Narrative Space (on Player Attention Span)

Regardless of what method you use to deliver narrative, your intended audience's attention span will determine how the story is received. When you develop narrative content for a game, it is very important to keep in mind how much time players give you to tell your story. This amount of time, or narrative space, varies for each genre.

Depending on your genre, the time you have to tell a story via text or noninteractive elements while having the player's full attention and engagement can be limited. This is mostly because players don't want to sit passively in front of the screen watching or reading something. Players play games because they want to interact with the world created for them. The narrative designer's responsibility is to support them on their journey as smoothly as possible and deliver the story through the gameplay or in conjunction with the gameplay as often as possible.

Another interesting aspect of game narrative space is that it contracts and expands. This means that sometimes you have more time to tell something important, and sometimes less. For example, in a boss fight in an action game, you have very little time to tell a story to the players via text or voice. The players are focused on defeating the encounter

TABLE 6.1 Narrative Space

Genre/Medium	Space (roughly)
Book/novel	A lot (hours+++)
Feature film	Some (~120 minutes)
TV episode	Less than film (~45 minutes)
Sitcom	Little (~25 minutes)
Sandbox game	A lot (hours, days)
Single-player RPG	Hours (contracts/expands)
RTS/MMO	Minutes (contracts/expands)
Action RPG/FPS	Seconds (contracts/expands)

and not reading whatever you toss at them. The worst thing you can do is start a cutscene or show a textbox in the middle of the encounter. Once the players have defeated the boss, the narrative space expands because the action is over, and now players will give you the time and attention to tell a more detailed story. This concept of contracting and expanding narrative space should inform the design for your game, showing where you can tell parts of your story.

A Narrative Tool: Graphical Perspective

Graphical perspective is another term for the in-game camera view (such as first person or third person). This view has a direct impact on your story, by helping to shape your players' assumptions of what actions they believe they have at their disposal to overcome an obstacle.

In a third-person view, the character is usually automatically introduced. The visual design of the character should allow the players to guess his or her abilities. Enough hints should be readily available through character design and the user interface, so the player can start off playing with little to no exposition introducing the character.

In a first-person narrative perspective, some players may assume that they can only do what they could do in real life in similar situations. This only changes if you have told them before that they do have special powers or something that enables them to execute special actions. So, for a first-person perspective, it is always important to establish the players' abilities before you require the players to execute them. Otherwise, their natural tendency is to only look for a solution in their personal set of abilities and experiences.

For example: You're working on a game which uses a first-person perspective. Right in the first level, players are placed on the top of a skyscraper, and the task is to escape the scene. With no further information, some players will not assume that jumping over the impossibly wide gap between the buildings is the solution—it's impossible for a human to make such a jump. So, with no further information, finding the solution will be near impossible. But if you tell your players before this scene that they are Spiderman or Neo from *The Matrix*, then the variables change accordingly. Now jumping becomes a very real possible solution.

Graphical perspective matters, not only in the way the players see the world that you've created but also in how you introduce gameplay solutions to them.

Narrative Types

Narrative types describe the way you tell a story in an interactive environment. This differs from what was covered in the story chapter because it defines the elements which need to be added to the structure to make it work in a game. There are many different types of narrative and even more different names. So, don't be surprised if you hear different terms from different professionals. One way to avoid confusion is to understand your tools and to be able to explain them, and not to insist on names. A hammer will always be a hammer by its function, regardless of whether you call it "hammer" or "thing with heavy head to drive in nails." At their broadest, the narrative types include those that use words (quest-based, mission-based, etc.) and those that don't (environmental narrative).

Quest-Based Narrative

In the previous chapter, quest-based stories and how they are structured in RPGs (though it is important to note that quest-based stories can be found in a wide variety of game genres) were discussed. Quest-based stories usually lead to a quest-based narrative type where the story is broken off in many small parts. These parts share one or more perspectives on the story and together make a complete story. With this type of narrative, the content is already designed with specific quest types in mind.

To make this type of story work in any game, designers must identify the story elements required for a satisfying quest. Most quests require the following elements: a problem, a character, a list of tasks, a list of obstacles/opposition, and a reward. By breaking these down to their simplest level, narrative designers can determine what assets are required to put their quest into the game.

For example, a character may need water for his animals, but the way to the river is blocked by crocodiles. The problems here are lack of water and crocodiles. At this point, that's all the player needs to know. In a traditional story, you can share a lot more details with these two problems, but interactive storytelling needs to focus on the essentials. A character who needs water for his animals will normally not discuss the origin of crocodiles as a species. He will just say something like, "I need water, but those crocodiles won't let me get close to the river."

Besides mentioning the problem in the quest text or dialogue, quest-based narrative usually requires that you summarize the players' task in the form of a short task list or journal. For this example, players might see the following task: "Bring water to NPC X." They don't see anything about crocodiles here because the crocodiles are not a task; they are an obstacle.

At this point, narrative designers must look at the actions available to players to get past the obstacles and accomplish the task. In a game with a combat system, this becomes simple: Fight the crocodiles to get the water. In a stealth game, the player's action might turn into "Sneak past the crocodiles without waking them up. Then sneak back with the water."

Finally, in a quest-based narrative, you always want to let your players know what they will get for the hard work they put into solving the quest. Yes, moving on in the story can be a reward in itself, but getting at least some experience points or money makes it even more attractive.

So, in executing a quest-based storyline, you will require documentation breaking down the quest-giver (or other way of receiving the quest information), the list of tasks, the obstacles/opposition for each task, the gameplay used to get past the obstacles/opposition, and the reward acquired. In cases where the player has the choice of how to complete a quest, you will need the complete plan for each branch worked out before it goes into the game.

A nice benefit of quest-based narratives is that they can be compared with typical TV formats, which make it easier to organize the story and to know what to tell when. Table 6.2 shows a sample comparison assuming that the average length of a quest chain is twenty-five to thirty minutes.

Mission-Based (or Between-Level) Narrative

While in quest-based narrative every new step in the gameplay might require more dialogue or text to advance the story, in mission-based narrative the text/dialogue-based storytelling mostly takes place in between gameplay missions. A mission is an objective (or set of objectives) the player has to achieve in the next map, and it is usually assigned during a downtime between two maps. You can think of these objective-giving scenes as being military-style mission briefings, before the soldiers leave to achieve the objectives. Missions can

TABLE 6.2 Length of Quest Elements

Quest Element	Equals in TV
Multiple quest chains	One season
One quest chain	One episode
One quest	One act
One task	One beat

contain story pieces and will usually have objectives and opposition that reflect the story. However, any major story progression or exposition requiring text and dialogue will usually happen outside the actual mission/map, either in cutscenes or in interactive-story environments such as the Hyperion (the big starship environment between the maps) in *StarCraft II: Wings of Liberty*.

Mission-based narratives very clearly reflect the principle of expanding and contracting narrative space. Between missions, you have a lot of narrative space, and you can introduce characters, conflicts, and plotlines. This is the time to share all the background and story information with the player.

Within the actual mission, you concentrate on the task the player must complete during the mission. There is little to no use of text or dialogue to convey character development or major plot twists. The story during the mission focuses exclusively on what the player can accomplish in gameplay, with a thin narrative veneer to provide motivation, for example, "Conquer the enemy base." During the mission, you have very limited narrative space, and thus you need to focus on the story elements that can be conveyed through gameplay, not on backstory or details that require text or dialogue to explain.

This kind of narrative is normally used within strategy and simulation games, which have a lot of narrative space between the missions and very little during the missions. A good example of this narrative type is *StarCraft II*.

Environmental Narrative

Environmental narrative (or environmental storytelling) is a story-delivery tool which can shine when used properly. This type of narrative immerses players because the world of the game itself communicates with players, giving them feedback. William Owen, in his thesis *Creating a Taxonomy of Environmental Narrative for Video Game Design*, defines it as "the story told via the world and its exploration by the player." Environmental narrative employs audio, visual, and design techniques used to *intentionally communicate* information regarding the game's world, its story, and its characters. The techniques could also be physical if the game's mechanics are connected to the controller's vibration feedback. The key here is that environmental narrative is a means of communication.

Information Environmental Narrative Can Convey
Environmental narrative is an important way to *show* instead of *tell*, and it can be used in any game genre and on any platform. It can reveal just about anything you and other team members can think of. Show players the state of the world. Use settings to help players progress through the story. Give players insight into characters. Environmental narrative can even be used in level design or as part of the game's mechanics. As you're considering implementing environmental

narrative, think about all of the ways your game uses aspects of storytelling. You'll discuss these with the team to come up with a plan of execution.

Worldbuilding

Environmental narrative can provide information about the world by illustrating characters' worldviews, expressing a society's values, and/or giving evidence for how a player's action (or lack of action) changes the world. These examples are by no means exhaustive, and there may be other key aspects about the world you'll want to express. The following questions will help inspire you to use environmental narrative:

- What are the cultures/societies in the story like?
- What types of locations can best illustrate these cultures/societies?
- Will the story or player decision-making affect the world?
- What locations can best show these changes, and how will they change?

For example, through plaques, statues, and graffiti, *BioShock* has constant reminders that Andrew Ryan founded Rapture on his objectivist principles, and there's a major power struggle that leads to mass mayhem. There are grandiose and opulent buildings, so players get a sense of what Rapture could have been like before it fell into chaos. From all of the gore and bodies lying around, players don't need to be told the utopia became a dystopia. They can *see* it.

The *Fable* franchise is known for choices and how they change Albion. In *Fable III*, those choices extend outside of Albion. Players have to make promises to gain allies and overthrow the player-character's brother. The player-character promises the City of Aurora it will be an equal part of the kingdom. However, if players decide to betray Aurora after becoming king or queen, this will open a mine. The mine unlocks a new dungeon in the game, through the players' decision to colonize the Aurorans. Players literally change the world's landscape by adding to it. At the same time, this choice makes life worse for the Auroran NPCs.

If choosing to use environmental narrative on this scale, make certain that the entire team is in on the decision, as creating a whole "post-state" area in a game world is an expensive decision on behalf of only a percentage of players. This is not a change that can be easily implemented at the end of the development process.

Story and Plot

Environmental narrative provides alternatives to delivering story and plot through cutscenes, animatics, or interactive dialogue. NPCs might give important information through ambient dialogue. Maybe they mention places players need to visit. Perhaps they act strangely, and players need to find out why. If several NPCs *run away* from an area, players may need to fight an enemy in this area or investigate it, for instance.

The level design might guide players in a certain direction or offer them a choice in directions, like a forked road. Environmental narrative can lead players to locations, reveal plot points, give hints, or foreshadow events.

Some questions that will help you deliver your plot through environmental narrative:

- What locations will you need to help tell the story?
- How will you get players to these locations?
- What do they need to find when they get there (NPCs, items, visual clues, etc.)?
- What other ways can NPCs communicate besides speaking directly to player-characters (ambient dialogue, behaviors, etc.)?

In the *Fatal Frame* franchise, the ghosts are very much a part of the environment. Players never know when one is going to appear. You may not see them, but you'll hear them, to let you know that they're a constant presence. Following ghosts is also important. They'll lead

Monsters escape the ice in *Cloudstone*. Screenshot from *Cloudstone*. Developed by Playsaurus, Inc. and Published by Nexon and protected by United States and international copyright law. © Playsaurus, Inc.

Monsters escape the ice in *Cloudstone*. Screenshot from *Cloudstone*. Developed by Playsaurus, Inc. and published by Nexon and protected by United States and international copyright law. © Playsaurus, Inc.

players to locations where important information is lying around in the form of letters, memos, and diaries. When players read this information, they can figure out mission objectives and get insight into the ghosts they'll have to fight. Following ghosts can also lead to cutscenes that advance the plot.

Players need to take photos of certain buildings with spectral glows— and this directly involves the game's mechanics. The photo will reveal another location in the game, and that's the next place players need to go to progress through the story.

Cloudstone uses its level design to foreshadow changes in the world. One map on a frozen island has several creatures frozen in ice, leading players to wonder what would happen if the ice melted. In the very next mission, the ice melts, and those enemy monsters are free.

Character Development and Characterization
The environments characters inhabit can say a lot about them. Where they live and what they own might tell players about their social status or what's important to them. Their actions might change places around them, giving insight about the character's development or characterization. Characters, whether they're player-characters or NPCs, can be unreliable. Environmental narrative is one way to expose the truth.

Some questions to get you thinking about how environmental narrative can support your characters:

- What locations are important to characters?
- If characters grew up or spent significant time at the locations, how did these places shape who they are?
- What does a location say about the character's personality? Do you have evidence to show how the environment helped foster a character's personality?
- Can it show how a character is progressing/changing?
- Is there anything at the location that's important to the character?
- What does that something reveal about the character?

The point-and-click adventure *To the Moon* develops a character through environmental narrative in a subtle, effective way. At the beginning of the game, players are introduced to an old man named Johnny, who's dying. Two scientists must travel back in time through his memories to grant him a wish. Before the scientists enter his mind, they find many origami rabbits in his basement. Then they find origami rabbits throughout the house in Johnny's memories. The scientists find this to be a little creepy. It turns out that the rabbits were made by Johnny's deceased wife, River, and he's kept them. They're her way of trying to get him to remember a promise he made her and an expression of her love for him. As the scientists go back in time, they find fewer and fewer rabbits. They reach a point where River is diagnosed as being on the autism spectrum. Now players can connect the dots: As River grows older, her condition worsens, and River and Johnny's communication also deteriorates. She uses all of these rabbits to show her affection for him because she finds it difficult to express it verbally.

Spec Ops: The Line uses environmental narrative to give insight into the player-character's mental state. Captain Walker and his squad hunt down Colonel Konrad, and Konrad's face appears on billboards throughout Dubai. But Dubai has been ravaged by continual sandstorms, and Konrad had traveled with his battalion to aid relief efforts before the game's beginning. The sandstorms have effectively cut off Dubai from civilization. With Dubai in this state, these Konrad billboards become nonsensical. When would anyone have the time or resources to erect them? Walker sees them, but are they real? If players think about the billboards, they can question Walker's mental state.

Level Design and Environmental Narrative
Any technique of environmental narrative can be included in a game's level design. The more techniques that are used, the more the player is engaged with both the story and the gameplay.

Examples: The level design in *Brothers: A Tale of Two Sons* encourages players to interact with the environment. Players guide both the older and younger brother through the world, and the brothers have different personalities. The older brother is more pragmatic and task driven, while his younger brother is playful and mischievous. Interacting with people and objects on the map will illustrate each brother's characterization. For example, when the older brother interacts with a woman sweeping in front of her cottage, he'll help her sweep. The younger brother takes her broom and balances it on his palm.

Fatal Frame II uses audio, visual, and design environmental-narrative techniques in its level design to advance the plot and develop characters. A ghost named Chitose leads players to important information, and she leads them to information about *her*. The player-character's sister is locked up in a room, so players need to find the key. Following Chitose brings the player to several journals. These journals give important clues. Chitose was always fearful and hid in closets when she was alive. Her brother gave her a bell to wear around her wrist that she could ring whenever she was afraid, and he'd come find her. He also gave her the key to his room—the key the player needs. She's still hiding in death. There are four closets in the house, so players must listen carefully for the bell to find the right closet, defeat Chitose, and take the key.

Game Mechanics and Environmental Narrative

What's true of environmental narrative and level design is also true of environmental narrative and game mechanics. Any technique of environmental narrative can be integrated into game mechanics. Fewer game manuals are being printed, and many players don't read them. Using a game's environment can instruct players about the game's mechanics while telling them something about the world.

Alan Wake (from the game of the same name) can't use melee weapons, and he can't pick them up. He only uses ranged weapons, while hostile NPCs only use melee weapons. Gamers have Pavlovian responses to items on the ground. They've been taught to loot. Imagine frustrated players as Wake gets ambushed and killed while they try to pick up a melee weapon. Showing players Wake can't pick up melee weapons is an effective way of teaching gameplay. Placing the melee weapons in the environment also says something about the world. It gives an in-game explanation as to where the enemies are finding *their* weapons.

But mechanics can add to the story itself. When players kill something in a game, they know that, eventually, the body will magically disappear. This is also true in *Bastion*—up until the end of the game. Towards the end, players discover the player-character's ethnic group is responsible for the mass genocide of another, called the Ura. The player must fight the Ura at the end of the game. The Ura's bodies don't disappear. They stay there—like real bodies. The very fact that this is bucking a convention in games is an emotional smack to the

To Text or Not to Text

Text is often used in environmental narrative in graffiti or other written forms. This is a way to get around using text in dialogue or cutscenes. Sometimes narrative designers are under pressure to use as little text as possible. This doesn't mean you should *never* use text. However, there are times you really don't need to. The environmental narrative can do all of the explaining for you.

When players are going to experience a major event or revelation, having a character comment on it or adding text to explain it *in that moment* can lessen the emotional impact. It may be better to let players respond to it without telegraphing what that response should be. Later on, you can explain how it's affected the world or story or have characters discuss it to show how they've processed what's happened.

Think about how you want players to respond emotionally to what they're

153

experiencing. That will help you decide whether you think you need to incorporate dialogue or text into certain situations. If what you want them to feel is overwhelming, or it's obvious that what they've just experienced is absolutely horrible or wondrous, talking or "texting" at them might break the mood.

Graffiti *is* text, and it can be just as bad as on-the-nose dialogue. If you're using graffiti, you really want it to add something. It doesn't have to be a "the cake is a lie" type of revelation, as it is in *Portal*. Some great examples of graffiti that enhance the worldbuilding are in *Left 4 Dead*. Scrawled on walls are conversations about the state of the world and moral and philosophical statements on humanity's responsibility for the Green Flu outbreak.

Also, be aware that if your game is released in multiple languages, it can be much harder to change text that is hardcoded into the art of the game world than to simply localize

head. It's symbolic. It reinforces the genocide happened—and *you*, the player, are now killing Ura.

This ties into the story, but it is also used to elicit an emotional response from the player. And the player is going to be faced with a potentially emotional decision at the very end of the game. Environmental narrative here is used through the mechanics to get the player emotionally involved and to contemplate the atrocities that have happened in this world.

Genre and Audience

When implementing environmental narrative, you *always* need to keep the genre and audience in mind. In action-oriented games, the visuals need to be large enough that players notice them. Sometimes they're not going to notice no matter what you do, but give them every opportunity to experience the information. With the Konrad billboards in *Spec Ops: The Line*, players can see them even if they're busy running by.

Not all players are explorers. If you're trying to communicate information players need to progress through the game, make sure it's obvious. Give them big, hulking neon signs, so to speak. Make sure that the core messages are accessible to and easily understood by all types of players.

Also, think about rewarding players who *do* like to explore. Visual puns, interesting ambient dialogue or sounds they might hear because they stick around, in-jokes, Easter eggs (in-jokes or messages that are well hidden and difficult to find), and other special insights are good ways to reward explorers.

Coming Up with a Plan

Executing a plan for environmental narrative is a collaborative effort that will involve all of the project's teams. The sound, design, and art teams will all have ideas. They may not be narrative designers or game writers, but having them be a part of this process will give them more appreciation for the game's narrative design. They'll have some ownership of the narrative design, and they'll be more invested in it as well. In working with other teams, you'll need to be very clear about how they can be involved. You may have to give examples of how sound can develop a character, for instance.

Again, these decisions about narrative need to be made early in development. Any use of gameplay, art, sound, or levels to communicate story means involvement from another department, and days or weeks of added time to that department's schedule. Environmental narrative isn't a way to fill plot holes late in development—it should be part of the plan from the beginning, giving you a fuller experience to play off when you try to fill last-minute plot holes with desperate text.

When you communicate with the other teams who are part of your environmental-narrative design, be very specific and detailed about your plans. Explain the following:

- What's the purpose of a location/setting?
- What can mechanics or level design say about the world and its characters?
- What is sound/art supposed to suggest? (For example, don't simply talk about a sigh. Is it exasperated? Annoyed? Bored? Weary?)
- What emotional responses are you trying to elicit?

Include references, just as you might help artists understand the attributes or personality of a character. These include:

- Photographs
- Image files from the Internet
- Sound files
- Sketches of your own ideas.

Don't assume everyone will know what you're talking about. If you don't have clear examples, your ideas may be misinterpreted. It's better to give too much information instead of not enough.

Be open to giving clarification. This may seem obvious, but it's essential, especially if you've never worked with the team before. Everyone has different writing and speaking styles. People are going to have to get used to the way you communicate orally and in documentation. The first time you share documents, encourage teams to give feedback and ask questions if anything seems unclear. Tell them to ask plenty of questions in meetings. This will make them feel more involved in the process and let them know they're free to share

words found in a book or spoken by a character.

Some games, though, just don't need text or dialogue. *Limbo* would become a completely different game with text or dialogue. Instead, it allows players' imaginations and emotional responses to explain what's going on. Players can come up with much more twisted theories as to why little boys are in cages or why they're trying to kill the player-character. If players ever get an explanation, they might be disappointed.

Writing Has the Flexibility

It's been discussed before how big an advantage it is to understand the requirements—and restrictions—of other disciplines. A lot of this is what will allow a narrative designer to better integrate narrative with gameplay, cinematics, and every other aspect of what makes a game. But this is also what will allow a narrative designer to know when and how to fight for a story point, or when to show the flexibility that narrative has and other disciplines may not.

It is important to remember that story is one of the most flexible elements of what makes a game. Sometimes last-minute catastrophes (or cut levels) mean narrative designers will have to go into overdrive to modify the story and associated elements to compensate while still providing a flawless experience to the audience.

On the flip side, it is just as important to remember that narrative isn't a fix for

their ideas when it comes to incorporating environmental narrative into the game design, sound, and art.

Execution: From Production to Narrative

All of the above covered how to prepare for the implementation of your narrative during preproduction. Going forward, the discussion will look at the behind-the-scenes operations, what players should ideally never see, that is, how the narrative itself functions and is communicated to the audience, and how the audience interacts with the game.

The actual crafting of a narrative for games is not just about the creative side of things. How to work with the team, how to balance the interdependencies of each department, and knowing when to prioritize your work versus the needs of other disciplines are all just as important as how you deliver your narrative to the audience.

If you can't work well with the other disciplines on the project (be they part of bigger teams as normally seen on a larger title, or individuals who cover several specialties as you may see on smaller titles), then the narrative delivery will suffer, and your story will not be conveyed as well as it should be to your audience. It is just as important to understand how the other members of your team work, what they need from you, and what you need from them as it is to know all the methods at your disposal to bring the narrative to life.

Narrative Design and Team Dependencies

AAA video games are a huge undertaking, which means that the more you know about how your ideas will affect other people's ability to do their jobs, the more welcome you'll be on a team.

The teams ahead of you in the process of development are called "**upstream**," and your job is dependent on them providing the tools you need, whether that means literal software tools, or just the go-ahead to work. "**Downstream**" teams require *you* to finish *your* job so they can do theirs. What is described in this section is a large team with specialists for nearly every individual role. Remember that in smaller companies, this process may change as generalists handle more aspects of development without involving other people.

This process may also change depending on when the narrative team begins work on a project and how fixed various elements such as level design, gameplay, and cinematics may already be. The more advanced a project is, the more flexible narrative will have to be to adapt to already locked-down content.

Upstream Teams

The things that you will require as a narrative designer to move forward with your work are:

1 **Working tools**. Before designers can start working, programmers must have selected or built a game engine and created (or bought or modified) the software in which you will be working. This can be as simple as "We're making a Flash game; write the dialogue in Excel," or as complicated as building a new game engine and dialogue toolset from scratch. This means that most programmers/engineers can be considered "upstream" team members, since their work is more likely to be a dependency for narrative design than the other way around.

2 **Approval of the overall concept**. Whether working from your own pitch or someone else's, *someone* will have to give you the go-ahead to actually make the game. Unless you're a sole proprietorship, in which case your investors likely will have to approve the funds before you can start.

3 **Core mechanics and "the loop."** Most games have a core "gameplay loop" that makes up the vast majority of player interaction in a game, something like, "Fight enemies, collect loot, use loot to upgrade equipment, fight better enemies, rinse and repeat." Until this loop is defined, very little can be settled about other parts of the game, such as narrative design.

4 **Initial level-design plan**. Before you start plotting, it's good to know how many environments you'll have available and what those environments will be. They won't be built yet, or even necessarily mapped out, but you should at least have a list of "three wilderness environments, one large city, ten dungeons" or "one swamp planet, one urban planet, one jungle planet," or "a high school, an office, and a park."

Those are the minimums you should try to have in place before starting this chapter's work. Depending on when in the process your company uses writers, there may be a whole lot of other work that's already completed that you have to work around. This means that:

- If levels are already designed and built, your plots need to fit within those levels, not require new environments and new art.
- If character models are already complete, your plots can't ask for a character with a distinctive appearance (a hunchback, or a burned face, or what have you).
- If character abilities are already set, you can't have a scene where the protagonist (or other controllable character) does something he or she won't be able to do in gameplay.
- If gameplay is entirely complete, your plot will have to fit in the spaces left between the gameplay scenes and serve to narratively

flawed designs, and attempting to cover up poor systems with bad exposition will generally end up being criticized as such—and rightly so—by players. For example, there is nothing quite as bad as being told by the character in a shooter to reload their weapon, because the user interface or animations that would show the gun being empty were not planned for.

string together gameplay levels that were designed without a shred of narrative in mind.

Downstream Teams

Once you *finish* your narrative overview, however, there are many other teams who should meticulously review your work to make sure you and they both know what it will take to build the game. The downstream teams include:

Level Design

If your game has any sort of action gameplay, someone will need to review your outline and figure out:

- **Where the fights go**: Level designers will be the ones sifting through your paragraphs of story and deciding, "Okay, after the heartwarming talk with the lost penguin, when you get ambushed by the machine-gun-wielding walruses, how many walruses should there be? Should they all use machine guns, or should one of them be a walrus mage? Is there going to be an iceberg nearby that the walruses can hide behind, or will they emerge out of the water?" And so on.
- **What loot the player finds:** When you write, "She offers the player a suitable reward for undertaking the quest," it is the level and/or game designers who decide what that reward is and balance its value and powers against everything else in the game.
- **Whether to include a boss fight**: Boss fights are more than just a difficult fight. They usually introduce some kind of new mechanic and require a specially designed area to showcase the fight. The decision of whether to include one is based partly on dramatic effectiveness, but also on budget and staff availability. Combat or systems designers also weigh in on this.
- **What areas are required**: If you say, "The player chases the evil walrus back to its lair," level designers and artists need to decide whether that lair is full of explorable ice caves and environmental hazards, or is just an overhanging cliff. If you write a plot requiring new environment art, that plot will be cut if there aren't artists available to build that level. On the other hand, if you wrote with the assumption that the walrus lair would be another boring snow set, the environment artists might surprise you by having a burst of inspiration and designing a fantastical floating ice palace. Or something. This walrus example is kind of playing itself out.

Production

"Production" really means "budgets and schedules." Again, if you're flying solo, this doesn't apply, but even at a two-person studio, the other person should be looking over your plan to see how much your grand vision will cost and how long it might take. Things that might cost more (in money or time) than you expect include:

- **New art**: Anything that requires new art tends to be expensive and time-consuming. This includes if you want to have any words in the art (like a sign on the door) that will need to be translated into other languages. If you're working with off-site artists, narrative designers may have the additional task of providing art references to the contractors for any new art they request (which can kill many an afternoon in the depths of Google Images . . .).
- **Animations**: Games are not hand-animated like movies. They tend to have a fixed menu of animations that are available (walk, run, fight, open door, etc.). Anything that goes outside this menu, like a kiss or holding hands, is enormously expensive.
- **Audio**: If you're recording dialogue, all decisions that involve voice recordings must be decided well in advance to be able to book, cast, and record the actors (not to mention translate them into different languages).

Cinematics and Audio

Any time you write a cutscene, the animators/cinematic designers will have to do a sanity check for how your script will work best within their budget and tools. Cultivate a good relationship with the people who will create your cutscenes—animators vary tremendously on how much input they want from writers, and you'll do best by asking your team directly what they prefer. Some animators want a script to work from that specifies exactly what physically happens in the scene, while others would rather just get the dialogue and be free to animate the rest of the scene however they want. Often, it depends on how overworked they already are. If your cinematics team is slammed, you'll get better results by including a description for them to work from.

If your game has VO, narrative design will also be a huge dependency for your sound department, requiring them to ensure that the audio is in and working correctly before the cinematics can be rendered.

Quality Assurance

Not every company has their QA team go over the narrative plans ahead of time, but it's highly recommended. Good game testers have played a lot of games. They're used to finding plot holes, and they think more like an average player than anyone else in a game studio. Having someone mentally playtest your plot and point out, "But walruses are from the North Pole, and penguins are from the South" at the very beginning of development can save you months of work and convoluted retconning later. (Hah! Got that walrus thing back in!)

There are also plenty of other teams who are neither fully upstream or down, but rather work in parallel to narrative design, and generally at the same time. Most art and narrative are created simultaneously, for example, since they are co-responsible for much of the game's content (as opposed to the game's design and structure). And no game development team can afford to wait until the design is fully complete to start creating that content . . . which often makes the writing experience feel a little like trying to fly a plane while someone is building it underneath you!

Conclusion

Although the two parts of this chapter, implementation and production, may seem to be separate, you can see how many topics bleed over from one to the other when it comes to communication and teamwork. That's because working as part of a team is essential to any large production, and it would be a mistake to think of good teamwork as a separate discipline from "real game design."

What has been covered in this chapter should give you a good grounding for future teamwork, in either large or small teams. While, as narrative designers, you can make use of a few or several narrative tools and invent more on the way as needed, it is important to remember that teamwork is not an optional variable. No matter how good a scene is, how cool an environmental element may be, or how amazing the story is, if you haven't worked out how to integrate the narrative design within the nuts and bolts of the game production, your story will not realize its potential.

Learning not just what the other disciplines need but also who your teammates are and what they enjoy working on is a huge advantage for any narrative-design work. You can't always work on what you prefer to, but learning how to balance the less interesting with the most interesting—and knowing how to interact positively with others— will be a huge asset in properly fulfilling your function as a narrative designer within your team.

Exercise

Exercise 6.1

Using the information detailed in the provided sample template at the end of the chapter, draft a narrative bible for your game.

Game design documents can take many formats, depending on the genre of the game, the needs of the project, the expectations of your lead, or your own personal preferences. The sample template shows the format such a document could take, with references to the chapter specific to each section. Initial narrative-design documents are usually high level, then gain more complexity as a project progresses. Each approval phase will open up more in-depth material to be elaborated upon. It is vital to keep a high-level summary of each section in an easily seen location for each of these chapters. People new to the project will not have the time to read a hundred-page-long document (unless they're on the narrative team, at which point it's mandatory). It's important to keep things high level and allow people from other disciplines to get a sense of what's going on while letting them choose which subject to read more about.

Note that more or even fewer sections can be used in the creation of a narrative bible, depending on the needs of the project and the information you need to put forth. Below is a baseline template to get you started.

Sample

Sample 6.1

Narrative Bible Document Template

Story Brief

Reference: Chapter 2, "The Concept"

Include your pitch, then your full story concept here. This should not be longer than half to one full page until the story has been approved, and you have the go-ahead to go into more details.

Setting and World

Reference: Chapter 3, "Worldbuilding"

This is where the high-level worldbuilding relevant to the game is located. During initial phases, keeping this high level is important. As the work proceeds, this section will become more in-depth, depending on what is needed to support the game's narrative.

Character List

Reference: Chapter 4, "Characters"

- Player-character(s)
- Major NPCs
- Minor NPCs

Expanded Story Breakout

Reference: Chapter 5, "Story"

A full beat-by-beat story breakout can cover multiple pages but should always focus only on critical-path content. Side stories, world exploration, and other such narrative elements can be located in this section. Or they can be covered in their own documents or in separate sections, per project preference.

Mission Breakdown and Pertinent Narrative Elements

Reference: Chapter 6, "Implementation and Production"

This section should cover critical-path story breakdown as missions. This is where you can use a program to do step-by-step breakdowns of each mission on a narrative level, using the information in Chapter 5 (see "Designing Quests") for high-level story breakdowns. Using the tools listed in the "Wireframing" section of Chapter 5, you can break down each mission in as much detail as desired. This will give you an easily consulted visual reference to pass on to the level design and gameplay.

Note that several of the elements mentioned in Chapter 6 can also be included in the introduction of this section (for example, graphical perspective), or where appropriate during the mission breakdown (environmental-narrative elements). If your game is meant to use environmental narrative in a consistent, omnipresent sort of way, then moving the topic to its own section has merit.

Addendum: Side Quests

Side quests are usually not contained in the main narrative bible, though any content that supports or is relevant to the critical-path story can and should be added after the main critical-path breakdown for the sake of transparency.

If you work in Confluence or any other similar web-based documentation archive, it will be easy to create pertinent pages and cross link as needed. If you're working in a Word-type document only, then you want to make sure not to bloat the document so badly that people are afraid to read it—that's when creating separate documents for ancillary material is a good idea.

Dialogue

As a writer in games, the first thing you must internalize about writing dialogue is that *its purpose is to keep the game moving forward*.

Dialogue can fulfill many other purposes, including:

- **Characterization**: Both through choice of words in plot-related conversations and by optional, personal digressions.
- **Worldbuilding**: Through discussions of history and backstory.
- **Pacing**: By providing "breather" moments between hundred-mile-an-hour action scenes.
- **Humor**: Which can serve to both lighten the mood after an intense action scene and to relax players in order to set them up for a "gotcha" moment when they're next attacked.

But the primary reason developers pay to add dialogue to their games is to help the player move through the game in the smoothest, most interesting, and most natural way possible.

If you keep this in mind, it becomes very clear when you:

1   *Must* use dialogue—There is a critical "plot juncture" that can't be explained to players any other way. In games with deep characterization, a plot juncture can also mean a crucial reveal of character.

DOI: 10.1201/9781003369332-7

2 *Should* use dialogue—The player needs a narrative motivation to proceed in the plot.

3 *Can* use dialogue—Everything else, but dialogue should generally remain optional and skippable for players.

IN THIS CHAPTER, YOU WILL LEARN . . .

- The difference between ambient and interactive dialogue.
- How to create all types of ambient dialogue, from grunts, to barks, to banter.
- The parts of an interactive conversation, from opening hook, to conversation hook, to conversation hubs, and the immediate goal.
- How to structure an interactive conversation so that player choices are respected but the information flow is consistent across all paths.
- How dialogue is typically used in RPGs, MMOs, action games, and casual/mobile games.
- How to work with other departments to breathe life into your words.

Types of Dialogue

While every genre of game and every company has its own specific dialogue type and terminology, they all fall into three broad categories: **ambient dialogue**, **interactive dialogue**, and **cutscenes**.

Ambient Dialogue

In this book, "ambient dialogue" means any talking that happens *during gameplay*, whether it's dialogue by the player, by AI companions, by a voice-over, a radio headset, or by characters the player passes in the street. This is dialogue that is prompted by in-game events and triggers, such as:

- **Entering an area**. For example, "Lay low! There are snipers around!"
- **Taking damage in combat**. For example, "I'm hit! Medic!"
- **Attempting an action**. For example, "This chest is locked. Give me a minute."

The player is free to listen to or ignore such dialogue, though frequently it does contain valuable instructions from NPCs or radio-headset voices, such as "That's a map of Guerville. We need to go west." Gameplay does not stop to accommodate the dialogue, and if the player-character speaks, the player is given no choice of what to say.

In many games, including most FPS and RTS games, ambient dialogue is the primary or only way dialogue is used in the game, and it is certainly sufficient to tell an engaging story. However, when your development team desires dialogue that is more responsive to the player's wishes, or that can function as a game system itself—by setting variables that change future game events or affect alignment or approval scores—you'll need to use interactive dialogue.

Interactive Dialogue

"Interactive dialogue" refers to any game system in which the dialogue pauses the action to allow the player to select responses from a list, wheel, or any other presentation of multiple options. Games that use this sort of player choice in dialogue vary from complex roleplaying games with multiple game systems, like *Dragon Age* or *Alpha Protocol*, to adventure games like *The Walking Dead* (in which much of the gameplay *is* the dialogue), to hybrid FPS games like *Deus Ex*, and even social games like *Game of Thrones: Ascent*. Even TV has gotten into the game of interactive dialogue in the past few years with Netflix shows such as *Black Mirror: Bandersnatch*.

What these systems have in common is that they allow the player to take an active role in the dialogue. By selecting what their character will say, players engage with the dialogue both for pure roleplaying purposes (to show that "their" character refuses to take money for helping those poor orphans), and to affect future game events (by setting conditionals that the game will later recognize with character reactions or tailored content). Narrative designers for games with interactive dialogue must take care to ensure that the dialogue choices they offer the player are meaningful. It is this choice between distinct options and outcomes that makes interactive dialogue a true game system and not just flavor.

And, of course, regardless of what style of dialogue you use in the rest of the game, there will usually be a few moments that require cutscenes.

Cutscenes

For the book's purposes, a cutscene refers to any dialogue that both:

- occurs outside of gameplay;
- does not offer player choice.

These are the "mini-movie" moments that usually occur to highlight particularly spectacular moments in the game. Cutscene dialogue is usually sparse and paired with extensive animated sequences that occur outside of the regular gameplay camera. This topic will be covered in-depth in Chapter 8, "Cutscenes and Cinematics."

Writing Ambient Dialogue

Ambient dialogue can be broken into a few distinct types:

- **Onomatopes/grunts**: Literally sounds with no words involved, used in the following situations (and more):

- **Screams**: Expressing fear, joy, rage, or any strong emotion which may be vocalized without words.
- **Sounds of effort**: When jumping, climbing, etc., of various degrees (jumping off a table to jumping off a wall ten feet high).
- **Surprise**: Indrawn breath, short huff of surprise, etc.
- **Laughter, giggles.**
- **Combat barks/soundsets**: These relate directly to combat situations and will have variables on them as to frequency of use, time of use, etc. It's recommended to have a healthy variety of each type, and to ask quality assurance (testers, QA) to keep an eye on how frequently they crop up. While writing ten variations for "Watch out!", "Over there!", and "Enemy incoming!" isn't fun for you, hearing the same line repeated every single time can quickly become a major annoyance to players. Writing these barks is also likely to be your first task as a junior writer in the industry . . . and is something your team will always love you for offering to handle.
- **Generic ambients**: Short lines of dialogue usually referring to an immediate situation, location, or event. Often just a one-liner. Can also serve as a hint for the player:
  - "I think we're in the right place."
  - "Over there."
  - "Go left."
- **Customized ambients**: These are one-liners that are used only once, usually for important missions, which serve as a clue for the player's navigation of the level. Where generic ambients are vague, customized ambients tend to be more situation specific:
  - "That's the key we've been looking for."
  - "There's no turning back after this."
- **Generic banter**: A few lines of dialogue between two or more characters (optionally including the player). They can either be situational (remarking on the new location you've just discovered), or they can be pure character development. These usually occur in-game and can be interrupted. Never place critical narrative information in a generic banter.
- **Customized banter**: As above, but may contain information relevant to the mission or narrative. Such lines need to be worked carefully into the level with cooperation from level design so they don't overlap or get cut off by other encounters.

Ambient dialogue is often detailed in a spreadsheet or other software that easily tracks many single, disconnected lines. As it is generally quick to write and easy for actors to record, ambient dialogue (especially the one-liner, non-banter types) may continue to be written up until the last moment of production, with quick lines added to fill holes (if there's a lot of dead time on screen as the player goes from place to place) or fix problems (by adding lines telling the player where to go during a section testers found confusing).

Dialogue in Action Games

Any game that is dominated by action gameplay must maintain the same kind of fast, driving pace, even in its dialogue. The player's attention span is short, and the narrative space is significantly smaller than in more story-driven games. Anything that interrupts the expected combat sequences will be viewed as a fun-killing obstacle. And since extended ambient dialogues are noninteractive, forcing players into the role of passive observers, action players tend to skip them no matter how well written they are. Therefore, to write "good" action dialogue, narrative designers need to consider not just the words they use but also the context in which the player will hear them.

Here are keys to writing a good action dialogue:

- **Keep all exchanges as short as possible**. Consider the player's attention span to be maybe fifteen to twenty seconds.
- **Consider where your dialogue occurs**. Shouts during combat can only contain the most crucial information ("Man down!"), while back-and-forth banter during cooldowns or while walking from place to place can generally go a little longer. Games like *BioShock* famously allow players to hear as much or as little dialogue as they want, by telling most of the story in ambient audio recordings that are entirely optional content.
- **Make all longer story blocks and backstory elements "on-demand."** This content is not a requirement for the gameplay experience. Let the players decide how much information they want and when.

If you find yourself getting wordy, imagine being in a situation where you're being hunted by something and you have to run away. How much time would you want someone to take telling you the best escape route?

Action Storytelling

When writing an action game, it's important to layer your dialogue into the gameplay without interrupting the flow of the gameplay itself. This means it should have a couple of characteristics:

- The dialogue does not force the players to stop what they're doing.
- The dialogue is supported by the gameplay situation.

Action storytelling normally requires games to use some form of voiceover because reading a text doesn't combine well with shooting a monster. Voiceover has the advantage that players can hear it even while focusing their attention on the combat action in front of them.

Consider a small example for a typical action RPG, such as *Diablo*. Imagine the following situation: A young couple is attacked by a giant toad while having a picnic in the forest by their village. The player arrives and finds only the woman because the toad has abducted her husband.

Since you want to avoid interactive dialogue here, this is a way to explain to the player what happened:

1   As the player approaches, the game can fire a short line from the woman to capture the player's attention. She might say, "Help me. . . . Someone help!"
2   When the player clicks on the woman, she'll tell him/her what happened, using voice-over—rather than text dialogue.
3   The player's journal now shows the quest to retrieve the woman's husband.

Unlike a less action-oriented RPG, the player never has to ask questions or accept the quest. Simply making the choice to click on the character automatically leads to the quest being accepted. This limited interaction in the dialogue allows players to continue fighting even if the giant toad shows up again while the dialogue is still running! Gameplay is not interrupted.

Now say you allow the woman to follow the player. You can share more information in the same way at key points on the way to the enemy. Once the player defeats the giant toad, the woman and her husband can thank and reward the player in the same ambient way.

Depending on the animations available, the husband could even run toward his wife in the background as the player loots the defeated toad. The entire story takes place as part of normal gameplay; players never have to wait and watch but can move on to new adventures.

Writing Interactive Dialogue

There are many different ways to create interactive dialogue, from hyperlinks in Microsoft Word and Excel, to proprietary dialogue engines created by many game companies. This book represents the dialogue structure as a flow chart, rather than using any individual program.

Interactive dialogue tends to be a costly feature for a game, in terms of both development time and time used in the game itself. So, in games with interactive dialogue, it is often the primary means by which the story and game move forward.

Each quest or story segment is introduced by a dialogue, frequently (and creatively) called the "quest-giving dialogue." Many mid-plot dialogues also function as quest-giving for the next stage. As such, when companies hire writers, quest-giving dialogue becomes *the* unit of measurement for quality.

A good quest-giving dialogue consists of the following:

1   **The opening hook**, which attracts players and prompts them to enter the dialogue.
2   **The first NPC hub**, in which the quest-giver explains the problem.
3   **The first player hub**, in which the player can pursue or leave the quest.
4   **Further NPC hubs**, in which the details of the quest are explained.
5   **Further player hubs**, in which the player asks questions and accepts or refuses the quest.
6   **The immediate goal**, the final NPC hub, in which the first step of the quest is clearly spelled out.

The Opening Hook

Many quest-giving dialogues jump right into the quest with an opening line like, "Ho there, adventurer! I have some adventure that needs doing!" However, this is clumsy and unrealistic. (How often have you walked up to a stranger and offered her a gold necklace if she'll fight the giant rats in your cellar?)

A better strategy, at least in games with voice-over and ambient animations for the NPCs, is to start *in media res*, with the quest-giver already involved in an action or conversation before the player arrives. Instead of standing and waiting for the player to kill the giant rats, the NPC could be laying down poison or dickering with a salesman over the price of his rat traps.

This opening line serves several functions:

•   It gives players an idea what the quest is about, to draw them into the storyline before they've even clicked on anything.
•   It makes the quest-giver (and thus her problems and storyline) feel more believable, since she clearly had an existence before the moment the player walked into view.
•   It makes the quest-giver more sympathetic. People are always more likely to help individuals who look like they're already trying hard themselves, not just waiting for a leg up.

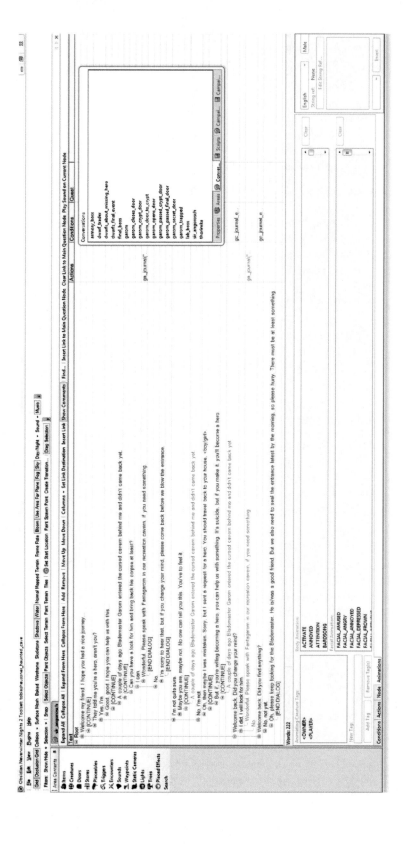

First NPC Hub

After the player enters the full dialogue, the next set of NPC lines is your opportunity to quickly tell the player the story of the quest. The key is to give enough to get the player interested, but not so much that they're overwhelmed. As a rule of thumb, assume players remember only a single detail per hub, and that detail is the *very last thing* stated. Which means that *this*:

> NPC: "M'lord, my basement is full of giant rats. I just bought this castle with my inheritance that I got from Mother when she died. I moved in last week, and my betrothed is coming tomorrow, and she hates rats, so now I'm scared I'll lose everything."

is not as good as *this*:

> NPC: "M'lord, my basement is full of giant rats. I just bought this castle with my inheritance, and now I'm afraid I'll lose everything."

which is not as good as *this*:

> NPC: "M'lord, I'm scared I'll lose everything. I just bought this castle with my inheritance, and now I find the basement is filled with giant rats!"

Since it is the last three or four words of a hub that players have ringing in their ears when they reach their own dialogue choices, the first two examples only present the player with a vague problem to go off: "I'm scared I'll lose everything." It's not immediately clear how the player's likely dialogue choices ("Sure, I'll kill the rats."/"What will you give me for it?"/"I don't care about your stupid castle.") relate to that problem. This causes a moment of disconnect for players. In the last example, the final thought players hear is "filled with giant rats," which immediately situates them in the problem they're trying to solve.

Many writers don't sweat the details when it comes to actually ordering the words in their sentences, but it can make all the difference to the players' understanding of what their dialogue choices mean, and thus their engagement in and satisfaction with the game.

First Player Hub

Every time you offer players a chance to respond in dialogue, you increase their engagement in the quest.

On *Star Wars: The Old Republic*, the rule for writers was that if players didn't get to comment on it, writers had to assume they didn't remember what was said.

All hail the Bard, Rat-Killer and Rodent-Bane, who has bravely made the cellars once again safe for

Screenshot from *The Bard's Tale*. Developed/published by InXile and protected by United States and international copyright law. © InXile.

This means you want to put a player-response hub fairly early in your dialogue. If you try to get all of the exposition out before players speak, they'll tune out and actually learn *less* than if you break each important piece of information into its own section and let players comment on it. *However*, a common mistake new writers make is to have a first-player hub that looks like this:

1   Hello!
2   Good morning!
3   How are you?

Or, if they're a little more self-conscious about trying to keep the choices distinct:

1   Hello!
2   How are you?
3   Why the hell should I think it's a good morning?

This has the exact same effect as not having a player hub at all. Players aren't making a choice; they don't engage emotionally or intellectually. So, essentially, all they're doing is acknowledging that, yes, they are in a dialogue. Skip it.

In every novel or screenwriting book, one of the first commandments is always *Thou Shalt Begin as Late into the Scene as Possible*. In film, this is usually accomplished by cutting to a scene after the greetings are over and the conversation has begun. In a game, conversations begin with the player arriving, so this effect can only happen *if the characters themselves cut to the chase.*

Avoid "Hello," "Goodbye," and "Thank you." They take up space without advancing the story.

The first-player hub is where players choose what approach to take to the conversation. You should probably include a minimum of one "Oh, boy, let me help!" response, one "I'm not interested" response, and one "Tell me more," or "What's in it for me?" If it's a dialogue in which the quest isn't clear yet, these can change into something like an "Oh, boy, I'm really sympathetic to you!" response, a "Tell me more" response, and an "I don't care about you" response. This covers the most likely player sentiments and provides a clear and distinct way to branch the next NPC hub.

Further NPC and Player Hubs

You can have anywhere from one (in a short side quest) to six or so middle hubs in your dialogue before it becomes a good idea to break the dialogue into two distinct encounters. For the exercise at the end of the chapter, you should stick to two or three. If you're planning to use your dialogue as a portfolio piece, it's far better to show what you can get across in a small space than to show how much space you can fill.

These middle hubs require you to show the NPC's reactions to the player's choice, but without losing the flow of the conversation. If using the player options above, for example, you would want divergent responses to each player choice. So, "Oh, boy, let me help!" might allow the player to skip past some exposition and go straight to "Great. Just go to the mountain range and bring me back a dragon head," while "I'm not interested" would either end the conversation or lead the NPC to plead, "But just listen to what happened! I swear this is important!" This line would then link to the same explanation of what happened as the one in which the player asked for more information.

GENERAL INTERACTIVE DIALOGUE TIPS

- Always have an "eager" option which lets players skip the details of what happened and go straight to what to do next.
- An "I'm not interested" option should rarely cut off all access to a quest. It's better to let the NPC plead her case or at least say, "Come back if you change your mind."
- Never use a player hub that's a single line. Don't make the player click if it's just a "continue" button.
- Never have an obvious false choice (i.e., 1. Yes; 2. Yeah; 3. Sure). A good way to lightly disguise that you're forcing a player to accept a quest is to offer the option between "Yes" and "What do I get out of it?" so that players can help either altruistically or for a reward.
- If you're at a loss for extra player options in nondecision hubs (i.e., places where you just want the player to say, "Go on . . ."), consider whether they might guess the next thing the NPC will say. One correct guess, one incorrect guess, and one "Tell me more" fills out a hub nicely *and* lets your players characterize themselves.

Skipping Dialogue

Some writers have a knee-jerk resentment of the idea that players can skip dialogue. They don't want to include a "Just tell me where to go and who to kill" option, if that means players end up slaughtering the orc hordes of Avergena'arg without understanding the complex history of their society. But when a writer fights to make sure that every player hears this backstory, what often happens is that the entire questline gets simplified, since even QA professionals get tired of listening to the five-hundredth explanation of it.

Allowing players to skip dialogue is a writer's best friend, because it ensures that *the only players who read your*

The Immediate Goal

In the last NPC hub, after players make their decision whether to take the quest, it's the writer's responsibility to resituate the player in the game. A long conversation generally takes the player out of the flow of the larger story. The final NPC line should ideally do three things:

- Remind the player where in the overall story they are.
- Tie this quest or conversation to the player's larger goals.
- Tell, in small and clear words, the next step that the player must do.

So, in a game in which the player is trying to stop an army of demons from rising, and a quest in which the player has just agreed to rescue someone's kidnapped girlfriend, you want to end the conversation with something like this:

I'm just afraid that the wizard who took Julie is in league with the demons. I know he has a castle in the mountains. I'll give you my mother's magic ring if you go there and rescue her from the dungeon.

Dialogues in MMOs

Most MMOs—with a few notable exceptions such as *Star Wars: The Old Republic* and *The Elder Scrolls Online*—present their dialogue in the form of **quest texts**. These are structured text boxes that include a short, written dialogue, a description of the task, a summary of the task, and the rewards players will receive upon completion.

In some MMOs, including *Drakensang Online*, these quest texts are the only tool for communicating story to the players. This presents narrative designers with the problem of keeping the texts short enough to fit and accommodate the expectations of the MMO audience, while still delivering enough information to understand the plot. But as the majority of MMO players skip straight to the summary and rewards without reading the quest text, it is the narrative designer's job to make plots that can be told effectively through those means.

Keep in mind that players in groups rarely have time to read long dialogues. Have you ever been in a situation where you wanted to kill the big, bad Raid Boss but were stuck waiting for your friends to read the quest first? Then you know what you want to avoid putting your players through.

In general, in quest texts, you want a laser focus on the problem the NPC is having. Players don't need to understand the background of how the problem developed, at least not at the moment that someone is asking them to fix it. To let players learn more about the backstory of the quest, narrative designers can use environmental narrative and/or on-demand storytelling, without adding extra bulk to the quest texts.

lines are the ones who want to hear them. If all the "I just wanna kill stuff" players have already chosen the first dialogue option, then the ones who are left with you as you leisurely explain the story are the ones who actually care about hearing it.

You will never force non-story players to like your story more by telling them more about it. The sooner you embrace that and structure your dialogues to *help* more gameplay-oriented players skip to what they care about more quickly, the better your work will survive playtesting.

* Screenshot from *Drakensang Online*. Developed/published by Bigpoint and protected by United States and international copyright law. © Bigpoint.

Using Tokens in Dialogue

In any game without a fixed protagonist, writers will need to become familiar with **tokens**, or **strings**, the tiny bits of code that let your game know when, instead of a single word, you need a word that refers back to something players chose about their character. Tokens will almost always be set early on in the game-design process by someone on the more technical side of design, and will look like this: @player_name, or _player_name, or [player_name_here].

For example, in *Game of Thrones: Ascent*, players could pick whether to be male or female, living in any of the Seven Kingdoms and sworn to any of the Great Houses of Westeros. This sometimes resulted in writing sentences like: "@address @player_name, the @fealty_plural want you to return to @fealty_city before @fealty_region gets invaded!" In the game, if you were playing, say, a female character named Jennifer who

This also helps keep players immersed in the game by making each individual dialogue and quest terse and urgent. Remember that you have the sum total of all the dialogues, books, journals, and ambient chatter to tell your story; it doesn't all have to be laid out up front in the quest text.

Dialogue in Social and Mobile Games

Advancements in mobile technology and social gaming made popular on Twitch and YouTube streaming allow for longer games with more complex mechanics. Social and mobile games can have voiced characters and interactive dialogue with player choices and NPC responses, just like traditional video games. More and more games in these spaces, especially RPGs, have dialogue that's increasingly story and character oriented. Other mobile games have some story elements, but they're more focused on gameplay. While concise dialogue is important in any game on any platform, it's especially true for mobile and social games. With smaller screens, these games have less space for text.

Specific Challenges

Dialogue boxes in social and mobile games usually give players some or all of the following information:

- Mission or quest objectives.
- A detail that advances the story or establishes the story scenario.
- Specific instructions to complete the mission.
- Hints to complete the mission.
- Reward(s) received for completing an objective.

Since all of this must fit in a dialogue box, the dialogue can come across as unnatural and clunky. People don't normally say, "Pick up five logs in the forest, and get 60 XP." So, it's a little odd when an NPC communicates this to a player. When written this way, NPCs come to feel like "signposts." In other words, they're less like characters and more like ways for players to track their progress in the game.

Social and mobile games also may not feature player-characters. NPCs might speak directly to the player. It can feel as if the player is completely *outside* of the world in which the NPCs live. The NPCs are simply there to help the player level and advance, and there's no relationship between the NPCs and players beyond this. In these cases, when the player is unable to actively interact with NPCs, the NPCs seem even more impersonal.

Whether to change this in favor of better characterization is something you'll have to work out with the rest of your design team, based on how important character and immersion are in your game, versus how easily you want the gameplay goals to be explained. However, strong dialogue with NPC characterization can make the game more immersive and entertaining for players *while* giving them important information.

Making the Best Use of Dialogue Boxes

First, determine what types of information you'll have in the dialogue box. Second, decide or find out how many total *characters with spaces*—not total *words*—you'll allot for each type of information. You might decide that dialogue can be 150 total characters or less, while the instructions may not be more than 50 total characters. The dialogue will give players an idea of what they need to do, so the instructions might be a succinct restatement.

The game's genre and target demographics will help you determine what kind and how much information you'll include. Casual social games tend to restate instructions three ways: during dialogue, in gameplay instructions, and through hints. RPGs with more traditional gameplay might leave more up to the player to figure out. Even traditional PC-based MMOs often have similar text-length restrictions for the dialogue or quest boxes.

Since you'll need to provide specific information through each dialogue interaction, create a template that you or the writers will use. The same type of information should always appear in the same places in the dialogue box, so players can quickly find it. A story-oriented bit of dialogue might be the first two lines, the details for what players need to do are covered in the second or third line, and the players' rewards are mentioned in the fourth line. Keep in mind that each NPC *does not* have to give the player all of this information each time. Put on your writer hat and consider: What would the character naturally communicate?

If one dialogue box with multiple lines is too much, you could alternatively break up this information in sequential boxes. The first box might introduce the story scenario, mission objectives, and characters in dialogue. Then when the player closes the first box, the next details explicit mission objectives and rewards.

Consider a scenario in which Fernando's daughter is lost in a town overrun by vampires. It's up to the player to find her. The player needs to learn the following details to complete this mission:

- The objective is to find Fernando's daughter.
- The search area will be in a particular town.
- The enemies on this quest will be hostile vampires.

All of this information can be expressed through dialogue:

Fernando: I–I've lost my daughter in Meritown! I don't want the vampires to get to her! *Please* help me find her! Maybe she went into a building to hide.

is sworn to the Starks, this would come out as "My lady Jennifer, the Starks want you to return to Winterfell before the North gets invaded!" While a male Lannister named Tobias would read, "My lord Tobias, the Lannisters want you to return to Casterly Rock before the Westerlands get invaded!"

MMO dialogue writing almost always requires the use of tokens, since the heroes come from a huge variety of genders, races, and backgrounds.

And keep in mind, while the English language doesn't make a distinction between the genders in the way words and sentences are formed, many other languages do. This can cause problems with translation if you end up with lines that are too long for your character limits!

The dialogue states the objective (find Fernando's daughter), tells the player where to find her (in a building in Meritown), and warns of the hostile NPCs in the town (vampires).

Broken down in your dialogue template, the information might look like this:

> **Mission Dialogue Part 1** (Character: Fernando): I–I've lost my daughter in Meritown! I don't want the vampires to get to her!
> **Mission Dialogue Part 2** (Part 1 of 1): *Please* help me find her! Maybe she went into a building to hide.
> **Instructions**: Look for Fernando's daughter in Meritown. Reward: 20 XP.
> **Hint**: Tap damaged buildings.

Notice that "Instructions" and "Hint" don't contain any dialogue. The "Instructions" line restates what players need to do while informing them of the reward for completing the mission. The "Hint" simply gives players a clue as to how to complete their objective, something a character wouldn't know.

Depending on the space allotted for dialogue boxes and how you design your template, you can combine any of these lines to take up less space. For example:

> **Mission Dialogue** (Character: Fernando): I–I've lost my daughter in Meritown! I don't want the vampires to get to her! *Please* help me find her! Maybe she went into a building to hide.
> **Instructions**: Click on damaged buildings in Meritown to find Fernando's daughter. Reward: 20 Copper.

Once players successfully complete missions, NPCs can give success dialogue, while text stating the rewards (or icons of specific rewards) can go underneath or above the dialogue. If the NPC is actually rewarding the player in-world, this should be a natural part of the dialogue:

> **Success Dialogue** (Character: Fernando): Oh, thank God you found her! I don't have much, but please take this.
> **Reward**: 20 [copper icon].

Characters might also address players in failure dialogue:

> **Failure Dialogue** (Character: Fernando): You couldn't find her? What if she's turned?!

NPCs Are More than "Signposts"

NPCs are more believable when dialogue reveals their personalities and relationships with the player. A lot of NPCs in social and mobile games are non-characters because they simply give players instructions. Their personality is "friendly"—they're supposed to be helpful. But when all NPCs are friendly and helpful, they're boring and might as well be melded into one character. Also, since so many social and mobile games are simulations, RPGs, or strategy games where players actually *change* the world in some way, it's odd that NPCs wouldn't have their own feelings on what players are doing to the place where they're living. *Animal Crossing: New Horizons* is an excellent illustration of this. Before players build stairs or inclines, animal villagers can't access the cliffs on islands. Once players add stairs, there's a random chance the player will have a conversation with an animal villager where they will express their appreciation for being able to reach the cliffs, when they couldn't before.

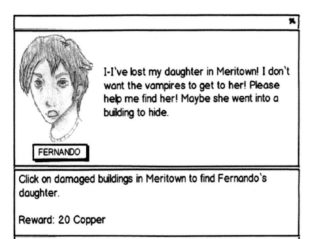

Mockup for a dialogue box in a social game. Mockups of UI and screens made in programs like Balsamiq Mockups are another visual tool you can create for the team. Mockup created by Toiya Kristen Finley.

Characters need to be just as developed as they would be in traditional games. This means they should have concrete personalities, likes and dislikes, merits and flaws, and clearly defined relationships with players or player-characters. Even if there's no player-character or avatar in the game, good dialogue can convey NPCs' attitudes toward the player. Good dialogue expresses how the relationships between NPCs and players/player-characters evolve as players progress. This makes the dialogue in social and mobile games something to savor as an immersive part of the game, not something to skip over to reach the gameplay.

Putting More Character into Text-Based Dialogue

Dialogue communicated through text instead of voice-over doesn't benefit from the personality, accent, emotion, tone, and inflection actors communicate. But you can use the dialogue's context and the player" convention in social and mobile gaming. A slightly in-world character who can say, "Hello, Toiya. Welcome to *Farm Town*. Now we need to buy a goat," gets you into the game more quickly than a fully realized character who needs to present her rationale for why getting a goat is important.

formatting of the text to suggest things like the character's emotion, tone, and state of mind:

> Fernando: I–I've lost my daughter in Meritown! I don't want the vampires to get to her! *Please* help me find her! Maybe she went into a building to hide.

Fernando is a terrified father worried about his daughter's safety. He desperately wants the player to find her. "I–I've" suggests stuttering due to anxiety and fear. Italicizing "*Please*" expresses that Fernando is putting emphasis on this word, and from the context, players can read into this his sense of desperation. Players can "hear" him pleading with them.

Personality can also come through clearly in dialogue. In the following scenario from the same hypothetical vampire game, players must work alongside a character named Ryan to repair buildings at a survivor camp. Ryan is highly intelligent and arrogant. He's extremely confident in his own skills, but not the player's:

> Ryan: Well, look who's not stumbling about like an idiot anymore . . . You ready to be useful?

Ryan's words hold nothing but contempt. He's demeaning: "Well, look who's not stumbling about like an idiot anymore . . ." And he doubts the player's abilities: "You ready to be useful?" Players can easily tell that Ryan does not like them, and the relationship with Ryan is strained at best.

With context and formatting, you can use players' imaginations to "hear" what is said and the manner in which it's said. Most games use the following formatting conventions for text:

- *Italics:* Stress or emphasis on a word, sense of urgency, irritation, sarcasm.
- **Bolding**: Raising the voice, emphasis on a word.
- ALL CAPS: Shouting.
- *Asterisks*: Onomatopoeia (representation of sound in words) suggesting coughing (*coughs*), throat clearing (*ahem*), etc.

If working on an established franchise, be sure to check with your team what conventions they use for emphasis. Not all games can handle bold and italic formatting, some disallow all caps, and some are all right with other forms of emphasis, such as *this*.

A NOTE ON EYE DIALECT

Eye dialect uses nonstandard spelling to mimic a character's pronunciation, accent, or regional dialect. "Wuz," "cuz," "wanna," "gonna," and "coulda" are all examples of eye dialect. Eye dialect can be difficult to read if you try to be too precise in conveying an accent: *Whar're y'all gowin' tuhnight?* Reading shouldn't be a chore. The overuse of eye dialect can also turn the character into a parody or caricature, or make the character come across as uneducated and simple. It's better to use a couple of words of eye dialect and use standard spelling for the rest of the words in the line. (Some words you'll use often in dialogue. Make sure that you spell these words consistently for each character, whether they're in eye dialect or not.) A couple of words in eye dialect will be enough to suggest the character's accent and pronunciation: *Where're y'all goin' tonight?*

General Dialogue Quality Tips

Once you've mastered the structure of your particular game genre's dialogue, it's important that the lines themselves be well written, engaging, and believable. There is a lot of advice on this topic in every screenwriting book, but a few game-specific tips include:

- **Consider pronunciation**. If you're writing a game with voice acting, have pity on the actors and only write sentences that can actually be read out loud. Check for tongue-twisters, alliteration, inadvertent rhymes, and other page-to-tongue mismatches.
- **Don't overuse made-up words**. Lots of science fiction and fantasy games are peppered with fancy place names, alien languages, and gibberish religious terminology. As a general rule, try to stick with one of these per line. The same goes for character names, even if they're English. "Jorvan the skirlingspawn went to Uverecht mountain pass to get the amulet of Oobergivish," and "Belinda, Jeremiah, and Franklin talked to Georgina and Roberta about whether Guillermo was sleeping with Jessica," are both equally unintelligible.
- **Stick with short words when possible**. Whether your game is voiced or read, shorter words fit more easily in both speech bubbles and actors' mouths.
- **Use sentence fragments, pauses, run-ons, and other bad grammar**. Perfectly grammatical sentences read like they're from an encyclopedia, not a conversation. In real life, people use slang, hesitate, stumble over their words, and talk awkwardly around things. The more you cut expository sentences into short chunks and pepper them with personal details, the more conversational they'll sound.
- **Include details about the speaker's life outside of the quest**. This makes them seem more like a person than a quest goal. There's a world of difference between saying, "Kind adventurer, I need someone to rescue my lost dog," and "Oh, no! Fluffykins is missing! My little sister gave me that dog on my sixth birthday. She's going to kill me!"

Text and Subtext

The art of dialogue writing is largely the art of turning text into subtext. **Text** is when characters say exactly what they mean, while **subtext** (literally "below text") is when a character says something else that the audience understands to mean an underlying emotion that the character does not want to voice. For example, "I miss you" is text. "Every time I see a flower, I think of your smile" is subtext. Both sentences mean "I miss you," but there are an infinite number of ways to express the same sentiment once you make it into subtext.

Most "good" dialogue stands out because it has turned the text of the character's emotions into interesting subtextual phrases. One of the best-known examples in science fiction is in *The Empire Strikes Back*, in which Princess Leia tells Han Solo, "I love you," and Han's reply is "I know." Had he simply replied, "I love you too," the scene would have been

Dialogue and Other Departments

As a narrative designer, you are far from the only person on the design team who needs to worry about dialogue. Some other departments whose jobs your dialogue will impact include editing (if you're fortunate enough to have formal editors on your project), localization/translation, and audio (if your game has VO dialogue).

Working with Editing

A good editor is the best friend and ally of narrative designers and writers alike.

Good editors will work behind the scenes to improve writing and tighten up the pacing and flow of both dialogue *and* plot. They will see what you've missed, not just on the word level but also on the story level. Good editors will fix that embarrassing typo that changes the entire meaning of a sentence. Good editors will ask for the intent behind a sentence or section of dialogue if they are not sure where you're going with it, before suggesting either a full rewrite, a partial rewrite to clarify, or general editing corrections.

If an editor is asking you about intent often, it is generally a sign that the dialogue isn't ready to edit, and you should offer to take it back and work on it some more. It is also likely a sign that what was clear in your head didn't turn out that well on the page. This is okay. Asking for a chance to write things over will earn you appreciation from your editor; it's a learning opportunity you should never pass up. And, if you're not sure how to make things clearer, a good editor will gladly help you do so.

Narrative designers and dialogue writers can learn from editors. You learn which mistakes not to repeat, which typos you make on a regular basis (and which you can fix versus which will be the death of you). You learn that, no matter how simple or clear something may appear to you, that doesn't mean it will be intelligible to others.

Good editors will—throughout your entire career—prove to be your best friends and allies. They make the writing look good. They polish diamonds in the rough, sort the wheat from the chaff. Be open to their notes and suggestions. Know when to hold your ground and when to take a step back, listen, and then ruthlessly kill your darlings. The writing and the narrative will both profit from this.

And if you do not have an editor and are working on a project with a large word budget, consider bringing up the possibility of hiring one for the project (or at the very least, of getting one on contract once the bulk of the writing is done). While "improving the quality of writing and narrative" is the most evident and direct benefit of hiring an editor, there are also many cost-saving-benefits arguments which may appeal to your management.

Working with Localization

Localization producers—just like good editors—are important allies for narrative designers. They will be translating your words for an entire audience that speaks another language. To help them accomplish their job (which is usually done at the very end of the schedule, after the deadlines have already slipped too many times), remember the following:

- **Keep notes on your writing that are clear and well organized**. Far too much of the budget can be eaten up in localization by bad organization, or by lines sent for translation without context. As the narrative designer, it is your job to make sure you pass along the best possible version of your dialogue and story content to the localization team.
- **Be ready to explain what you meant in a sentence or by an idiom**. Be ready to explain this several times, until the localization producers are certain they've understood it properly. Explain every time, no matter how much you feel you're repeating yourself. If you don't, you're the first one who will be responsible for a bad translation.
- **Realize that not all expressions have equivalents in other languages**. There will need to sometimes be an adaptation rather than a direct translation.
- **Realize that not all jokes translate successfully and may also require adaptation**. This has to be worked out between writer and translator. Same thing with swearing.
- **Consider that some names may seem innocuous to you but mean something else in another language**. Sometimes you'll have to change the name of a character because of this, depending on the languages your project will be released in (or you may have to accept that in *X* language, the character name will change).

Geographic and Political Review (GeoPS)

In one shape or another (either with a person who is part of the localization team, or via external services), large games will hopefully go through a round of review by Geopolitical Services, also known as GeoPS.

forgettable and rightly criticized for being trite and "on the nose." Instead, by delivering that sentiment in a sympathetic, surprising line, it made both the scene and the characters infinitely more memorable.

However, in games, clarity generally trumps quality. So, how can you use subtext while still ensuring that the player knows what to do and where to go? A simple rule of thumb is to assume that "how" and "what" questions (such as "How do I defeat the bad guys?" and "What do I have to do to complete this quest?") must be answered using text. "Why" questions (such as "Why were you targeted by the Mob?") are safely—and more entertainingly— answered with subtext.

Considered to be "deep localization," GeoPS is more than translation. It has to do with understanding the nuances of regional dialects, cultures, and perceptions, and delving into what may be taboo to a specific group of people or a country—and also whether the context in which it is presented in-game may aggravate or actually attenuate meaning and effect. This is achieved by exploring how people think or interpret what they see, and what regional, cultural, religious, or other variables may affect players' reactions to game dialogue and situations.

Carefully handling sensitive themes and determining whether they should be in a game according to the intended audience and region of distribution is not censorship, nor should it ever be perceived as such.

GeoPS exists so you can avoid unpleasant surprises. It's much better to learn during development that a problematic scene is likely to alienate your target audience than to lose those sales (or endure a scandal) once the game is out. GeoPS review will cover the entirety of the game, from options in the menus to the writing, the graphics, the packaging, the audio, the branding—anything players may encounter. GeoPS will also try to account for your unintended audience, ensuring that not only will your target market be satisfied but also that a potentially wider market will open to you.

GEOPS EXAMPLES

- **Thumbs-up**: In the US, it means "good job." In West Africa and Greece (among others), it's an obscenity.
- **Waving your hand goodbye**: In the US, it means "hi" or "bye." In Greece, it is a rude gesture.
- **Crooking finger to call someone over**: In the US, it means "come here." In the Middle East, it is rude and insulting.

Conclusion

Dialogue for games is both art and craft. By following the principles in this chapter, you will master the craft of structuring both ambient and interactive dialogue. By understanding what purpose the dialogue in your game serves for the player, you can ensure your conversations are the right length, pace, and clarity to let the player seamlessly enjoy the experience of the game. Once structuring complex dialogue trees or working around high-octane action scenes becomes second nature to you, you can spend the rest of your career improving and perfecting the art of writing the flawless, quotable line that will be replayed in endless GIFs, email taglines, and T-shirts.

Dialogue Sample

The following sample is an example of interactive dialogue as it might be written for a game quest set in a generic medieval fantasy world, using a dialogue-tree structure.

The player comes upon the quest-giving NPC mid-spell, overhearing the end of what he has been saying to himself before the player arrived.

Exercise

Exercise 7.1

Write one scene of interactive dialogue from your proposed game, using any available program. Dialogue should include at least one (and no more than three) characters besides the player and should be at least two player responses long (and no more than four). Use a scene in which the player is being told a new objective, whether a new quest or a new step in your main plot—there is far more value in a writing sample that shows you can clearly communicate plot steps to a player than one that just shows off your grasp of spoken language.

After finishing the exercise, check for the following:

- Is it clear to the player what their current objective is? If this objective is given early in the dialogue, is the player reminded in the final line?
- Is the objective clearly stated on all paths through the dialogue? Are there any options the player can take that will end up with a Quest Accepted state without actually hearing what the objective is?
- Do optional player lines (like extra questions) contain only optional information, or do later responses assume the player has heard this information?
- Are player options all clear and distinct from each other (the difference between "Yes," "No," and "Tell me more," not "Yes," "I guess," and "Why not?")?
- Do the player's choices actually get a reaction from the NPC, or does s/he plow through the exposition as if the player never said anything? If you can remove the player lines from the conversation and the NPC's story would still make sense, that's a sign of a passive player-character—rewrite.
- Does the NPC give any personal details about his/her life, or is s/he completely focused on the quest?
- Do player options reflect a variety of player types and responses players will want?
- Do all the lines sound good when read aloud?

Once you've revised your scene to fit the requirements above, you're ready to go on to Chapter 8, "Cutscenes and Cinematics."

Scene # 001   Shot # 01

ACTION: Zoom out from Samantha and Jamal in window and slowly pan down. Building
collapses in background. Simone's boot comes down in extreme foreground when pan
finishes. BEAT and then collapsing building lands behind captured enemies.

Scene # 001   Shot # 02

ACTION: Simone laughing
maniacally.

Scene # 001   Shot # 03

ACTION: Simone shouts up to her
allies in the building.
DIALOGUE: "Hey guys! Guys! We're
good down here! Full surrender!"

Scene # 001   Shot # 04

ACTION: Samantha and Jamal stare

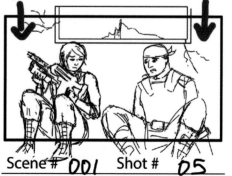

Scene # 001   Shot # 05

ACTION: They slide down to the floor.

Cutscenes and Cinematics

It can be frustrating when progress in a game is interrupted by a cutscene. When done poorly, it feels like the designer walked into your living room, grabbed the controller, and said, "You're not playing this right. Let me show you the cool parts!" Which is unfortunate, since the philosophy behind cutscenes is that they're a *reward* for players—the moment, after everything they've done, when they see their actions rendered in full-cinematic animation, complete with partying Ewoks (or not).

In some games, cutscenes may be the only vehicle for conveying story moments of any kind, whether exciting, intimate, or simply expository. So, knowing that cutscenes are a pretty blunt tool, how does a narrative designer make the best use of them?

IN THIS CHAPTER, YOU WILL LEARN . . .

- How to determine if a cutscene is needed and what to include in it.
- The difference between cutscenes and cinematics, and how/when to use them.
- What makes a cutscene fun.
- How to use cutscenes in RPGs (and higher-budget games in general).
- How to use cutscenes in lower-budget, social, and mobile games.
- How to use cutscenes in MMOs.

DOI: 10.1201/9781003369332-8

Scripted Scenes and Animations

Cinematics and cutscenes are just a couple of types of scripted scenes or animations used in a game. Here are types of scripted scenes/ animations you might use:

- **Postures**: Short animations using NPCs, creatures, or the environment to help set a scene. Can be reused across levels to bring the game world to life.

- **Sequences**: Very short scenes, sometimes with repeatable dialogue, that can loop without becoming (too) tiresome for the player.

- **Animatics**: Noninteractive sequences of still images edited together.

- **Cutscenes**: Noninteractive scenes, scripted by narrative and usually done "in-engine," which do not allow dialogue options to the player.

- **Full Motion Video (FMV)**: Heavily scripted scene in which the player

Is a Cutscene Necessary?

The first thing narrative designers should ask when planning a cutscene is "Is this necessary?" Since too many cutscenes have a crippling effect on pacing, it's wise to consider alternatives before committing to them.

The alternative to a cutscene is generally some kind of ambient dialogue, voiced lines that take place during a time the player is performing normal gameplay tasks. This could include players overhearing a quest prompt while walking past two background characters ("I heard the king is being held prisoner in his own castle!"), or just learning about a new city by listening to folks on the street ("It's almost time for the harvest festival!"). Lastly, the player's own character can take part in ambient dialogue by talking to a partner or group of companions. When using ambient dialogue to convey important information, it is helpful to follow these tips:

- **Don't give exposition during combat**. Yes, characters generally shout during combat, but few players pay attention when they're frantically hitting buttons or issuing orders. And many game audio engines aren't great at prioritizing sounds, meaning any given line will disappear into a mass of yells and grunts.
- **Don't give crucial information**. If the player absolutely *must* learn something in order to advance, ambient dialogue is not the place to learn it. The whole point of ambient dialogue is that you're in gameplay while it happens, so players are free to walk past a conversation before it ends. If the rest of the game won't make sense without this one crucial line, a cutscene is still the place to put it.
- **Use interparty ambient dialogue when there is a natural pause**. If players are on the wrong side of a locked door while the party's thief is picking the lock, they have both the time and the mental bandwidth to listen to the party's mage talk about the brewing war in Faerie. But if the mage is still talking once the door is open, players are likely to ignore her while charging ahead.

Cutscenes vs. Cinematics

While cutscenes can be used throughout an entire game and are often done "in-engine," they are usually not on the same level as cinematics in budget, quality, or length. Cinematics (always noninteractive) are usually much higher in both budget and quality, and the narrative content they cover is usually an intrinsically vital part of a game's narrative. When budget allows, cinematics are traditionally placed at the start of the game, used as an introduction to push forth essential expository content with a goal towards drawing the player into the narrative and, at the end of the game, used as the final "big moment," rewarding the player for having played through all the content. Sometimes they can be used at midpoints of a game as a reward, depending on the allotted budget on a project.

While the process is similar for both, planning a cinematic can sometimes be even more collaboration-intensive than a cutscene, due to the large budgets involved and the amount of unique assets and animations that are often required.

As has already been stated many times throughout this book, narrative design is not an island. Clear communication and good teamwork are essential to the production of cinematics:

- **Don't be afraid to add setting notes to the script of a cinematic**. The more information you pass on to your storyboard artists and animators, the more likely the cinematic will be what you want it to be. No one will see the scene as it is unfolding in your head—you are solely responsible for making sure others can see it as you do.
- **Go over the scene with the writing team (if you're working with one), the animators, and whomever is involved in creating it**. Proof it by the relevant leads. This is where you want iteration to happen—the animators are your experts in *setting* a scene, and they know exactly how far they can push their skills. Their input is vital for the quality of the end result.
- **Storyboard**. Give the scene to your art team. See how the first storyboard turns out. That's when you'll see how your vision is understood by others, and what you may have forgotten to include because it seemed so obvious to you at the time.
- **Iterate on the above**. Keep iterating until all participants are satisfied that the scene is ready to be handed to animation.
- **Keep communicating with the animators as the scene is being created**. This ensures that the initial vision remains steady throughout its execution.

Sometimes major changes occur to a script or a level, which may even require changes to a major cinematic. After they're produced, cinematics are usually not revised due to budgetary reasons alone. But be ready for this to occur anyway. You never know what will happen during the course of a production, and flexibility in the face of major changes is imperative if you're going to produce consistent narrative design, no matter how much duct tape may be behind the scenes. As long as what the player sees is solid, that is what matters.

is offered a limited range of options by pressing buttons at the right time, or other similar game systems.

- **Interactive cutscenes**: Interactive scenes, scripted by narrative and usually done "in-engine," allowing the player dialogue options.

- **Cinematics**: Fully pre-rendered in-game movies, with no player interaction and high production values. Cinematics usually have the highest budget.

Storyboarding in Video Games

A storyboard is a series of drawings (think old-school animation) which, in lesser or greater detail, will show the events occurring in the scene while including the key elements important to narrative and cinematics. Camera angles, relevant characters, items needed for a scene, expressions only the player may be privy to—all these things and many more can be included in storyboards. Each panel should have a line or two describing what is happening in the scene. Sometimes these lines are lifted from the script by the artist; sometimes the writer provides them.

Depending on the project you are working on, budget, and the size of the team, there may or may not be storyboards created to assist the rest of the team in bringing a scene to life. Sometimes you will be lucky enough to have an artist who actually does specialize in storyboards, but more often than not, any of the artists on a given team may multitask for this role. Again, communication will be vital to ensure the success of this process. It's not enough to just send off your script and expect the artist to be able to reproduce your mental image of the scene to perfection. Sitting down and discussing the scenes and allowing artists and cinematics to contribute their expertise are essential parts of the process.

Scene # 001   Shot # 01
ACTION: Zoom out from Samantha and Jamal in window and slowly pan down. Building collapses in background. Simone's boot comes down in extreme foreground when pan finishes. BEAT and then collapsing building lands behind captured enemies.

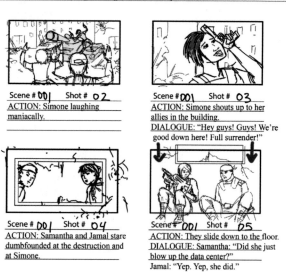

Scene # 001   Shot # 02
ACTION: Simone laughing maniacally.

Scene # 001   Shot # 03
ACTION: Simone shouts up to her allies in the building.
DIALOGUE: "Hey guys! Guys! We're good down here! Full surrender!"

Scene # 001   Shot # 04
ACTION: Samantha and Jamal stare dumbfounded at the destruction and at Simone.

Scene # 001   Shot # 05
ACTION: They slide down to the floor.
DIALOGUE: Samantha: "Did she just blow up the data center?"
Jamal: "Yep. Yep, she did."

A sample storyboard. This image was made by Tonia Laird and is protected by United States and international copyright law. © Tonia Laird.

What Makes a Cutscene Fun?

If you decide cutscenes are necessary, try to keep them as focused as possible while ensuring the maximum reward for the player once they do kick in. Cutscenes should be a moment of awe and enjoyment for the player, not the sign for a coffee break:

- **Ideally, keep a cutscene short and impactful**. The general rule is no more than thirty seconds. Obviously, sometimes this rule is broken. Make sure your reasons for doing so flow into crafting a good reward for the players, and that the planned scene will be a good reward despite the timing (i.e., don't let the player get bored).
- **Show things that are more impactful as a cutscene.** Such as things that would have less impact if done in the gameplay camera and by the player's own actions.

- **Never contain in a cutscene moments that would otherwise allow for player agency and interactivity**. Taking away player agency won't be a reward but an annoyance. This is particularly pertinent for RPGs or games where there are many dialogue choices throughout the entire narrative experience; it can be alienating for players to suddenly have their ability to control their character's dialogue taken away right at a key moment!
- **Don't use a cutscene as an obvious work-around for game-engine limitations**. Showing a huge explosion during a massive battle is fine. Showing a more flamboyant final attack based off something doable with the game mechanics is also fine.
- **Ideally, always make cutscenes from the player's point of view**. Something the player-character is seeing unfold, rather than the cutscene booting players away from the player-character's frame of reference and making them watch what she does. However, this is a rule that is often broken, and it will be up to you to judge whether you should do so or not and if the payoff is a good one.

As with writing and narrative in general, the rules of cutscenes aren't unbreakable—but it's good to know and understand them, as well as how they affect the player, before you decide to play around with them.

Cutscenes in RPGs (and in Higher-Budget Games in General)

Particularly in RPGs, players should feel that the cutscene flows smoothly out of choices they've made in gameplay and at a time when they are naturally unclenching from the controller.

When writing a cutscene, you should:

- **Wait for a natural break in the action**. Players like cutscenes more if they don't interrupt something they want to do. A cutscene upon loading a new level, or opening a new door, is far more tolerable to players than one that comes just as they're pulling the trigger for battle.
- **Keep dialogue short**. Cutscenes are not the time for long exposition. Especially if you have the option of using ambient or interactive dialogue to tell your story, cutscene moments are best reserved for those cinematic visuals you don't get in the rest of the game. Spaceship battles, arriving dragons, and the sweep of an entire army—those are the cutscenes that players get excited about. An inspiring speech from the player-character can be a good fit as well, but don't show the entire State of the Union address. A few lines from the beginning or the end are enough to encapsulate what will be said. And outside of speech scenes, dialogue should be terse and action oriented.

Voice-Over Comments

If we're talking about cutscenes, it's a safe bet we're describing games with a large budget for cinematics and voice-over. Which means if you're reading this chapter, your words will likely go to actors well before they're ever seen by players.

Since actors won't play the game or record their dialogue in chronological order, it is important for the writer to include information in the script describing how and why each line is said. Things to remember when writing these comments include:

- **Mention all relevant information**. This includes pronunciations for any foreign/fantasy words, meanings for words or names the actors might not know, and any plot details that might be relevant to the actors' performance, like "This character is lying. She's actually planning to kill the player."

- **Don't put words in the player's mouth**. If you're working on a game with dialogue choices everywhere else, don't suddenly give lines to the player-character in your cutscenes that presume to know what's important to him or her. If the player had the option to be a greedy, self-serving jerk in all previous dialogues, don't suddenly write a cutscene in which they grandly announce they ask no reward for going alone into the dragon den to save the young prince.

- **Have the scene come directly out of actions the player just took**. If players select "Take me to your leader" in an interactive dialogue, that's a good prompt for a cutscene of their arrival into the capital. If players defeat a boss monster in combat, they will welcome a cutscene showing the beast in its death throes. The same scenes coming because someone else walked up and said, "Come meet my leader," or someone else slew the monster, might be rejected soundly.

- **Know your budget**. Knowing what the budget is for each of your cutscenes is vital information that will affect how you write the cutscene and what the animation plans for it will be. Talk to your cinematic department and make sure everyone is on the same wavelength before you plan out how many cutscenes you will use and how big they will be.

- **Share the details**. Writing dialogue is essential, but knowing the elements which compose the scene and what is needed beyond the dialogue will affect the end product in considerable ways. If you're writing a combat scene with tanks all over the place and your characters are commenting on this but animation has not a single tank on hand to place in the scene . . . then you have a problem.

- **Cooperate**. Knowing which animator(s) will work on your cutscene will allow you to coordinate with them as you figure out what needs to be in your cutscene. If you need an emphasis on a visual to pass a narrative point across, if you want a really fancy explosion, it is to your advantage to ensure your animator(s) are just as excited about the cutscene as you are and are willing to invest the time, assets, and effort required to bring your cutscene to life. There should be a regular back-and-forth between the narrative design and the team producing any given cutscene, in order to ensure a proper realization of the story the cutscene is putting forth.

Cutscenes in Lower-Budget Games, Social, and Mobile Games

Cutscenes in lower-budget games, social, and mobile games can all be voiced. They can have sweeping scores to highlight the action. They can have momentous scenes that alter storylines or unveil shocking revelations. In other words, cutscenes in social and mobile games function just like cutscenes in traditional video games.

However, many social and mobile games are meant to have short gameplay sessions. When players expect to be in and out of the game in ten to twenty minutes, their sessions can't be taken up by long cutscenes or cinematics. But with short cutscenes, you can give players valuable information about the game and add some visual and auditory interest.

Cutscenes in these types of games are best used at the beginning and end of levels, stages, zones, or worlds, for winning and losing conditions, and at the beginning and end of the game.

Beginning and Ending Cutscenes for Levels/Stages/Zones/Worlds

Levels, stages, and worlds usually have specific themes. One world in a game might be based on candy, while another world might be based on vegetables. Cutscenes quickly give players a glimpse of the world they're about to enter and a simple story scenario about what's going on in the world's levels. Players can anticipate the types of obstacles, NPCs, abilities, and even weapons they might find as they watch a shot spanning the vegetable landscape. An ending cutscene might show the victorious player-character leaving the vegetable world and heading for the candy one. The cutscene might include defeated enemies, grateful NPCs, or obstacles the players might have overcome to remind them of their achievements.

These cutscenes at the beginning and end of levels, stages, zones, and worlds transition players from one part of the game to the next. They show players how they're progressing through the game. They might hint at possible rewards for completing levels to entice players to keep playing. In mobile games where the story is very separate from the gameplay (like the many match-3 games that use their story and setting to set themselves apart), these brief cutscenes may be the only place to tell your story, making them vital for keeping your game distinct in a crowded field.

Winning- and Losing-Condition Cutscenes

Cutscenes can be used any time players meet a winning or losing condition. These can show player-characters or NPCs celebrating players' wins, or they might encourage players to do better if they lose. They need to be very short. They also need to be images or animations players won't get tired of seeing, especially if they're playing games where they can meet winning or losing conditions often. Long or annoying cutscenes might make players put the game down.

- **Make sure your comments have a single, clear meaning.** Saying a line is "sarcastic" isn't useful, because sarcasm can range from cuttingly cruel remarks from an enemy to affectionate teasing from a friend. Instead, try for more specific descriptions, like "jealous and spiteful" or "gentle mocking."

- **Make double-checking your commenting part of your revision process.** If you change a line, make sure you change the notes for the actors as well. Otherwise, you end up having the comment "Ready to kill him at a moment's notice" on your new dialogue of "I want to have your babies," and everyone gets very confused.

- **Make sure to allot time in your production schedule for a VO-comment pass.** There's nothing quite as disheartening as hitting your writing deadline only to realize you need to get VO comments done in an impossible frame of time. Badly commented lines may very well affect performances.

- **Attend VO sessions if you're given that possibility**. It will allow you to make sure you can correct misunderstandings if one of your VO notes is unclear, and will allow the voice director to consult you on line delivery if so desired.

Animatics: A Stylized Alternative to Cinematics

Many developers can't afford the elaborate cinematics you see in big-budget titles. Handheld consoles, like the Nintendo Switch, and mobile devices have limited storage capacities; cinematics can take up a lot of memory. There's a solution to both limitations: animatics. Animatics are sequences of still images edited together. They can also be multiple-panel sequences, as in comic books. You can add texts, voice-over narrations, and/ or soundtracks to these sequences to use animatics for cutscenes

Opening and Ending Cutscenes

In games that are light on story, opening cutscenes can introduce player-characters, NPCs, the world, and gameplay. The cutscenes give players quick scenarios of what the game's about. Ending cutscenes might reward the player for finishing the game. They can include reminders of NPCs players defeated or rescued, levels they may have beaten, or other feats they accomplished in the game.

For example, in under a minute, the arcade game *Wooli: Return to Ploppington* uses its opening cutscene to hint at gameplay and enemy NPCs while establishing a simple story scenario. Player-character Wooli is a prize-winning sheep. He's left behind at an international sheep show. As the wagon speeds away, Wooli chases after it down a road for miles. He chases the wagon until he can't keep up with it anymore. As Wooli rests on the road near a wooded area, he realizes he's being watched. The silhouettes of three hostile animals peek out at him from tall grass. Terrified, Wooli "plops" a little present onto the road and speeds off into the woods.

This opening cutscene gives players all of the following information:

- **Wooli's motivation**: He's trying to get home, since he was left behind.
- **Wooli's abilities**: Wooli is superfast, and his little "plops" can slow down any predator chasing him.
- **Enemy NPCs**: Each of the three silhouettes is of an enemy NPC that will pursue Wooli in the game.
- **Zones and settings**: The woods are one of the first zones players will encounter.

Wooli's opening cutscene tells players who they're playing as, what they're trying to do, how they'll accomplish their goals, and what will attempt to stop them. Cutscenes that give players these kinds of tidbits can be used at the beginning of a game or at the beginning or end of levels, stages, zones, and worlds.

Cutscenes in MMOs

Normally, cutscenes are a noninteractive form of storytelling meant for a single-player experience. During a cutscene, there is usually no way to interact with other players, nor is there any other kind of interactivity (except for aborting the cutscene). This is why cutscenes need particular handling in MMO environments, as huge parts of the play experience are based on interaction with other players. This doesn't mean that cutscenes won't work at all in MMOs. But when implementing or even considering cutscenes for an MMO, you also need to gauge what impact it will have on the multiplayer experience.

Here are some practical questions that may help to determine if and when to use cutscenes in your MMO:

- What is the current main gameplay activity in this moment?
- How big a group is expected for this part of the game?
- Is the content for player-organized parties or random groups?
- How essential to the overall experience is the story at this place?
- Are there other ways to tell the story that preserve interactivity?

What Is the Current, Main Gameplay Activity in This Moment?

This is the most important question when planning a cutscene, not only for MMOs but in all genres. Telling a great story is awesome, but only if it doesn't block or hinder the gameplay. As mentioned before, most players don't want to watch a movie when they turn on a game. They want to play.

Another example is a big boss fight. No one wants to see a cutscene while involved in a huge, intensive battle. The main activity is fighting, and a cutscene would block the flow of this activity.

As a rule of thumb, the more gameplay is prevalent, or the more that interaction is required among the players, the more you should move away from using a cutscene at that moment. Always ask yourself if a cutscene would end a certain gameplay activity, and if you as the narrative designer want the activity to end at that time.

How Big a Group Is Expected for This Part of the Game?

In MMOs, a part of the content, especially towards the end, is designed with the idea of having groups of players cooperating together towards a single end goal in mind (usually defeating a major encounter). When planning cutscenes, it is important to consider the size of the group at the given point in the game that you want to use for a cutscene. The conflict that can arise between players that want to watch it and those that don't can harm the game experience and, in the end, could lead to the players logging off or bypassing important narrative content, something which is undesirable.

If they stop playing because of a cutscene, then you failed your mission to create a great narrative experience within the genre of your game. Simply keeping in mind that the bigger the group, the more you should avoid a cutscene—or be very particular about its placement—can help when designing a story and cutscene for an MMO.

For example, in *World of Warcraft*, some cutscenes are used before a major encounter, both to give the raid a last moment to prepare and also to introduce the boss before the encounter begins. Major group

and in the place of cinematics.

If you decide to use animatics, this doesn't mean you're giving up quality. Sometimes animatics make more sense for the style and feel of the game, despite the budgetary and technical limitations you're working with. A game might use a combination of cinematics and animatics. For visual novel/adventure games like the *Ace Attorney* and *Zero Escape* franchises, animatics are a genre convention and make sense for the text-heavy parts of the games. Lots of movement in animation can distract from the player's reading experience.

Animatics also encourage stylized and detailed art because much attention is placed on the art itself, not action and movement. *Deadlight's* animatic cutscenes are dark and gritty, like something out of a horror graphic novel. In the AAA franchise *inFamous*, the animatic cutscenes evoke the feel of comic books, fitting for a series where the protagonist is akin to a superhero or supervillain.

Whether you must find a way to stay within budget, are concerned about technical limitations, and/or want to express a certain "feel" of the game through its art, animatics are a strong option to meet your needs.

battles are also followed with a cutscene at the end of a raid instance, where the timing of the cutscene isn't so crucial to the group's activities anymore.

Is the Content for Player-Organized Parties or Random Groups?

If players organize groups on their own or simply just play with their friends, then it is less of a problem to wait at cutscene moments; it becomes a shared experience with friends. In random groups, the level of tolerance for delays is usually a lot lower. Everyone joins the group experience for different reasons, which makes it very likely that some just do it for an achievement or loot and may not want to experience any story. Or they may have already seen the relevant cutscene before. Here, it really helps to have a look at Bartle's four player types.[1] In random groups, you must assume that all four types are present and that there may be no agreement on whose preferences the group follows.

How Essential Is the Story at This Particular Moment to the Overall Experience?

Narrative design must decide whether or not there is a need for a major storytelling moment at any given time. It is important to consider if placing a cutscene at a different time in the story would work even better, or if just leaving the moment to the player's imagination would create deeper immersion for the player. Whatever it is, the story of your game should make the moment important without hindering the gameplay. If you do a good job, gameplay and story become one. If you don't, players will abort one story moment after the other. Telling the right things at the right time helps to create a deep and memorable experience.

Are There Other Ways to Tell the Story That Preserve Interactivity?

Finally, a cutscene doesn't always need to be designed in such a way that it's a full-screen movie. Sometimes it's better to use **sequences**.

Sequences are another form of cutscene that work with any form of dialogue and can be repeated an endless number of times. Some can have dialogue, but as sequences can be repeated ad infinitum, they should be written in such a way that they do not become overly repetitive and annoying. Normally, a single sequence is a lot shorter than a cutscene.

Sequences are one of the most cost-effective ways to implement animated, visual storytelling into a game and can save hundreds of words that otherwise need to be written and read to explain a certain situation. Imagine a village that was just overrun by orcs, and now everyone is scared. Without a cutscene or sequences, you'll need quite a lot of text to convince the players that the villagers are afraid. With sequences, you create a few short animations such as cowering, hiding behind a door or a barrel, etc., and let level designers place them in your scene. Now the players don't need a long explanation. As is the case with environmental narrative, they can understand the story by looking at what's going on.

Also, the posture of an NPC can tell a lot about him and how he perceives the world. **Postures** are short animations or, in other words, sequences. Planning those sequences carefully and together with the art and animation department can be a very effective way to tell more with less.

Besides saving words and visualizing your story, sequences also have the benefit that they can be used to bring your world to life. Imagine NPCs walking around the city, chatting with each other, or buying things. Or a cat running on a roof or chasing a mouse. . . . All of this will make your world more believable, and the more players care for your world, the more they will be interested in experiencing the story.

Sequences will cost the animation department time and work, but since they are visual and not text based, they will save time on the text, voice-over, and localization (unless you use animations not suitable for a certain culture). They can also be reused in different areas/scenes.

Questions for the practical use of sequences:

- What do I want to tell?
- How would I move/stand/behave in this situation? What is believable, and what's not?
- Can I reuse some animations that were created before?
- How often can I make use of a certain sequence?

The last two questions are critical. If you can reuse animations, it will save time and money, which will factor in the production decision of whether to create a sequence or not. The last question in particular will help you to find out if creating a certain sequence is worth the money and time it costs. In general, you don't want to create a sequence that can be played only in one specific situation, especially if it may not be visible to all players. The more benefit a sequence has for the players and the story—while still being reusable, and thus saving on the project budget—the better.

While sequences can be used in any game genre, they are an excellent tool in MMOs because they support the multiplayer environment. They can be played in such a way that they don't interrupt any gameplay. Due to the fact they can be repeated, players can enjoy them whenever they have the time to do so.

Conclusion

The information in this chapter can be adapted to cover cutscenes, cinematics, or animatics for any genre of game, team composition, or budget. The length of the cutscene, the assets involved, and the production quality can be scaled up or down as needed, if you decide your game needs cutscenes at all.

Remember that while the first reflex of a narrative designer may be to rely on a cutscene or cinematic to pass along vital information, this is not always the best option. Flexibility in how you deliver your story and the ability to rely on other means to carry on narrative in a game will make your decision to use a cutscene or cinematic that much more valid and, ultimately, more rewarding for both designer and audience.

Interview with Brian Kindregan (while at Blizzard Entertainment, Now NetEase Games)

What Would You Say Are the Biggest Challenges in Telling a Story in an RTS?

The biggest challenge of crafting narrative in a real-time strategy game is that the genre does not lend itself to character-driven story. RTS games are about resource management, multitasking, and fighting with entire armies. There is nothing inherent to the gameplay that requires a story. However, players benefit from having a context to their actions, and the same holds true of RTS and narrative.

So, narrative is vital, but not an easy fit. The first challenge is simply finding the right place to tell your story. Most RTS games have a briefing at the start of a map, designed to explain the core gameplay mechanic. You can try to slip a little narrative about the map in here, or some character conflict. Maps often have a brief victory cinematic, which celebrates the player's achievement. Perhaps you can put story there as well. In *StarCraft II*, the campaign mode gives players the opportunity to interact with various characters while upgrading their armies.

Another challenge is the player's divided focus. The player is engaged in any number of activities, including frenetic firefights. You can't take control of the camera, so you cannot show players a specific visual. You can only have characters speak, and those lines often go unnoticed amid the chaos of battle and resource management. We compensate for this by repeatedly communicating our important story elements to the player in several different ways so that as the level progresses, a player will get the gist of what's going on.

The third big challenge is dealing with late changes. Because of voice-over and localization, story and writing must be locked several weeks, if not months, before release. But design can—and often needs to—change maps very late in the process. That sort of thing can play havoc with your story, so it's important to stay in tune with design so you can avoid having to find creative ways to reflect these changes in your narrative.

What Changes If You Have to Write the Same Story for an Action RPG?

For an action RPG, I would consider telling a different story. Game narrative is not genre-agnostic. Action RPG, by its very nature, is about one larger-than-life, overpowering character. Even with a multiplayer component, the core fantasy revolves around the player-driven character being (or becoming) incredibly powerful.

To use an analogy, if games were history books, RTS would be about a great war. There would be characters—generals and spies—but the focus of the book would be the war. Stratagems, famous battles, logistical difficulties, and how the ensemble cast of characters influenced events. An action RPG, on the other hand, would be a biography. Very likely set during wartime, but the focus would not be who won the war. It would be about the protagonist player-character, her rise to prominence and power, how she influenced events, and how she conquered her nemesis.

What Are Your Top Three Tips for Designing a Great Cutscene?

First, be visual. Two characters standing around talking just isn't enough, even with compelling dialogue and subtle facial expressions. This doesn't mean the cutscene must be a kung fu extravaganza. The visual part can just be spectacle, an amazing location, an important prop. But there must be something in the scene that is better seen than heard.

Second, be brief. This applies to all game writing, but it's even more important in a cutscene. While the cutscene runs, the player is passive. Gaming is active, and the player is in a different mindset at the computer or console than in the movie theatre. She will sit still for a brief period if the writing and cinema are good—but there is still a timer counting down in her head. When that timer expires, she will escape out of your cutscene, and likely every other cutscene thereafter. Don't let that timer expire before your cutscene ends.

Third, does it need to be a cutscene? Would the story still work, and achieve its goals, if the player could experience the moment through gameplay? If you are going to ask a player to stop and simply watch, you'd better have a great reason for it.

How Do You See the Relationship Between Interactive and Noninteractive Storytelling?

Many of the basics still apply. Strong conflict, rising tension, tight pacing, compelling characters who grow and change in response to the conflict they endure during the story. Love, friendship, betrayal, all that sort of stuff. If it applies to storytelling in a traditional medium, it applies to interactive storytelling.

However, you have no control of the protagonist in your story. You might want that protagonist to turn left inside the door, but the player may choose to turn right instead. Or perhaps the player doesn't go through the door at all. It's best to embrace that lack of control, and learn how to evoke the feelings and reactions you want. In some ways, you build the world and story to be a stage for the player. You set the scene, you supply surprises and twists—like a stagehand suddenly throwing a bucket of water on the lead actor. You can usually guess how the player will react, but you cannot control it.

This can lead to some very powerful moments. Because the player is part of your story, and because her identity is tied to the actions she takes, she will have a level of investment that books and movies can only envy.

What Is Your Number One Tip to Get Players Emotionally Involved in a Story?

It's all about character. If the player is invested in the protagonist, she's involved in the story. Every accomplishment, every setback, every slight will be felt as if the player experienced it.

How does one get the player so involved in a character? That's a very complex task. The short version is, make your character exceptional—everybody wants to be the smartest person in the room, the object of admiration and jealousy. Everybody wants to make witty remarks, or be funny, or wise, or insightful. Beyond that, nobody is interested in perfect characters. We've all made mistakes, we all have a history, and people will buy into and believe in a character who has made mistakes—and perhaps still has a few left to make.

Note

1 *Wikipedia*, "Bartle Test," accessed July 10, 2014, http://en.wikipedia.org/wiki/Bartle_Test. Bartle's Player Types are a simple classification of player behaviors and goals in games.

Exercise

Exercise 8.1

Write a cutscene for your game. Use the sample script at the end of the chapter for reference.

There are many ways in which you might work formatting-wise, depending on the company you work at and how their internal tools are configured. This may range from working in Excel to working in a completely in-house tailored engine. It is important to conform to in-house formats if they have been long established and work well, though improvements can always be suggested once you have properly learned the current method.

For the purposes of this sample, however, traditional script formats seen in such tools as Final Draft or Scrivener will be used. An example of traditional script formatting can be found here: www.oscars.org/awards/nicholl/scriptsample.pdf.

Some Basic Terms and Rules

- **Scene headings:** Needed every time your script changes locations.
- **INT:** Used to indicate the scene is indoors.
- **EXT:** Used to indicate the scene is outdoors.
- **Character names:** Always in all caps the first time used and in dialogue headings.
- **Dialogue:** Always centered (along with the name of the character speaking).
- **Dialogue-specific descriptions:** Right above the dialogue and in parenthesis. Parentheticals are only used for very specific and short details pertaining to the dialogue and character. Anything pertaining to scene descriptions or longer general actions of the character (more than four lines) during that dialogue scene should be right before the character name/dialogue.
- **CONT'D:** Used to indicate that a character keeps speaking after an interruption in the scene due to action/events.
- **Scene transitions:** Such as "CUT TO," "FADE IN," or "FADE OUT."
- **Font:** Use Courier, size 12.

Sample

Sample 8.1

Composed in Word, this example in script format is of a cinematic that segues to gameplay, then a cutscene.

INTRO CINEMATIC 1.0

INT. DAMAGED BUILDING, GENERIC ROOM

SAMANTHA and JAMAL are hunkered below the window of a building, on the second floor. Both are out of breath, and are listening to the sounds of shots being fired outside. They are armed and wearing combat gear. Jamal finishes tying off a bandage on his leg and looks at Samantha. He is not happy.

> JAMAL
> This is a joke. They had to know we were coming.

> SAMANTHA
> Of course they knew we were coming. We have Simone with us. Simone is the one who likes to blow up things to let people know we're there, remember?

There is a huge explosion. The walls rattle, several of the windows shatter inward, though the one our heroes are hiding under is already broken, and thus safe. Samantha and Jamal don't even react to the explosion. They might be used to this.

> JAMAL
> (sighs, nods)
> Yeah, okay. Simone being along means stealth isn't a variable in a mission. But this is stupid!

There is another huge explosion, followed by shouts of fear. Maniacal laughter also can be heard in the distance—this is SIMONE. She is having fun. The shooting has stopped.

> SAMANTHA
> Well. At least they always surrender quickly when she's around.

Both turn and slowly peer over the window.

CUT TO

EXT. TOWN SQUARE

The camera slowly pans from the open window, from which we see Samantha and Jamal slowly peer out, to the scene of utter devastation in a town square.

A Jeep is embedded in the side of a building. The fountain is demolished. One building slowly teeters, then collapses. The bad guys are all on their knees, weapons to the ground, having clearly surrendered.

A woman, SIMONE, is standing on the roof of a tank, laughing cheerfully. A lot.

> SIMONE
> Hey, guys! Guys! We're good down here! Full surrender!

> SAMANTHA
> (looks annoyed)
> Jamal. Did she blow up the data center building?

> JAMAL
> (looks resigned)
> Yep. Yep, she did.

> SAMANTHA
> (shouting)
> Simone!!!

> SIMONE
> What? Oh no, hey, it's okay!
> (she smiles happily)
> Look, I got the drive before I blew up the building!

Simone holds up one arm, holding a completely intact and pristine computer drive in one hand. Jamal and Samantha both smile slowly. A shot rings out, but Simone hops back while yanking the drive out of the line of fire. She turns a slow, annoyed glare towards the roof from which the shot came.

> SIMONE
> Not cool, man. Not cool.

Simone raises her other hand and pushes down on the trigger of a remote. The building explodes and collapses, the sniper on top comically waving his arms in dismay. The building Samantha and Jamal are in also starts shaking due to the explosion.

END CINEMATIC 1.0

GAMEPLAY SEQUENCE: The player must survive the aftereffects of the explosion sequence, dodging debris and pieces of ceiling while finding a safe place to stand in the room.

START CUTSCENE (NONINTERACTIVE) 1.0

INT: DAMAGED BUILDING, GENERIC ROOM.

In the aftermath of the tremors, Samantha gets up and hauls Jamal to his feet.

SAMANTHA

Well, looks like we're done here.

JAMAL

Yeah, let's go get Simone before she blows up THIS building.

There is a sudden series of small explosions, and then the building begins to shake. From outside, they can hear Simone say one word.

SIMONE

Oops.

Samantha and Jamal look at each other as the building they are in starts to tilt slowly, and then both turn and begin running for the window and leap out without a second thought, shouting.

SAMANTHA

Simone!!!

END CUTSCENE 1.0

Troubleshooting

Congratulations on getting this far! If you've been following all the exercises, you now have a pretty decent portfolio of game documentation, writing samples, and maybe even a good idea of what game you want to make. You've probably thought through what audience you want, and visualized the scenes that will leave your players staring slack-jawed. You're ready, you're eager, and you can't wait to make this thing happen!

Great. Now throw it all out, and start again. The money just came in, and they only want to invest if you can turn your text-based romance into a military shooter. Or your shooter into a hidden-object game. Or your HOG[1] into a platformer starring Barney and Friends.

Or maybe they love the concept but just don't think your plan lives up to its promise. Or they want exactly the scenes you've planned, but all in a single environment, and with the only animation being opening a door.

The reality of game development is that games have a *lot* of moving parts. And if anything changes in any one of them, the repercussions are felt all down the line. And writing is often the first thing targeted for change. It is far easier to rewrite the words of a dialogue than to painstakingly reanimate the scene that goes with it. A picture may or may not be worth a thousand words, but it certainly takes a thousand times longer to make.

So, if you're a word person in the games industry, be prepared to do a lot of revising. And while this is often done to make a game better, it

DOI: 10.1201/9781003369332-9

is just as likely to make the game *worse* . . . but cheaper, or easier to produce, or easier to market, or another factor that outweighs the loss of quality.

IN THIS CHAPTER, YOU WILL LEARN . . .

- To make the most of criticism to improve your work.
- To parse vague or contradictory feedback.
- To give useful and meaningful feedback to other writers and designers.
- To work effectively with testers, QA departments, and focus groups.
- To design an effective testing plan for your game stories.
- To minimize your emotional reaction to feedback and criticism.
- To apply the above strategies both as an in-house designer and as a freelancer.

Feedback

There are two steps to the revise, rinse, repeat stage of development that are equally important: 1) receiving the feedback and 2) acting on it. The first is an emotional challenge (how do you handle having all your hard work torn to shreds in a review?), while the second is a technical challenge (how do you address the concerns, while still preserving the parts of the writing that *do* work?).

Accepting Feedback

Rule number one in game development: You can't argue someone into having fun.

If someone on the team plays your game and doesn't enjoy it, it does no good to get defensive or tell them that you just followed the plan. Every time someone says they didn't have fun playing the game, you have to listen—because they represent some portion of your audience. And your audience won't care how much effort you put in. If they're not having fun, they'll walk away.

(Note that "fun" doesn't just mean laughing and partying. "Fun" entertainment has always included less obvious emotions, such as weeping in gut-wrenching sorrow over a tragedy.)

This doesn't mean you should try to please all the people all the time, which is impossible. Some of the feedback you receive won't represent the specific audience you're aiming for (anyone saying that your preschool game lacked challenging action sequences can be politely dismissed). But you should always listen, and try to tease out *why*. Did they not understand it? Not feel motivated? Were they just put off by the unfinished graphics, and you're confident their criticism won't apply to the finished product?

As a narrative designer, you must understand the difference between feedback (players' reactions to your material) and suggestions (what they say they would like better). All feedback is legitimate because it is people reporting on their own feelings—"I didn't like X." But most suggestions—"I'd rather see Y"—are extremely suspect because the people making those suggestions are far less familiar with the material than you. They don't know that you already tried Y in five different ways earlier and ended up with X because it worked better.

When trying to find the *why* behind a negative reaction, always check for:

- Did they understand what to do? Confusion is a top killer of fun.
- Did they feel free to make decisions? Most players hate being railroaded almost as much as they hate not knowing what to do.
- Were they uncomfortable with the depictions of any characters, particularly any unintended gender or racial bias? Only when people outside the development team start to play the game do the unconscious assumptions of the team get suddenly exposed.
- Are they expecting a level of polish you haven't reached yet? Often a game is first played in an early stage before all art and animations are in place, and it can be hard for people to imagine the gaps in the narrative that the finished art will fill. For a simple example, if someone says, "Go over there," and there's no pointing animation yet, a good part of the information of the line will be lost. In this case, it's important to resist filling in the gaps with words, since once the missing elements are in, words become clumsy and redundant, for example, having a character say, "I am so sad!" when in the finished animation they will be crying.

How to Handle Feedback

Receiving feedback—from another writer or someone in a different discipline—is at least a weekly part of working as a narrative designer. It is important to keep in mind who is giving you the feedback; then review the quality of the feedback you received, and react accordingly.

A WORD OF ADVICE

Learn to discard feedback which relies on personal attacks or excessively insulting commentary. While writers are often told to look through abusive feedback in case there's something useful there, frankly it is demoralizing and can be psychologically damaging, and no one should be required to put their mental health at risk for their job. If there is a genuine issue hidden by the vitriol, there are others who will notice the issue and frame it in an appropriate way. While honest feedback can be invaluable, abusive feedback is poison.

A tester's feedback (tester meaning anyone testing the game, not just those officially employed in that position) will inevitably reflect his or her interest in and knowledge of what you do. Interest and knowledge aren't always paired together, and one of the tricky tasks for narrative

What If You're the One Giving Feedback?

If you're the one reviewing another writer's work, it's important to find the right balance between a critical eye and a supportive attitude. Constructive criticism focuses solely on the work you're reviewing, not your opinions of the person who created it. Never engage in personal attacks or use derisive language when reviewing a document. Do the following instead:

- **Find out what kind of feedback is wished for and tailor your comments to this**. While sometimes it will be "comment on everything," often people are happy to clarify what they are looking for, which will help you give more useful feedback.

- **Read everything carefully**. Don't skim a text in order to give feedback—it isn't useful, and your lack of attention will show in the comments you give.

designers is to learn how to weed out the useful feedback from the less useful feedback. The following tips can help you make sense of the times when you're faced with a notebook full of hastily scribbled review notes:

- **Sort the feedback you get into different groups**. Useful, Not Sure, and WNU (Will Not Use).
- **Sort by how long it will take you to do, once you know which comments you'll be addressing**. Do on the spot anything that will take less than five minutes to fix (and that isn't in a section that is likely to be gutted due to other comments), and get it out of the way before tackling larger issues.
- **Note and use positive review comments to gut-check yourself when you're not sure if you want to change something**. On the other hand, one positive comment should not be an excuse to dismiss other criticism; it's more important to double-check something than it is to dismiss comments out of hand.
- **Balance the criticism you receive with your view of the entire narrative**. Sometimes people aren't in a position to take a holistic view of the narrative, while you should be.
- **However, be sure to keep in mind that feedback may come from someone who has a better view of the project**. Someone else may have a better understanding than you do of the project as a whole (this will be common when you are a junior team member). Adjust accordingly.
- **Check to see if enacting changes based on this feedback will affect other disciplines**. If yes, make sure to clear this with them first (by email, Slack, Discord, or other platforms where you communicate and get things in writing, not just verbally), and get the approval of everyone involved (especially your producers or anyone else responsible for budget and scheduling) before moving ahead.
- **Always say "Thank you."** Regardless of whether you'll use the feedback or not, or whether it was respectful or not, you are in a professional environment. Thanking others for engaging in your content regardless of how they choose to do so reflects on you as a professional, just as their method of discussing criticism of your work will reflect on them.

Sometimes you can't act on feedback, even if you agree a change needs to be made; the cinematic is done, the level has been approved and will not be changed further, etc. Whatever the reason, there are alternatives that you can resort to in such instances, such as adding a game artifact or book/letter that can help patch the holes. Look for such alternatives when those situations crop up, or try to think of creative and low-budget solutions. Call on others and see what suggestions they may have. Troubleshooting in narrative design is often an exercise in creativity for the team as a whole, not just an individual.

Making Revisions

Different people have different revision philosophies (some writers prefer to throw everything out each draft and start over!), but generally, it is wisest to make the minimum possible changes to address the feedback. Every time you write a new version of a scene, it is essentially a first draft all over again, so the more of the existing work you can preserve, the tighter and cleaner each draft will be. This makes the previous part of this process—understanding exactly what the problem *is*—extremely crucial.

When you begin revisions, the following suggestions should make the process easier:

- **The first thing to do is to step away for a moment**. Take a break from the script before you go any further, be it for a day, a weekend, or even a full week, should you have the leisure to do so. Stepping away from your work and giving yourself time to detach before sitting down for a full revision will give you the distance you need to properly evaluate your work and spot mistakes you couldn't see while in the midst of writing.
- **Once you've taken a break, reread the entire script to make sure it still makes sense**. During a first revision, you'll often find yourself wondering what you were thinking when you wrote that scene or this line. This is entirely normal.
- **As the one writing the story, you already know what's going on**. This can often lead to important details being left out, since they seem so obvious. The most important thing to do once your first revision is done is to **find a "new" reader/tester** on the team, someone who has never read any part of your script *or* heard you talk about it overmuch. Do not explain anything. Let them come at the story without any of the knowledge you have. This will allow

- • **Remember the feedback you gave earlier**. Sometimes a plot hole is actually taken care of later in another scene (and thus wasn't actually a plot hole). It's good to leave earlier notes intact and to later comment, "Oh, I see you resolved point X here!" instead. It lets the writer know you notice what is going on.

- • **Explain why you are pointing out an issue**. For example, your feedback should not be "You should use orange because I hate pink." It should be "You should use orange because that is the complementary color for blue."

- • **Be sure to point out what you like just as much as what you feel needs improvement**. Giving the writer a good notion of what does work in a narrative is just as important as pointing out potential flaws.

- • **Add a "general comments section."** Sometimes, line-by-line feedback may not cover other issues in the script, or something

215

may be a recurring problem through the script that would take too much time to note every time it crops up. When that happens, add a "general comments" section at the beginning or end of your feedback, and go over the high-level issues you want to bring up in a neatly categorized fashion.

Note that even if you're the kind of creator who doesn't mind harsh criticism, respectful feedback means suiting yourself to the other person's preferences. Keeping your feedback honest but constructive and respectful means everyone wins. If you want to help improve the material, it's your responsibility to deliver feedback that the original author will accept and be able to act on.

you to discover fatal plot holes, information flow problems, etc. This is a *vital* step in the revision process.

BETA READERS AND NDAS

It is crucial to make sure you do *not* break the company NDA when finding a beta reader. (Most companies require anyone viewing their unpublished material to sign an NDA promising not to show anything the company hasn't already cleared.) Do not give your script to a "writer friend" who isn't already working for your company, or even a good friend whom you're sure "won't tell anyone." It's far too easy for someone to slip up and mention something potentially damaging, through no fault of their own—if any details of your script leak due to you sending it to an external source, it is entirely your responsibility, not theirs. You broke your NDA first.

- **Keep a copy**. If you aren't using game software that keeps a revision list, start every revision by copying the original file into a new draft named [Filename].[date]. This will help you easily revert if your changes don't work out. In shared storage, such as Google Drive, keeping a date in document names also helps other people sort which one is most recent.
- **Find out what resources are available**. If you're making changes because another department couldn't execute your script ("Sorry, we can't do a giant ship-to-ship space battle on this side quest."), find out what they *can* do (a fight in a cockpit, yelling at the opposing captain on the radio?) that will serve your needs.
- **Throw out your outline**. All that documentation you spent so much time on? It's only valuable up to the end of the first words-on-paper draft. After that, unless you spend a lot of time updating, it's only going to tie you to outdated theories instead of the actual player experience. Look at your original logline and goals for the game to see if you're still on target. If not, clarify with your leads whether it's the logline or your script that needs to be revised to meet the team's current narrative goals.
- **Check your original wireframe**. Make sure you're still on target for the scenes and cinematics that are being worked on and the events level design have crafted their levels around.
- **Kill your darlings**. This common piece of advice is often applied to individual lines that a writer has made overly poetic and baroque. But it can also be valuable when applied to the overall narrative. Are you having trouble getting from A to C because you need to stop at B? Try eliminating B, even if it's the best part, and see if the sequence of events flows more smoothly. If you can cut something without changing the story progression or the main narrative, do so. But remember that different games have

different needs: A scene that is purely character development may be considered more important for an RPG than for a shooter. Keep your genre (and project budget) in mind when doing this pass.

- **Review your characters:**
  - Make sure the dialogue flows readably for each character.
  - Make sure the dialogue is consistent for the character in question, in both tone and style.
  - Make sure your characters remain true to their motivations.
  - Make sure your characters aren't being forced into nonsensical choices or acts for the sake of moving the narrative along (players will quickly spot this flaw).
- **Check for player agency:**
  - Make sure your choices are real ones, which bring value to the narrative.
  - Make sure you do not railroad the player.
  - When in doubt, ask yourself, "What does the player *know* or *want* right now?" In the end, everything you do serves those two purposes. Make sure players know what to do next, and make them want to do it.
- **Table read.** For a game that will use VO, gather enough people to cover the characters in a given scene, mission, or narrative arc; book a meeting room; and do a table read of the script. Assign each person a character, and work your way through what you are reviewing. This will help you figure out weird pacing in dialogue or scenes, bad word choices or sequences (and make life easier on your voice actors), and, in general, help you fix your dialogue one line at a time. If you can include actual actors or your VO director/audio designers in this meeting, all the better.

Once you've gone through all of the above steps, take another break . . . and then repeat the steps once more, until you feel the script has reached a state polished enough to be reviewed by your lead, your editor, your producer, or whomever your work is answerable to.

Keep in mind that a rewrite phase is likely to occur after each and every one of the points above. As time goes on, and you go over the list (again and again), there will be fewer rewrites. Until someone else finds another plot hole, anyway!

Cutting the Umbilical Cord

A lot of writers call their work their "baby," and for good reason. Writers spend months nurturing their stories, usually one-on-one, and we tend to love them intensely, to the point of being blind to their flaws. Video game writers (along with writers in most fields who aren't self-publishing) don't get to keep their babies. Like all parents, they have to eventually let them out on their own, and it's important not to rush to the rescue if they get a few cuts and bruises on the playground. Remember, whatever hard knocks your baby sustains during internal testing, it'll be nothing compared to when you let it loose into the crime-ridden slums of the Internet!

Working with QA

QA is the industry shorthand for quality assurance, the department responsible for testing (and breaking in new and creative ways) all of the levels and plot points you've spent so much time on. QA will be the department submitting most of the bugs you're called upon to fix, and they'll be the ones who verify that your changes don't break the game or narrative flow under any circumstances after you've made the fixes.

The QA department is an invaluable resource in ensuring that your content has the desired level of quality and that everything works the way it should. Be grateful if the studio you're working for has its own in-house QA because it gives you the chance to work with them often and as soon as possible. If your studio doesn't have an in-house QA, it's not the end of the world, but you should make sure that there will be regular people—who weren't part of the design process!—who can test the game well before it goes out the door. You don't want the day the game releases to be the first time you hear "I just don't understand anything that's happening."

Regardless of whether you have an in-house QA department, part of your work as narrative designer is to create and support testing plans for your material.

TESTING PLANS

A testing plan is a document outlining all of the ways to play through the content of your game, for purposes of ensuring that every branch is tested.

Those test plans define not only the desired level of quality you aim for but also what kind of feedback you expect from the QA department. A good way to start working on these documents is to sit down and ask some questions:

- What do you want the players to know after a certain part of the story?
- Did the tester easily find all the required information?
- Which parts of the story are essential? Which are optional? Could the tester tell? If the tester skipped all the optional parts, did the story still make sense?
- Which game mechanics are taught, introduced, or used heavily in this part of the game? Did the tester understand what to use and how to do it?

Consider what other questions are specific to your game. (For example, with a party-based RPG, QA should test for different party makeups. Can this be accomplished with a party of all mages? Without anyone who can pick locks? Without any healing magic? And so on.)

Testplan for "The Witch Hunt"

Step Nr.	Quest	Condition	Choice/Result	Implementation Test	Dialogue Test	Task Test	Reward Test	Balancing Test	What is the key Information I received?	How does it fit into the story?	Comments
1	Travel to Village X			OK	OK	OK	OK	OK	Someone got killed in Village X		
2	Find out what happened			OK	OK	OK	OK	OK	The beloved and possible future mayor villager Z was murdered by poison		
3	Find clues in the nearby forest			OK	OK	OK	OK	OK	Villagers shared about someone living in the forest. I found a small hut		
4	Kill the witch		Killed witch	OK	OK	OK	N/A	BUG	Witch says she is innocent, but couldn't convince me		The encounter with the witch is too hard
			Listen to her story	OK	OK	OK	N/A	BUG	Witch says she is innocent	Somehow it seems that no one is trustworthy in this world	
5a	Receive reward	Witch killed = true		OK	OK	OK	BUG	OK	Mayor was thankful and peace should return now to the village	I don't know. Seems not to be important. Side quest?	No reward received
5b	Proof innocents of the witch	Witch killed = false		OK	OK	OK	OK	OK	The mayor of Village X met a stranger two days ago and gave him something	The mayor was the one who gave me the task to kill the witch and also the victim was a possible candidate for becoming mayor in the future	
6b	Find the murder			TODO	TODO	TODO	TODO	TODO			Needs to be tested

Test plan for "The Witch Hunt"

Make It 25 Percent More Awesome

Unless you're working at a company with a large writing staff, most of your feedback will be coming from people who aren't writers. This means that they don't necessarily know the jargon writers use to discuss their work, and they may not understand what a writer can accomplish with simple changes. This can result in your receiving some feedback that, on the surface, seems pretty ridiculous. (Often, the worst comments come from higher-ups on the team, since, unlike QA, giving feedback isn't the main focus of their job.)

So, what do you do when you receive a comment like "Make this opening 25 percent more awesome"? While it's obviously not the pinnacle of constructive criticism, there actually are real issues that you can parse from such a comment. By saying "25 percent," the commenter is telling you that they don't see the problem as systemic or requiring a complete rewrite—it's

Another important variable to consider is how often you want to have new testers test the story. After a while, everyone will be blind to minor story glitches if they already know what's supposed to happen.

Once you've laid out your questions in a testing-plan document, you'll need to meet with the lead QA manager or whomever is in charge of testing your work, and talk about your requests and ideas for testing. QA will ultimately be in charge of developing their own final testing plans, but they should welcome your help in clarifying what is important to test in your content. It's also always a good idea to ask the QA manager for a date by which you can expect the feedback, and whether you can review their final test plan before they start working.

QA Feedback

Assuming you and your QA lead designed a good, thorough testing plan, don't be shocked if you get a *lot* of feedback in the result document. Welcome any criticism you receive at this stage—after working so long on a project that it's all become a blur to you, a fresh perspective from QA can be your best way to make the game better. And remember, anything QA complains about now would just become angry forum posts or Internet memes if you let your game go out the door without addressing it!

At this stage of development, while it's still possible to fix things, it's extremely valuable to see how someone who does not know your story perceived it, and what they understood and what they didn't. Use this feedback to polish the glitches and trim your content until you're sure that what you've defined as the core of the story will be clearly communicated. If you can, take the time to sit down and talk with your testers to see what comes to mind in a less-formal setting than the feedback form.

It can help to view the QA process as a ball game, where you toss the ball to the testers and then they toss it back to you. Remember, even if your testers give you a hard time and tough feedback, they want the same thing you do: To create the best and most fun experience for the players.

Focus Tests

But what if you work for a small indie studio and barely have enough developers, much less a QA department? Luckily, in this case you still have a tool you can use to receive good feedback before shipping your project. This tool can be used by studios large and small and will provide the best down-to-earth feedback you can receive: Focus Tests.

For a focus test, you invite a group of people from outside the company and ask them to play your game. It's important that you don't explain to them how to play or what they should look for. They should play the game exactly as if they had just received it as a birthday gift, with no previous information. By observing the players' reactions, their struggles, and their experience, and asking them afterwards how they experienced certain elements, you will get a good picture of how real players will react to your project.

Two things to make sure of before running out of the door to invite people to play your game are:

1) You have permission from the publisher and project management to show the game outside the company.
2) Your company prepares a good NDA for every tester to sign, swearing that they will not release any information about the game before you're ready for it to go public.

With these in place, you can either run your own focus test, or work with a focus-testing agency to find players in your desired audience, book time and space for the test, and interview the testers.

For Freelancers

As a narrative designer, you have more opportunities than ever to work on games. Some of these opportunities may extend to working with clients who aren't in the game industry. These individuals or companies may want to make a game for many different reasons. They may feel a game will increase brand loyalty or bring them new customers. They may see the mobile/social market as a way to make money. Or they may want to use educational games to train employees or teach children academic or life skills. Whatever their reasons, these clients can always use a narrative designer.

Working with non-developers can bring its own set of challenges, however. Even if they've done a lot of research into making a game, these clients may not understand everything that goes into game development. They might understand that game designers and artists are involved, but not know about specialized roles like "systems designer" and "character rigger." They might have hired a developer to make the game, or be working with several freelancers. Whatever their method, these clients will count on you to evaluate the game's narrative design and make critical changes and revisions.

Educating the Client

Just as with game developers, a non-developer client can hire a narrative designer at any time during the development process. It's not unusual for the narrative designer to be the first person the client works with, as the narrative designer might wear several hats. Sometimes the narrative designer is also the game designer and the game writer! Whether you're taking on one role or several, consulting with and educating your client will be important, because you may be long gone from the project by the time the official "QA phase" begins. Knowing

just not quite as good as they were hoping. And even the word "awesome," vague as it is, does communicate something. "Awesome" instead of, say, "fabulous" implies that the commenter was looking to feel powerful and in command, and the game didn't give them that feeling.

With that understanding, you can return to your work and look specifically for whether there were places in the dialogue or gameplay where the player-character felt passive or was upstaged by NPCs. Often, with just a little restructuring of a scene to put the player in command, such a comment can be addressed without the original commenter even understanding what you did to make it better.

Attending Focus Tests

If you have the opportunity to be present at a focus test, do so. There is nothing to compare with watching through one-way glass as real people play your game. Too often in larger companies,

221

actual in-the-trenches developers aren't present at the focus tests. They only receive the written summation of the testers' reactions. This can lead to a tendency to dismiss the feedback as not representative or mere marketing nonsense. But it's hard to deny the effect of watching real people struggle for 45 minutes to get past gameplay that you thought would take 30 seconds.

you may not be around to course-correct, you have to act early to prepare your client for the testing process.

As a narrative designer, you should always consult with your client directly, even if they are already working with a development team.

You need to understand your client's concept and figure out the best plan to make that vision come to life. The idea may be extremely underdeveloped ("It should be a platformer with a prince who's trying to find a lost scepter"), or it could be well fleshed out with concept art and a prototype. Evaluate the idea, review whatever documentation the client might have, and discuss with the client your suggestions for the game's narrative design. Help the client understand why you'd like to make certain implementations. Remember that you'll probably have to explain concepts like narrative space, environmental narrative, and other aspects of narrative design.

Here's a checklist of the documentation you'll want to review with an eye toward future testing:

- High-concept document
- Pitch document
- Game design document (GDD)
- Game/universe bible
- Narrative bible
- Anything else the client has that will give you a sense of the game, including assets and prototypes.

Don't be surprised if the client doesn't have some of this information. Explain why the documentation is important—for both the client and any developers who'll be working on the project. If it's in your realm of expertise to write any of the missing documentation, share this with the client, and negotiate a fee for drafting the documents as part of the scope of your work.

Communicating the Plan

It's of the utmost importance that the client agrees with and understands the narrative-design plan for the game because they will often be the one communicating it to everyone working on the game. The client may have hired several freelancers who can't meet together in the same building or same time zone, which creates an unnatural environment for collaboration. The clearer the plan and the better you and the client can express it, the easier it will be for other team members to contribute their own ideas and execute the plan, or for QA to test it after you're off the project. Sometimes clients will only be able to afford you long enough to work on the documentation. They won't be able to pay you to work with other team members as development continues. In that case, you want to make sure that the client can explain the game's narrative design and all of the documentation.

QA and Non-Developers

The same tactics narrative designers use on AAA titles can be applied to smaller games. Talk with your client about the need for beta testing. Discuss how to gauge player experience and the kinds of questions to ask beta testers. If you're working with a team, be sure to get their input. Does something need to be cut from the game or changed? Why, and how will this alter the narrative design and writing?

Keep in mind that the game's narrative design can also solve problems that arise during testing. You can find story or worldbuilding explanations for glitches, for example.

Working on Your Own Projects

There are several engines now that will help you make a game. You don't have to have knowledge of code, and you can make simple (or even not-so-simple) games with a variety of mechanics. However, when you're working alone, it can be difficult to evaluate your own work. You might catch some of your design's weaknesses, but you can be blind to others.

Ask developers you trust to evaluate your documentation. Sometimes it can be difficult to ask because it feels like you might be taking advantage of people's time. There are many in the industry who wouldn't mind helping when their busy schedules allow it. Don't just reach out to other narrative designers or game writers. Programmers, artists, sound designers, game designers, and even marketing specialists will be able to assess your strengths, weaknesses, and possible technical limitations from perspectives you don't have.

There are also many developer communities online made up of hobbyists, students, and professionals. Some include the International Game Developers Association (IGDA), GameDev. net, forums dedicated to software and game engines, and various mod communities. These communities come together specifically to support each other. You'll find individuals there who'll be willing to evaluate your work to improve their skills and get better at evaluating their own work. If you're worried about people taking your ideas, you can always ask them to sign an NDA. Since these are standard in the industry, people are used to signing them.

Before you hand over your work for feedback, determine what you believe are its strengths and weaknesses. Don't share this with whomever will be evaluating your work; you don't want to plant seeds. Let them assess your design plan with an open mind. Once

When Someone Else Takes Over Your Work

Sometimes when working as a narrative designer, something you wrote will end up being passed off to another writer or designer to finish. The reasons behind this may run the gamut. Sometimes a writer on the team may find it easier to write certain types of missions, sometimes a learning opportunity that was given to a junior writer turns into a major emergency on the project and requires the hand of a senior writer to bring it to completion, sometimes tasks are shuffled about and reassigned, etc.

Whatever the reason behind the changes, your responsibility is to ensure that you are doing everything you can to pass on your work to the other writer in an organized, clear, and concise fashion, answer any questions the new writer has, and then be ready to take up your next task. It would be inaccurate to advise you not to take this personally, as in an industry with

they've given you feedback, see if they've identified the strengths and weaknesses you recognized. If they didn't, ask about these. You may find that others feel differently. What you might feel are strengths may not be coming across as you'd anticipated, or your perceived weaknesses may not be problematic.

Taking into account your readers'/testers' feedback, discuss with them how you might implement their ideas to make your narrative design better. Ultimately, it will be up to you whether you take their advice or not. But it's a lot easier to make these decisions when your testers understand your vision and what you're striving to do.

Tools for Personal Projects or to Build Your Résumé

Here are suggestions of narrative-focused tools you may use (for free) to create your own interactive stories as you work on your résumé:

- Twine: For writing text-based, branching narratives, http://twinery.org/
- Storyloom: For writing visual novels, www.pixelberrystudios.com/storyloomlandingpage
- StoryNexus: For creating choose-your-own-adventure interactive stories, www.storynexus.com/
- Ren'Py: Used for writing visual novels, http://renpy.org/
- Fungus: A Unity add-on and visual coder created specifically for visual novels, adventure games, and hidden-object games, https://fungusgames.com/
- Choice Script: Programming language for designing branching stories, www.choiceofgames.com/make-your-own-games/choicescript-intro/
- inklewriter: Another tool to write interactive, branching stories, www.inklestudios.com/inklewriter/
- Inform: a design system for creating interactive stories, http://inform7.com/

These are some of the more commonly known and used narrative tools available to you, but if they don't fit your needs, do not hesitate to research other tools to work with.

More complex, but no less interesting, tools available to you are as follows:

- The Electron Toolset (included with *Neverwinter Nights 2*)
- GameMaker: https://gamemaker.io/en/gamemaker
- RPG Maker (one-time purchase): www.rpgmakerweb.com/

While it may be harder to figure out how to make your first game in tools that require more cross-disciplinary knowledge, it's always a good idea to try. You will learn new things and also gain appreciation for the work and skill sets of your colleagues.

Important note: In some companies, you may not actually be allowed to work on personal projects without gaining company approval, leading to the loss of your intellectual property. Make sure you know what the internal policies are at your company before you begin working on something outside of the office.

Conclusion: Working with the Imperfect

Often, by the time you reach the end of the testing and polishing phase of development, you'll be left with the feeling that no one really understood your story, or that what's left after all the changes is just a mere shadow of what it could have been. Don't worry. This is normal. All game writers (and all writers!) have been there before and will be there again.

As storytellers, writers have the tendency to seek perfection in their work, but game development is a collaborative process, with many people contributing their ideas to a single end product. And with an increasingly broad audience, games must serve the tastes and needs of a wide variety of people, not just a single author. As games have become a more important part of the culture, gaming academics have invented terms like "ludonarrative dissonance" to explain the conflict between what works best in a story vs. what is the most fun in gameplay. All of these things can contribute to a growing gap between your initial conception of the story and the finished product.

This isn't to say that you should stop trying to reach your ideals, only that you should expect that what actually makes it into the game won't be the same as what's in your head. It may even not be as good as you'd like, or have terrible plot holes that are returned to you as WNF (Will Not Fix), because it's too close to ship to start making non-crash changes.

Once you realize this and accept that it's better to have a lot of people playing this version of your story than nothing at all, you'll be able to think about better ways to use the parts that ended up on the cutting room floor. Maybe there will be the chance to continue your story in a novel or comic—transmedia is a huge market today and is definitely something to keep in mind when designing and telling your story. Another great thing that could happen is that the fans of the game will start writing and telling their own stories based on what you developed. It can be incredibly gratifying (and sometimes horrifying and disgusting!) to see where fans take the world, and characters, and events you developed.

Even if, in your eyes, the story that you release is not perfect, once it hits the community it can turn into something more than you could

as many layoffs as game development, having work taken away can certainly be a warning sign that your team views you as nonessential. However, you have to gauge how realistic this worry is. If it happens more than once, definitely talk to your lead about why the work is getting shifted. But if it's a one-time thing, try not to be possessive, and definitely don't take any issues out on the new writer who's taking over—they need your help to make the game the best it can be. Any issues need to be resolved with your lead, not someone else who's just doing what they're assigned.

ever imagine. Many of today's big game properties started very small, and it was years of work by developers and fans that made them what they are today. Do you remember the first *Warcraft*? Or the first *Legend of Zelda*? Publishing your first game is only the first step on what can become a long, long journey, and some of those cutting-room-floor bits may end up in places you never expected.

Interview with Editor Cori May (While at BioWare, Now Onlea and Freelancer)

How Would You Describe Your Approach to a New Script?

I read through the conversation—preferably the whole plot—once first, trying to get a sense of what the characters are about, what the plot is about, and the general themes. Then, ideally (given enough time, which admittedly is rare), I'll do a basic copyedit and then, finally, a voice/consistency pass, trying to make sure the lines flow well and the voice is consistent.

What Can Narrative Designers Do to Help You with Your Work?

Get things in on time! Actually, the most important thing is to have good voice-over notes; it's hard to edit something properly if you don't understand the emotional state of the characters involved—but they also need to be short enough to be easily conveyed to the actor. It's a balance.

What Advice Would You Give to Someone Who Wants to Become an Editor?

For video games? Read. A lot. Write stories. Play games, particularly word-heavy games. See words not just as a system of letters and symbols that can be correct or not correct but also as art used to convey emotions and intellect, convictions, and ideas. The stories we write are about people, and people do not always use language correctly . . . but it's important to use that to convey aspects of their personality, not just be sloppy for the sake of it. Every word should have meaning.

What Are Great Exercises for Narrative Designers to Improve Their Editing Skills?

I'm not really certain. For me, the most enjoyable writers to work with aren't the ones who make no mistakes; they're the ones who are open to discussion about the text and the impact they're trying to make with it.

But cooperation and peer review is already a large part of our process here, so almost all of my experiences have been positive in this way.

What Is the Most Annoying Thing You Have to Fix Over and Over Again?

I don't know about "over and over" again, but the hardest thing for me is when edits get overwritten without being told why; the work between a writer and an editor is best when it is give-and-take, a conversation where you both explain and try to understand each other's position. Editors need to explain their edits, and writers need to explain why they may or may not disagree.

I suppose, actually, the "over and over" idea does remind me of something: Every writer has a few "tells," a way of writing conversations—catchphrases, ways of starting sentences, particular adjectives—that they use with almost every conversation. Part of your job as an editor is to make sure they're not being overused, for one, and that they're being used in ways that would be appropriate for that character. It might be all right for one character to start every conversation with "And so . . .," but it shouldn't be appropriate for all of them. Canadians in particular like to downplay their language, to use adjectives/adverbs like "simply," or "very," and so on to pull back on the impact, make things more polite. We very rarely want to make things more polite in video games.

Exercises

It's impossible to actually read your work and offer you valuable criticism on your structure or dialogue. Therefore, here's a simulation of some of the more crazy and pointless changes you might get asked to make during development. So . . .

Exercise 9.1

Rework your sample dialogue, but change all the characters' genders. What other effects does this have?

Exercise 9.2

Rework your narrative bible by completely redesigning the climax of the game. If it is a combat-oriented climax, change it to have no combat elements. If it has no combat currently, change it to a boss fight. If this affects your sample dialogue, rewrite that too.

Exercise 9.3

Rewrite your narrative bible, but change the genre of your game to the following:

- If FPS → RPG.
- If RPG → HOG.
- If HOG → MMO.
- If MMO → single-player adventure.
- If single-player adventure → casual social game.
- If casual social game → RTS.
- If RTS or anything else → FPS.

Good luck!

Note

1 Hidden-object game.

CHAPTER 10

Visual Novels

In the past few years, visual novels . . . and the demand for visual novel writers . . . have exploded into the game writing market. If you're early in your game writing career and looking to break in, contract writing for visual novels is likely to make up a large portion of the job openings you see. So, what *are* visual novels?

In the simplest terms, visual novels (or VNs) are story-driven games without the gameplay, like the old "Choose Your Own Adventure" books. Generally, they play out as a text story told in both narration boxes and non-voiced dialogue, accompanied by static or minimally animated backgrounds and character art. This is accompanied by music, sound effects, and occasional special custom art or animation moments, but for the main part, all action in the story is sold by the writing alone.

This, of course, makes it a bonanza for game writers who master the form!

Like in many story-driven games, players are offered choices of what to say or do throughout the story. These choices separate visual novels from, say, an online comic book, as they offer the key video game experience: Player agency. As in other games, these choices can range from mere color—Are your first words to your kidnapper cautious or defiant?—to large, game-changing decisions—Will you side with the vampires or the werewolves in their centuries-old war?

The bulk of visual novel apps are romance focused, with an intended audience of women between 18 and 45, but many also support other

DOI: 10.1201/9781003369332-10

Incarnō: Everything Is Written character sheets featuring different poses and emotional states. When working with existing art, writers can request sprites with expressions and body language most accurately fitting the dialogue and tone of a scene. Images protected by United States and international copyright law. © Schnoodle Studio LLC.

genres of stories . . . especially if you can fit in a good romantic subplot! Some base their stories on adaptations of existing novels (which still requires a strong game-writing skillset to do well!), but the majority use original stories (either provided by the writer, or provided in outline form by the company for writers to flesh out and complete).

So, now that you have a basic understanding of the market, what exactly makes a good visual novel, and what do you need to know to write one?

Stories and Outlines

As we've emphasized elsewhere, the main difference between writing an interactive narrative compared to more traditional story formats is that you must create the illusion that the player's choices shape what happens. This means that the key behind-the-scenes scaffolding for your VN plot will be **player agency** and **fantasy fulfillment**. Fantasy fulfillment is what makes the player *want* to play the story, and player agency is how you make it a satisfying experience when they do.

Fantasy Fulfillment

This is often part of the "high concept" for your story—the way to boil down all the details into a sentence or two that make it easy for the player (or the publisher!) to understand what they're getting. For example, say you're writing a Regency romance: You probably want a title that evokes nobility and elegance, maybe with a hint of the simmering passion underneath the proper exterior. In your first chapter, you'll want to set up a world in which manners and social class are paramount, and give players the chance to chafe against or embrace the many traditions of that time. You'll also know that by choosing this genre, you're evoking certain tropes and expectations in your players—they're going to expect beautiful dresses, numerous unsuitable suitors, and fancy balls undercut with political tensions.

At the outlining stage, you can use the fantasy to shape the initial menu of story points, to make sure you include all the plot beats that players expect. For example, if outlining a spy thriller, you might have a checklist of beats like: go to exotic location to meet with contact, contact betrays you, get hunted by your own agency, prove your innocence. This doesn't mean that your story should be reducible to tropes, but you should definitely recognize when players might *expect* a certain trope—that way you can consciously make the decision whether to subvert or fulfill it.

Then, while writing, you can turn back to your original fantasy to use as your bar for answering questions about what to cut and what to keep. If a scene is core to the main fantasy, it can usually be fixed, even if there are large execution problems, but scenes that don't serve the fantasy can often be axed without anyone missing them.

This is why it's so important not just to know what the fantasy *is* but also to understand why it's meaningful to its fans. Even if S&M shapeshifter romance isn't what does it for you, if that's the story you're assigned, you need to understand why your players clicked on that title and what they're hoping to get from it. A lot of writers think they can hold their nose and write something that they personally look down on, but that distaste usually comes through. If you don't understand the appeal of a particular fantasy, explore fanbases for similar properties until you find some point of connection that gives you an "in" to what those readers/players enjoy.

Fantasy Fulfillment and Worldbuilding

While visual novels tend toward contemporary, realistic settings, many game writers prefer stories with supernatural elements. So, if you're working on a story that requires you to design a fantasy world, or add fantasy elements to the real world, you can also use the fantasy fulfillment as a blueprint to guide your worldbuilding. Many traditional fantasy games use an "inclusive" approach to worldbuilding, including many different types of magic and magical creatures that all coexist in a large and complex universe. This serves an important function in games: It gives players a wide variety of enemies, numerous possible powers to learn, and many fascinating new areas to explore.

In visual novels, though, instead of a large, sprawling, explorable world full of monsters, you tend to just end up with a large sprawling wall of exposition. The original fantasy fulfillment can therefore be a valuable yardstick for determining what supernatural elements belong in your story. If you're writing a sci-fi action adventure, do you need multiple alien races who have an intergalactic society (*à la Star Trek*), or are you writing something grittier, where the first discovery of alien life is a horror for humanity (*à la Alien*)? If your fantasy fulfillment is being the first human to explore an undiscovered galaxy, then having multiple alien species there just clutters things up.

Player Agency

Player agency in VNs works similarly to other game writing. As always, when planning a story, you should start with the following questions:

- What role does the player-character (generally referred to as the "main character" or MC) play in this scene?
- If the scene involves important things that happen to other characters, how can the player play an active role in making that happen?
- What does the player learn in this scene that compels her to move on?

Motivation and Clarity

Unlike most games, players can't "get lost" when playing a visual novel. There is no self-directed movement or exploration, so it might seem less important to be clear to players about what they're doing and why. After all, as long as they just keep tapping, they'll end up in the next scene no matter what, right?

But because VNs have such limited interactivity, it actually becomes even *more* important that players always understand their goals. After all, other games with confusing stories might be able to coast on players' enjoyment of their combat or exploration, but with a VN, players who don't understand what they're doing are likely to just drop out.

Most players don't consciously recognize that their frustration comes from something as freshman-lit-sounding as "I don't understand my character's motivation." Instead, they'll feel "the story was boring," or "I didn't know what was going on." But as a narrative designer, you should understand "boring" or "confusing" to mean you need to clarify and increase the agency around the main character's motivation. Ask yourself whether every scene provides the player with the following information:

- What their character is doing next.
- *Why* the character is doing that.
- What the character's goal is, in that specific scene and in the book overall.

Goals

As implied above, characters always have at least two goals at any given point in a story:

- Overall story goal.
- Immediate scene goal.

Again, players don't have to be able to write a paper about their character's goals, but they should have a gut sense of what they're trying to accomplish. For example, in a mystery, the overall story goal would be something like "Find out who killed the elusive heiress," while the immediate scene goal might be "Find out why the old drifter visited the heiress's estate the night before she died."

But a mystery is a cheap example, since the story goals are so clear. It's equally important as a writer to understand the player's goals in a story that is less obviously goal-driven. For example, consider a romance in which you are trapped into an arranged marriage in order to get enough money to support your ailing father. Your overall story goal *might* be to win your new husband's love, *or* it might be to find a way to support your father without having to marry. Then, in each scene, you can have a more immediate goal—take your fiancé on an interesting date, decide whether to pursue a job to have independent income—that ties in to advancing your main goal.

When you're having trouble planning or writing a scene, you can usually jumpstart a solution by asking: "What is the MC's goal in this scene?" and "What is getting in the way of her accomplishing that goal?"

Structure and Pacing

Visual novel apps are generally played on people's phones, which means there is a lot competing for their attention. This gives you a very short window to engage players before they lose interest. Since literally every tap (i.e., every line of text or dialogue) is a chance for players to choose to leave the app instead of continuing, you need to ensure every line either moves the story forward or deepens the player's connection to their character.

A fairly standard breakdown of how pacing works in many VNs is something like the following:

1. **Opening scene:** Most chapters start with either an exciting cold open (in a Chapter 1) or a lead-in coming off the previous chapter's cliffhanger. This scene serves to orient the player (giving them the basics of their new story's world, or reminding them what happened last chapter), establish motivation (either for the story overall or for the current scene), and give a taste of the story's fantasy fulfillment (to initiate or continue their engagement in the fantasy).
2. **Two to five scenes:** This can vary from company to company, but generally chapters with fewer than two scenes feel pretty short, and longer than five scenes often means you've gone beyond the scope of your contract. These middle scenes should generally be connected; there can be some time passage conveyed by transitions, like "A few weeks later, . . .", but the thread of the player's motivation should stay clear. Players should understand

why they moved from scene 3 to scene 4 and what they're doing in scene 4.

3. **Cliffhanger:** Most VN chapters end with a cliffhanger to encourage players to stay engaged. Cliffhangers can be story-driven (We just found out my brother is the murderer!/The Russian mob have us cornered in the alley!/I woke up gagged in the back of a van!) or character/emotion-driven (Two boys both asked me to Homecoming!/Do I say yes to the Bachelor's proposal?/I never knew that my mother had an affair, and my father isn't really my father!).

Narration

Narration (also called "descriptive text" or just "text") refers to all non-dialogue writing in your VN.

Point of View

How to write your narration depends on two things: Who your MC is and from what point of view you want to tell her/his story. Visual novels tend to default to a female MC, but depending on the specifics of your contract, you may also be writing characters of other or player-customizable genders.

In description, English-language visual novels tend to default to the second-person narrative ("You walk into the dark alley and hear a footstep behind you . . ."), but can also be very effective in first person ("I wished for years that the cute barista would notice me, but now that he said hello, I'm just gaping like a fish!"). Third-person narrative is less common because the goal in a VN is for the player to identify strongly with her MC, and third-person narration ("She went to the bathroom, searching for any clues left by the mysterious woman . . .") can put up a barrier between the player and the character.

If you aren't given guidelines for POV in your contract, you can help make this decision by asking whether your story is about a particular person or whether players should feel like the story is about *them*. Second-person narration works well for self-insert characters; it gives players more control/possession of the narrative, which has advantages and disadvantages for the writing. Most narration for self-insert stories tends to be in a neutral voice, focusing on giving players the information they need to form their own emotional response. This can take away some authorial tools for writing high-emotion scenes.

For characters with a specific background or interest that players may not share, it can be more effective to use first-person narration. Players in first-person stories can forgive more obvious guidance telling them what their character wants or feels. In romance, this is particularly useful if players don't get a choice in their love interest. Even if it turns out he's not someone they find attractive, they can still enjoy the story of how Emma the shy high school student gets brought out of her shell by the bad boy punk drummer she falls in love with.

First-person narration can also use a less neutral voice, since it's supposed to mimic the voice of the MC who is narrating. If you like a strong personality in your narration, or there are long stretches in your story where the MC has no one to talk to and needs an interesting inner monologue, first person might be an easier choice.

EXAMPLE: NEUTRAL SECOND-PERSON NARRATION

Text: As you enter the classroom, he looks up and smiles. You glance down at your feet, then peek up again. He's still watching.

EXAMPLE: VOICE-HEAVY FIRST-PERSON NARRATION

Text: As I enter the classroom, he looks up with that special smile that I like to think is just for me. My heart starts to pound, and my mouth gets dry. Not wanting anyone else to see, I look away and go to my desk, but when I sneak a glance, he's still watching me.

Exceptions

Of course, sometimes you can't keep your narration neutral, particularly if you want to write a sex scene that doesn't feel like it's with a robot. (Oops. Did we mention that many VNs contain explicit sex scenes? YMMV on whether that's a net benefit or drawback for your personal writing style.) For an effective sex scene, you need to use a closer point of view, so players experience the emotions and sensations the MC is feeling. If your narration to that point has been generally neutral, though, try to stay consistent by using mostly physical (not emotional) descriptions that allow the characters' reactions to convey their emotions.

EXAMPLE: NEUTRAL SECOND-PERSON SEX SCENE

Text: His hands run through your hair, sending shivers down your spine as he pulls you closer.

Text: You drop your head, lips making contact with the pulse at his throat. A low groan vibrates his chest as you run your tongue across it.

MC [Smile]: You like that, do you?

237

Dialogue

Dialogue is the heart of the visual novel experience, and you should strive to use it whenever possible to convey the story. On dialogue screens, players get the visual reinforcement of seeing their own character and the people they are interacting with, not just static art and text.

But there are some important rules of thumb to keep in mind for the best player experience.

- **Avoid large blocks of dialogue:** To reinforce for players who is in the scene (and also to just keep the dialogue as active and cinematic as possible), try to use quick back-and-forth between characters, rather than having a single character speak in large paragraphs.

EXAMPLE OF POOR USE OF VN DIALOGUE

Character A: All my life, I wanted to be president one day, but my parents always said I was worthless and wouldn't amount to anything. They said all politicians are crooks, but I think it's possible to go to Washington and still keep your values. That's why I moved here and took this internship, but now I'm worried I made the wrong choice, because the senator I'm interning for is such a sexist pig. What if he hurts my career instead of boosting it?

Character B: You shouldn't work for someone who makes you uncomfortable. Maybe your parents were right. I mean, you don't usually hear anything *good* about politicians. Maybe there's a reason for that.

EXAMPLE OF BETTER USE OF DIALOGUE

Character A: All my life I wanted to be president one day, but my parents told me I couldn't do it.

Character B: Why not?

Character A: They always said I would never amount to anything. And they *hated* politicians. Said they were all crooks.

Character B: Did you ever think they were right? I mean, you never hear anything *good* about politicians. Maybe there's a reason for that.

Character A: I don't know. I thought it was possible to go to Washington and still keep your values. But now . . .

Character B: Now that you're there?

Character A: I don't know. The guy I'm interning for is such a sexist pig. What if working for him hurts my career instead of boosting it?

- **Minimize the number of characters in a scene:** Because players only see a character when they are speaking, it can be difficult to replicate the feeling of a large crowd scene in a VN. The "extras" in the background will only register as present if they're speaking, so ensemble scenes need to have every character speak to remind the player that they're present. This can be difficult to balance and end up with a lot of "And another thing . . ." type of dialogue. Because of this, it's best to proactively try to keep your scenes small and focused. If you do end up having a large group of characters in the same place at the same time, consider the following strategies to make your dialogue flow smoothly.
  - **Let unimportant characters leave:** This can be as simple as a single line at the beginning of a scene to let anyone superfluous bow out gracefully. ("You, stay here and keep watch. The rest of you, come with me."/"I don't like where this is going. I'm getting the cops!"/"Ew, I'm getting out of here. PDAs make me barf.")
  - **Break it up:** Sometimes a big ensemble situation is inevitable—who's going to play a high school story where no one ever goes to a party? In cases like this, consider breaking your larger scene into smaller vignettes. As long as each encounter flows logically, you can manage it without players having to ever interact with more than a person or two at a time.

EXAMPLE OF BREAK IT UP SCENE PLANNING

- MC arrives at a Hollywood party and immediately sees the agent she's hoping will notice her.
- MC tries to get the agent's attention but instead ends up embarrassing herself in front of him.
- As she flees, she runs into an up-and-coming movie star (her future LI), who comforts her about her embarrassment.
- As the movie star is called away to sign autographs, the player is confronted by her rival for his affections, who threatens her.
- But before anything worse can happen, the host of the party announces the reason everyone was invited. This is the kickoff to a new reality show, and everyone there will be taking part. Whether they like it or not!

  - **Establish factions:** In a big ensemble scene leading up to a major player decision, it's often easiest to think of the characters as representing factions. That way, each of the player's potential decisions has one portion of the group arguing for it, and the other portion arguing against it. By having a single figurehead who represents each point of view, you can quickly establish how the group's overall opinions break down, then write the rest of the scene as a dialogue between the MC and the two figureheads, with minimal involvement by the rest of the group.

EXAMPLE OF FACTION SCENE

Faction Leader 1: We should go fight the werewolf pack ourselves!

Faction Follower 1: Yeah!

Narration: Name 1 and Name 2 nod weakly, obviously worried that you'll be outmatched.

Faction Leader 2: Look, you may have a death wish, but not me! Attacking a werewolf pack is suicide, and I'm not doing it. What's wrong with catching the next bus out of town?

Faction Follower 2: Yeah, I say we run. Better part of valor and all that.

MC: Is there some way to negotiate with them?

Faction Leader 1: They're a bunch of rabid animals. And even if we run, that's just giving them license to kill everyone else in town.

Faction Leader 2: I don't want anyone to get hurt. I just don't think we have a choice . . .

- **Keep the MC Active and Driving the Scene:** Players need to feel like their character is the one making things happen in your story. That means she should be present and visible in every scene. Visual novels generally don't use "cutaways," so even when a scene revolves around someone else (best friend gets arrested/love interest (LI) overcomes his stage fright and finally performs his song/LI is out with his ex, and the MC is spying on them), try not to go more than about a dozen lines without seeing the MC's face. This is particularly tricky if the MC is hiding or otherwise not speaking, but a combination of whispers and thoughts can go a long way to keeping her centered in the player's experience.

KEEPING A HIDDEN MC VISIBLE

Text: You watch through your binoculars as LI walks down the street with some strange woman. Cracking the window, you can just hear what they're saying.

LI: . . . tampering with voting machines . . .

Woman: . . . investigate . . . make sure no one suspects us.

MC: What the hell . . . ?

Text: Your roommate looks up and sees you at the window.

Roommate: Something going on?

MC: I don't know . . .

Text: Outside, the woman hands LI something, and you zoom the binoculars in far enough to make out the letters. They're Cyrillic.

MC (thought): Is . . . is LI a spy?

- **Respect the Player's Voice:** In most visual novels, players don't get to choose their MC's *every* dialogue line. Instead, you'll be writing sizable stretches of forced (autoplay) dialogue for your player's MC, so you'll need to be careful that whatever she says, it doesn't interfere with the player's self-image of the character. Most often this means that the MC's forced lines must be generic enough to fit any voice . . . but without crossing the line into bland or uninteresting. So, how much personality *can* you put into a forced MC line? Some rules of thumb:

  ○ **Give new MC backstory only in the first few chapters:** In a book or movie, a writer may hold back key details about their protagonist in order to milk the reveal at the most dramatic point. But in an interactive narrative, this is incredibly alienating to players, who feel like they *are* the protagonist. This means any important backstory details need to come out as early as possible. After about Chapter 2, any new backstory should probably only be given inside a choice, to allow players to decide on the details that best fit "their" character. So, if it's important to know that the MC is a runaway princess/once worked on a farm/can translate Arabic/has prophetic dreams, that needs to be established right up front, or be revealed in a way that the MC herself is surprised by it ("I'm sorry I never told you that your father is the king of Fakelandia. He made me swear never to talk about our affair").

  ○ **Don't have the MC know things the player doesn't:** This is related to the backstory rule but can also refer to smaller things, like knowing how to ride a horse/recognizing the symptoms of a poisoning/guessing where LI ran away to when he got upset. If the player didn't learn something *during* the story, try to put it in a choice, or give an NPC the knowledge instead. Since the most important characteristic of an MC is her emotional connection to the player, you can't also use her as a source of exposition.

  ○ **Don't express controversial opinions:** If your MC was abducted by bandits and is currently screaming "Let me off!" from the withers of a speeding horse, that's generally a fine use of a forced line. But it's probably going too far if she adds "Otherwise, I'm going to cut off your balls and make you eat them!" Why does that change things? Because you can assume that all players are angry about being kidnapped, but not every player will want violence as the solution. In forced lines, try to only say things that the vast majority of players will agree on; if you're not sure, that may indicate you should offer a choice. This includes any time that the MC is saying how she feels about another character—even if *you* intend that character to be hot/romantic/annoying/terrifying, don't assume that they come across that way to all players. That sort of opinion is almost always best offered in a choice.

Choices

Player choice is what makes interactive fiction *interactive*. This means if your choices aren't **meaningful**, **memorable**, and **satisfying**, the rest of the VN won't be either. So what makes a good choice? Generally, a good choice is one that will either:

- Change the story.
- Characterize the MC.

Let's take a look at the difference between those.

Story Choices

These are the big choices that come to mind most easily, things like, "Do I side with the gang or the cops?" or "Do I go to Homecoming with Emily or Peter?" But you can't have too many of these choices in any given story, because to honor them means that you're adding a significant narrative branch. With novice writers, you'll often see this sort of choice offered and then immediately rescinded with narration like, "You try to side with the gang, but the cops say, 'over here,' and you obediently get into the squad car." Or they *try* to respect the decision but end up having to write two almost entirely different stories after that point: one about Elise Chu, police informant, and the other about Elise Chu, gangster girl on the run.

Most VNs can only support a few large, plot-changing decisions like this per book. Things like picking a side or choosing one LI over another work better as short-term moments (whom do you side with in *this fight?*/whom do you sleep with *tonight?*) while letting players choose differently in later scenes if they want.

You can also offer even smaller choice points that branch the story in minor ways. Things like: Do you fight with the knife or the gun?/Do you wear something sexy or professional for your first day on the job?/Who do you take with you to negotiate with the gang leader? But even these smaller choices are relatively uncommon; most choices don't actually change the story at all.

Roleplaying Choices

So, if most choices don't change the story, what's the point in offering them? What do they *do? The vast majority of choices in a VN should allow the player to characterize her MC's beliefs, emotions, and reactions within the story.* Story choices may be the spine of your interactive narrative, but roleplaying choices are the flesh and muscle that let it move.

And unlike story choices, you can use almost an infinite number of roleplaying choices! They just let players say, "Hey, this scene makes me feel X," so they won't change any plot developments. Yet making the choice is still empowering to players because it shows that the game recognizes and validates their reaction to the story.

You can offer roleplaying choices about almost anything, but some common ones include:

- To define the MC's background (She was a student/bored housewife/washed up former pop star before getting recruited by the top secret spy agency.)
- To decide whether the MC knows how to do something (change a tire/stitch a wound/fire a bow and arrow) or needs an NPC to show her how. This is a simple way to branch something that pays off big in letting players identify with their MC.
- To offer an opinion. This can range from momentary and unimportant ("I think Joe put gum in your hair because . . . He hates you./He has a crush on you"), to important characterization ("As a Magical Agency enforcer, I think it's important to always . . . Follow the rules./Do what's right, even if it goes against regulations.").
- To have an emotional response to something that just happened. "Robbing that train with you was . . . Exciting./Awful./ Romantic."
- To choose whether or not to flirt with an LI or make a minor choice between LIs in books with more than one love interest.
- To make a stylistic choice ("I want to go . . . To Paris!/To Disneyland!"/"For prom, I'm going to wear . . . A dress./A suit.")
- To make sure players remember what you just told them. Every choice reengages players and makes them think about what they're reading. So, if the MC learns an important clue that you want them to remember, make sure they get to choose an opinion or emotional response to that clue so that the information is more likely to stick in their heads.

When *Not* to Offer Choices

Choices are only fun if the game respects what you choose. When playing a game, we all know this instinctively—it's often rage-quit time if you make a choice that the game immediately undoes. Yet offering choices that the story doesn't honor is an extremely common mistake for novice writers. A lot of times, these problems are fairly simple to fix. For example, say you've offered players a choice of whether to accept the prince's proposal, when the story is all about what happens *after* the MC marries him. You can fix this kind of problem by changing the choice from a **story choice**—do you accept the prince's proposal?—to a **roleplaying choice**—*why* do you accept the prince's proposal? Then, instead of a simple yes/no, you can offer players a range of reasons—from the passionate to the practical—of why they want a life as a princess.

So let's look at some common places where writers might use choices that don't work:

- Allowing a choice to opt out of a situation that the story requires the MC to engage in.
  - To fix this, try refocusing your choice on how the player *feels about* engaging in the situation, instead of the option of whether to engage at all.
- Offering choices that are all variations of the same answer.
  - This mistake is often a new writer's first attempt to fix problem 1. Realizing that they can't offer the player an honest chance to say "no," they try to fix the situation by offering a choice of different ways to say the same thing, for example, "Will you marry me?" "Yes!/Yeah./Sure." A better solution is to embrace that the MC will be saying yes, and offer either a range of emotions (thrilled to be getting married/relieved that she won't have to tell anyone she's pregnant out of wedlock/resentful that everyone expects she won't turn down a prince), or a tone choice ("Of course, Your Highness./Oh, thank God! I thought you'd never ask!/Well, you're the prince. I guess you can just command me to say yes.")
- Offering a choice that is boring or insignificant.
  - Sometimes, in an attempt to keep players engaged, writers might offer moments that *seem* like choices but are too minor or uninteresting (what to order for dinner, whether to stand up or sit down at a party) to actually accomplish that goal. To improve these moments, consider how to make them showcase characterization for the MC. Does ordering dinner give a chance to define her as fancy or down-to-earth? Can that choice then be noticed by the prince/her best friend/the dashing but distant LI and give them an interesting insight into the MC? Or can you imbue the moment with greater emotional significance? Instead of just whether to sit or stand, can the player be choosing whether walking into the sensory overload of the party is difficult for her or exhilarating and whether her MC wants to get to the center of the action or hang back and watch for a while? And what is the response of other characters to that decision?
- There's been a long time with no choices, but there's no obvious place to add one.
  - This problem is often a sign that the MC is not driving the scene, and while that may be necessary (she is in the audience at the prince's coronation; she is watching from hiding while she finds out that her lover is really a secret agent), you should always consider any long stretch without her participation a red flag. To find the best way to insert the MC into the action of the scene, the best thing to do is to figure out why watching this event is significant to the MC's personal arc, then offer an emotional reaction to let players characterize how the

scene affects them. This works even if the MC can't speak.
For example: She sees her LI kissing another woman but
can't barge in and confront them because she knows the other
woman is a master assassin. You can still give her the choice to
vow that "When I get home, I will . . . Force him to tell me the
truth./Take my things and move out./Beg him to come away
with me, so we can both be safe.")

Branching and Reactivity

Not every visual novel has the technology to track and branch for
player choices. And even in projects that do, trying to remember every
choice quickly grows too complex to manage. So, as a writer, how do
you make the call for when and how to acknowledge player choice?
This is best answered by remembering that if you're going to make
more work for yourself by making the writing more complex, you
want to make sure that the player will notice and appreciate that work!
Far too often, novice writers make their own lives harder by tracking
choices that players have no idea they're tracking. So, keep in mind: if
the player doesn't realize that the story is branching based on what she
picked, then you might as well not have put the branching in at all.

So if you're working in a game that can use branching, consider using it if:

- **Branching is easy.** Letting the player decide something like what
  career they had before deciding to become the vampire artist's
  captive muse is low-hanging fruit for writers, because you can
  often write three identical branches, just swapping out a single
  word as the vampire waxes rhapsodic on his love of your poetry/
  ballet/accounting acumen.
- **Not branching would be highly noticeable.** Conversely, you
  should try to branch any time a player makes a choice that is large
  enough to immediately notice and be confused if the story ignores
  it. These are things like whether she slept with an LI, whether she
  sided with the Jets or the Sharks in the gang fight, or if she lied to
  her best friend about spreading rumors about her.
- **The choice was recent.** Other than really character-defining
  things from the very beginning of your book (like whether a
  player prefers male or female LIs), usually the choices you should
  be concerned about are the ones that happened within recent
  memory. Players forget things fast, and it's often a waste of effort
  to acknowledge a choice they made more than a chapter ago. This
  is especially true if you're dealing with a multiple-love-interest
  situation and trying to track whether the player ever flirted with a
  character. If it wasn't in the last two times they saw that character,
  it's best to assume they don't remember doing it.
- **The link between the choice and the branching is clear.**
  Your biggest payoff with players comes when you can easily

communicate exactly how their choice prompted the branching (i.e., "So . . . this is the boy who snuck into my office yesterday . . ."). If it's harder to include that reminder ("Hey, remember you told me you were tired a few hours ago? Maybe that's why you're now falling behind in this chase scene we're currently in!"), you may want to skip the branching and stay in the moment.

- **The choice isn't likely to change.** Many dialogue choices are momentary emotional responses that may mean something different to the player than to you. For example, you may have intended that snapping a rude response to an LI means that the player doesn't like him, whereas to the player, she may have just been roleplaying the stress of that moment of escaping from the gang. Trying to honor that sort of choice long-term won't feel validating to the player, just confusing. If a choice will result in significant branching down the line, it's best to telegraph to the player that the choice will be more meaningful than normal dialogue, either by framing it with a suggestive text line ("I knew, whatever I said now, he was likely to remember it forever . . ."), or by making the choice lines themselves very black and white ("I love you no matter what!"/"I never want to speak to you again!").

Other times, when branching is hard to put in and the player won't miss it if it isn't there, you're better off just focusing on the here and now, instead of spending effort on branching the player doesn't want or need.

Premiums

The majority of visual novel apps are supported by selling **premiums**. These are usually either outfits/props that can be equipped on the MC to change her appearance, or **premium choices** that charge players in-game currency to make a choice outside the bounds of their standard choices. Every app handles premiums differently, but from a writing standpoint, there are two overarching approaches:

- **Pay to not screw up the main story.**
- **Pay to access additional content.**

Pay to Keep from Screwing Up

This type of premium generally manifests in a situation in which, for example, the MC is on a date with the bachelor on a matchmaking reality show, and she's been told to do something that will bump up the ratings. The free path allows her to just walk along the beach with the bachelor, doing nothing in particular, while there are either one or two premium choices that allow her to, for example, kiss him for

12 coins or skinny-dip with him for 16. By picking the free option, the player isn't actually allowed to accomplish the goal the story set (do something to bump up the ratings), so players are paying to avoid messing up.

This can also be even more blatant, such as only offering a free path option to eat with your hands when at a fancy Regency dinner, or to be rude to the arresting officer who just found you red-handed over the murdered body you stumbled on.

Some things to keep in mind when writing this type of premium:

- **They generally don't result in significant branching.** The goal in these premiums is generally to dovetail back with the rest of the dialogue quickly. Since players are paying to avoid a bad outcome, they don't necessarily expect an entire distinct scene.
- **The free branch shouldn't be so bad that it creates more branching.** Even though we're defining this as "pay not to screw up," this doesn't mean that your free branch should be so terrible that it would, say, get the MC thrown out of the party she's at. You still want to keep your branching manageable, so make sure that whatever unappealing free path you offer doesn't actually make your writing more difficult.
- **The free branch is often more "bland" than "bad."** By the same token, you don't want to fall into the trap of making the free branch so bad that it makes players curious what will happen if they take it. There's a certain subset of players who will *always* want to pick the "spit in your face" option if it's presented. Since the goal of your game is to make money by selling premiums, the premium options not only have to be better than the free path; they have to look like more fun too!
- **These are frequently roleplaying choices, not story choices.** A premium story choice usually results in more significant branching and unique scenes (see **Additional Content**). This style of premium is more likely to come in the middle of an otherwise normal dialogue and offer the player a better way to present/conceive of their character, rather than a different action to perform in the story.

Additional Content

The other style of premium choice is one where players pay to access exclusive content. Most often this will be something like "Pay for an exclusive date with the prince" or "Pay to spend extra time with your bestie and help her plan her wedding." The good news is that, because players are just buying additional content, writing the premium scene isn't all that different than writing any other scene in your VN. But following these rules of thumb in addition will help you make premium scenes that players don't resent paying money for.

- **Premium scenes should not have negative consequences:** Depending on the overall tone and genre of your book, premium scenes may range from pure fun (go on a date to the carnival) to something that might put the MC in danger (explore the secret dungeon/find a new magical weapon to use against the usurper/ sneak into the evil scientist's lab and steal his prototype). But since players are paying real money to access these scenes, they should never end in a negative effect on the plot. This means no fighting with/getting dumped by an LI, no injuries that aren't healed within the scene, no getting arrested for stealing the scientist's prototype, etc. In terms of her overall goals, the player should end the premium at or ahead of where she was before it.
- **Premium scenes should mesh well with your overall pacing.** Additional content premiums, by definition, take place outside of the momentum of the main plot. Therefore, to maximize how many players buy them, you want to make sure they aren't choosing *between* the premium and success in the larger story. For example, in your action-adventure VN, never offer a romantic premium (or other distraction from the main plot) at a time when the MC is still under threat from the bad guy. Wait until she has a moment of relative safety, *then* offer a chance to celebrate with her LI. But if the premium is something that relates directly to the plot/could give her an advantage in achieving her goals, like a side quest to get a special weapon or find a safe house with secret information, then by all means, put it right in the middle of the action.
- **Premium scenes shouldn't paywall something core to the story's experience.** Premium scenes should offer enticing and fun bonus content for players, *without* making the rest of the story incomplete if players don't participate. This means that anything that's a core part of the fantasy fulfillment your story is offering probably doesn't belong exclusively in a premium. So, if you're writing a romance VN, the LI's proposal shouldn't be for sale in a premium; at best, you should get a much more detailed and romantic version of the proposal (including a steamy post-"Yes!" hookup), while still offering a shorter version of the moment in the free path. Same for things like "defeating the villain" in a more action-oriented story. Don't let free path players miss those moments, but *do* consider whether a more elaborate version of that special moment might make a good premium.
- **Premium scenes shouldn't happen too frequently or back-to-back.** Players don't like feeling like they're being milked for money. So, try to keep to no more than two or three premiums per chapter (depending on the length of your chapters), and try to have at least one full free scene in between each premium you offer.

The Upsell

The most important part of writing premiums is selling them to the player; in other words, presenting them in such a way that they feel enticing and important, and that players feel like they will be missing out if they don't pony up. The art of where to put the lead-in to your premium, and how to write it in the most compelling way possible, is called **writing the upsell.**

The first step is to consider where to place your premium to give it the most urgency.

If your premium is something that either gives you an advantage in the main plot, or prevents you from messing something up in the main plot, you want to put it at the most pivotal moment possible. Don't offer players a chance to buy a fancy sword on their way *into* the deadly dungeon; wait until they're already in the battle with the dragon, then give them a glimpse of a sword embedded in the cavern wall, and offer them the premium choice to pull the sword from the stone and slay the dragon! If the MC is at the royal ball and meeting the prince for the first time, don't have her introduced first and immediately give her a premium line to catch his interest; instead, wait until the rival princess is already flirting with him and *then* offer a premium to interrupt in a way that upstages her!

If your premium is additional fun or romantic content outside of the larger plot context, do it right after a moment of triumph in the plot, when the player is in the mood to rejoice. The MC just got voted prom queen—does she want to take a special premium to celebrate in private with her LI? Or offer it as an antidote to a downturn. The MC lost a big court battle, and now it looks like she'll never prevent her ancestral home from being turned into a mini mall—does she want to go with her LI back to the house one last time, so he can comfort her?

In-dialogue premiums that simply give the player a better line don't necessarily require a lot of upsell, but when selling items/outfits, or offering additional-scene premiums, writing the lead-up can be tricky. You need to straddle the line between advertising and narrative writing, with the writing working to create a desire for the premium without actually breaking the player's immersion in the narrative. You want to plan to spend at least 5–10 lines leading up to the premium choice, and those lines should be used to establish the question that the premium will be the answer to: What can I possibly wear to the king's ball? What is LI going to want to do after prom? Are there any important treasures hidden in this dungeon?

Then show the MC's investment in answering this question and have her or another character suggest the premium as the best way to do it.

EXAMPLE OF UPSELL

Narration: You toss restlessly in your bed, still too keyed up from that last kiss to sleep. LI kissed *you*, not Rival! Maybe he likes you!

LI: Hey. You awake?

Narration: You bolt upright at the soft whisper from the window. There he is. LI. Tapping gently on the screen.

MC: Hey. What are you doing here?

LI: I . . . just couldn't stop thinking about— You know.

MC: Me too . . .

LI: So, I was wondering, maybe you want to . . . go somewhere? Take a walk, maybe?

MC: In the middle of the night?

Narration: Your heart is pounding. Could you really climb out the window and run off with LI? What would your parents think?

LI: Please. I . . . I just want to be with you a little longer.

Game Text: Take a romantic walk in the woods with LI in an **Exclusive Premium Scene** to get to know him better and take your crush to the next level!

Player Agency

So, how do you use all of these new tools to make sure that the player always feels like she is driving the story? Use the following questions as your litmus test to make sure you're centering your stories on the player's experience.

- **Does the player know what she's trying to accomplish in the scene?** When someone doesn't know what they're trying to do, it's just human nature to skim everything until they reach a point where they have a reason to invest in what's happening. And if they have to make choices before that point, they'll be picking randomly, because they can't weigh how the options will affect them. To ensure you're always giving players motivation, make sure that every scene ends with something that sets up the MC's goal in the following scene (learn who is leading the gang/find out if my LI is cheating on me/have a good first day on the job).
- **Is it clear when the goal for a scene has been accomplished?** As a corollary to the above, once the player has accomplished that goal, make it very clear and then immediately set up the next one, so she spends as little time as possible without a goal. For example: The MC is trying to find out who assassinated a prominent judge. She knows the judge met privately with a lawyer the night before he died and goes to the law firm to find out who. But when she gets there, she learns that he never showed up for his appointment, even though security footage shows him entering the building. So now she has to find out where he disappeared between the front lobby and the thirteenth floor!

- **Who is speaking first?** The first character to speak in a scene tends to feel like the person in control—everyone else is responding *to* her. If you can arrange the dialogue so the MC is the first one to speak, then you shape the feeling that the story is reacting to her and not the other way around.
- **Who is giving important information?** Try to put key information into physical evidence (Look! This note says that he went to the graveyard alone!) or the mouths of trusted NPCs. But don't use the MC herself to communicate exposition. Let her dialogue be there for action, characterization, and story purposes, not to tell the player things they didn't know.
- **Does the player always have a choice of how to feel?** Your MC should never *have* to have a specific emotional reaction that may be different than the player's. Even if the character has to *do* or *act* a certain way because of the demands of the plot, try to give players a choice of how they feel about it. As importantly, when giving options of how the MC can feel, try to offer ones that are empowering. Instead of letting them choose between undergoing the initiation enthusiastically or reluctantly, try making it a choice between enthusiastically and *defiantly* ("Fine! If you're going to force me to join your weird coven, I'm going to make a few changes around here . . .")
- **Who is coming up with the plans/solutions?** Don't let an NPC suggest a plan or guess the solution to a mystery if there's a way to let the player have a choice to do it instead. It's always more empowering if the big ideas come from the MC and not her entourage. To avoid putting words in the player's mouth, it can be helpful sometimes to have an NPC suggest a worse version of the plan and then let the MC respond with, "I don't think that will work. But maybe if we did it *this* way . . ."
- **What is causing the events of the story?** In your stories, try to make sure that NPCs' actions and big plot events are actually triggered by the actions of the MC. The rival king isn't building his new castle now because he finally has enough stone from the quarries; he's building it because the MC just took the throne after her father's death, and he thinks she's too weak to hold the border. The rival reality show contestant doesn't just win the bachelor's attention because she's hot; he's pushed into her arms by his jealousy at how the MC upstaged him last episode, and now she has to win him back.

The Unbearable Lightness of Fan Tears

Don't confuse giving players agency with never having anything bad happen to their character. Of course, if you only went by social media comments, you would definitely be left thinking that players never *want* anything bad to happen to their MC. But if you made the mistake of taking them literally and just letting their MCs go through their day without encountering any challenges or disappointments, that's breaking the basic tenet of good writing: Things get worse.

Which means the trick of your job is knowing how to make things worse in a way that keeps players glued to their seats, not storming off in a huff. And if you're thinking that's a fine line to walk, you're right. And there's honestly no way to walk that line that will satisfy everyone. But the following tips should help keep the majority of players only angry at you in a *good* way.

- **Don't force players into decisions that backfire.** In other words, if the MC gets dumped because she stole her LI's phone to spy on his texts with his ex, make sure that it was actually her bestie who stole the phone and gave it to her. That lets the player have a "You shouldn't have done this!" reaction initially, and an "I told you so!" after the breakup.
- **Keep downturns short.** Negative consequences for players shouldn't last more than a few scenes. They generally work best if they're either resolved within the same chapter where they are introduced, or are introduced as cliffhangers with an immediate chance to resolve them in the next chapter.
- **The MC should always make a comeback.** And try to have it be a comeback that vaults her head and shoulders over where she was before the setback. (Run for school council against her ex–best friend and win student body president!/Escape the alien spaceship with a prototype of their technology!/Win the heart of the rival king and prevent the war between your kingdoms!)
- **Romantic downturns should be followed by an escalation of intimacy.** Setbacks can be particularly challenging in romance stories, as many players use VNs as escapism where they can expect a perfect and unceasingly devoted dream boyfriend. Yet romance stories, by their nature, require some degree of running hot and cold to sustain a narrative. You can offset player resentment after an LI pulls away from them as long as when they come back, they reach a new level of intimacy (from crush to dating, or lovers to a marriage proposal, for example).

What You Can Expect Working with a Mobile Studio

Established mobile studios frequently hire freelance writers to work on VNs, and other developers are entering this space, as it's proved to be profitable. Each studio will have different workflows and writer responsibilities. Depending on the IP you're working on and the needs of the developer, you will either be following established documentation and using templates, or you will be required to write this documentation. Some studios have a very precise formula and/or formatting technique; others leave everything up to writers, with some parameters in place.

Here are scenarios you may find yourself working in and the likely responsibilities you'll have in each:

Working on established IP: These are series or universes that have some measure of success on the app. Your client will provide you a bible and character bios, and possibly timelines to illustrate the evolution of the world and story. They may also provide you with background assets representing the story's locations.

Along with writing the script, your work will include:
- Fleshing out the story's outline.
- Designing choices and premium choices.
- Choosing appropriate background assets and pairing them with scenes.

Working with templates: Some studios have detailed and structured templates for all of their VNs. These templates can include both outlines and scripts, which can be Word docs or spreadsheets. Templates may also include scenarios, plot points, and story beats that you will be responsible for fleshing out. They may dictate choice points, which choices include premium content, and the background asset used in each scene.

Details you will need to provide in these templates:

- Outlines
  - Scenarios for scenes or chapters/episodes.
  - Character bios/descriptions and references, if you're responsible for creating the MC and/or NPCs.

- Scripts
  - Exposition, narration, and dialogue.
  - Secret scenes and other premium content players unlock through microtransactions.
  - Prompts for choices.

Developing the scenario and/or outline: While your client will give you some parameters, like the maximum number of words per line of dialogue or chapter, you might have great flexibility in designing the VN's story. Here are some of your possible tasks:
- Writing character bios and providing references for artists, if the studio isn't reusing character assets.
- Writing descriptions for locations, including the times of day in which scenes take place, if your client is making new background assets.
- Providing chapter summaries.
  - This includes explaining the chapter's plot, noting which characters appear in each chapter and which background to use in each scene. Whoever reviews these summaries should be able to understand how each chapter will transition into the next, how you're handling character development for multiple

characters, and how you're designing the main plot and subplots.

- Providing choice summaries.
  - Describe the choices you're giving players, detail where choices will branch, and summarize the results of these choices, like how they will affect the plot or change relationships for better or worse.
- Summarizing premium choices.
  - Indicate which choices are meant to be premium and what kind of special content these will give players access to, like secret scenes and/or dialogue and hairstyles and outfits the MC can wear. If NPCs will have more favorable responses or interactions as the result of premium choices, be sure to explain this and how these choices will affect the story and relationships.

Working with Art Assets

Some mobile studios have libraries of assets that they reuse for multiple VNs, including sound and art assets (character sprites and backgrounds). While you're not likely to work with sound assets or character sprites, you may need to choose the backgrounds that will feature in scenes. These backgrounds represent settings and locations in both established franchises and new stories, as they're flexible for use in multiple genres.

Sometimes, you'll have the task of choosing the backgrounds you want to appear in the VN you're writing. You might be limited to choosing among a few backgrounds, or you might have access to most or the entire library. Ask to review these before you start writing or outlining to see what assets you can use in the story. (Even if your client doesn't mention backgrounds, ask them if they would like for you to choose the art. They may not realize this is something you can do.) You can have a lot of fun with this, as you're also planning the visuals of the world to enhance your writing and worldbuilding. If you're working from a detailed outline, you may have very few backgrounds to work with. In that case, think carefully about what will work best for the scene, and consider the tone and atmosphere of the background's art.

Always Follow the Guidelines!

And—it goes without saying, but it's always a good reminder— whatever guidelines you're given, stick to them! If the client asks you to have 3–5 choices per chapter, don't plan for more or less. If chapters must be between a particular range of lines or words, don't go over or under, etc.

Developing Your Own VN: An Asset Checklist

If you're writing your own VN and looking for collaborators to create assets (or maybe you're making some or all of them yourself), you are the project's lead and in the shoes of a creative director. So, you'll need to not only consider the writing part of the game but also its narrative design. This means that you will be developing storytelling told through your VN's art, sound design, and UI. You're probably aware of some of the assets you'll need to have produced, and there may be some you have not yet thought about. If you can, start planning for these assets during your preproduction, so you'll have a cohesive vision that you can communicate to your team members.

Visual novels can have any aesthetic, whether it's photorealistic, simple, or influenced by anime and manga. The assets' level of detail will be determined by the game's aesthetic, the story's needs, and your budget. For example, there's a cryptid hunting club at a high school. A few of the school's background assets are generic, like the entrance and a classroom. And there are stock sounds you can find on royalty-free websites, like walking down a hallway, a ticking clock, or writing on a desk. But the classroom where the club meets provides more details through environmental narrative and sound effects. There are Bigfoot, Loch Ness Monster, and Chupacabra posters on the wall, along with a map of cryptid sightings. On the map are crossed-out places where sightings have been debunked and question marks over places where sightings still need to be investigated. There's soft scratching and gnawing in the background, as if a small critter is trying to escape from its cage. These may not *seem* like a lot of details, but each detail will be more expensive, as it takes more of the artist's and sound designer's time. On the other hand, those details can make your world feel more complete.

Here is a checklist for common assets found in visual novels and other interactive fiction games. Every project is unique, so your game may require additional assets that aren't mentioned.

Art

Characters
- MC sprites
- NPC sprites
- Off-screen portraits

Think about the character sprites' camera angles, emotional states, and whether they will be half (from the waist up) or full body. Camera angles include front, side, back, 3/4, and rear 3/4 views. Emotional states are the range of expressions characters can convey in scenes. And half or full body affects how much of the character the player can see behind text boxes and other UI assets.

Keep in mind your characters' change in physical states as well. If it's important to the plot or the character, you might include a sprite variation for it. For example, a character gets a cut on their cheek.

Offscreen portraits are headshots or partial images appearing near or with a dialogue text box and are a representation of the speaking

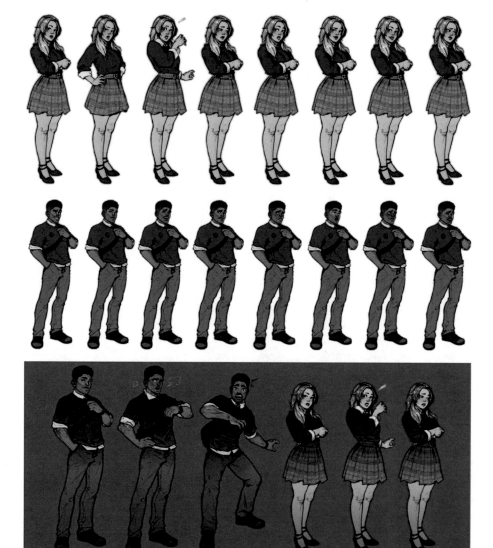

Some of Sindy and Vincent's character sprites from *Incarnō: Everything Is Written*, including different poses, emotional states, and wet variants representing a change in physical state after they're caught in a water main break. Images protected by United States and international copyright law. © Schnoodle Studio LLC.

character, usually the MC. These portraits illustrate characters' emotional states and reactions when they don't appear on screen. You may have this type of portrait for each of a character's emotional states.

Locations

- All places players will visit
- Variations for times of day (morning, afternoon, night)

Keep the purposes and functions of locations in mind when designing them. Who uses the space and why? Even if the backgrounds are static images, players can gain insight about the world by looking at them.

Remember that if your story takes place during different times of the day, you need morning, afternoon, and/or night variations for backgrounds used in scenes during those times of the day. The lighting in the morning is very different than at night, making the same space look very different.

The background may change for other reasons. Going back to the cryptid hunters, a variation of the classroom background might have piles of books on desks and the floor during an intense research session.

Computer Graphics (CGs)

- Unlockable illustrations/art that appear in-game

CGs are rewards for befriending or romancing certain characters, finishing a certain route or getting an ending, or reaching a significant moment. They can also be used as images for cutscenes. If you include CGs, you want them to feel special and worth the wait when players unlock them. CGs are often in different styles than the sprite or background art or illustrated by different artists. This gives you the opportunity to show characters and situations from a different perspective, where you can capture moods, atmospheres, and levels of intimacy (both romantic and spatial).

UI

- Text boxes
  - dialogue (MC and NPC)
  - choices (action and dialogue)
  - narration
  - "previous" text (the player can go back and look at the last few lines of the story, including dialogue or narration based on their choices)
- Choice buttons
- Skip button
- "Next" or scroll button (advance to next text box)

- Main menu
- Settings
- CG gallery
- Unlocked music tracks
- Menus for other collectibles

The UI needs a unifying aesthetic that ties together all UI elements, menus, and fonts. That doesn't mean the UI design can't be simple and clean, but it does have to be consistent. It, like all of your game's components, can be incorporated into the narrative design and a part of the game's storytelling.

Music/Soundtrack

- All tracks in the game
- Character and location themes
- Tracks for pivotal moments

Your game's music deserves as much thought and care as art and UI. It not only creates atmospheric soundscapes, but it also engages players emotionally in ways that art and text cannot.

Your game's overall themes, characters, places in the world, and plot points can serve as inspirations for the soundtrack. Think about what tracks will play during certain scenes, at certain locations, when certain characters are on screen, or during certain moments. Music is part of your storytelling too, so focus on how a track can highlight, communicate, or set a vibe.

Sound Effects

- UI interactions
- Ambient sounds
- Dialogue text sound effects
- Emotes/onomatopes
- Screen transitions

Player interactions with UI elements tend to have a click or soft chime/ding accompanying them. Screen transitions can also have simple sound effects like a "swoosh."

Ambient sounds make the world feel dynamic and inhabited. They also build atmosphere in scenes, like suspense, solemnity, or whimsy.

Most VNs are unvoiced, or a portion of the dialogue is unvoiced. Each character can have their own dialogue text sound effects that distinguish them. You can express a lot of personality through these and make them unique. For some games, like *Undertale*, players can identify which character is speaking just by the text sound effects.

Emotes and onomatopes can be used with unvoiced dialogue. A gasp or a sigh at the beginning of a line of dialogue establishes the tone and emotional state of the character.

Also, think about major moments that can be enhanced by their own sound effect, like an NPC running from a werewolf and banging frantically on the door, getting the player's attention to let them inside a room filled with silver.

Game Logo

- Marketing representation outside and inside the game

Sure, the game logo is a marketing tool, and anyone who sees the logo should get a sense about your game's themes, story, and/or aesthetic. It does not have to reference any one character or plot point, although it could. *The Letter*'s player characters are entangled with the hauntings at an English estate. The logo evokes a sense of horror and features a silhouette of the ghost.

The Letter's logo. Image by Yangyang Mobile and protected by United States and international copyright law. © Yangyang Mobile.

A Word on Being the Boss

While the role of creative lead may be a new challenge for you, it gives you a lot of command in determining what gets into your game. There are a lot of moving parts in game development, and it might be difficult or a little overwhelming to keep track of them all. If you have experience working on games (whether that was a student project, game jams, or with a studio as an employee or freelancer), think about all of the different departments or team members who had a hand in storytelling and making assets. That will give you a good idea when planning your own storytelling and narrative design.

If you *don't* have this experience, it's not a hindrance! Play a game that's similar to yours—it may be the same story genre. Analyze the scene building, what makes up a scene, how characters are designed, what you hear, how you interact with the screen, etc. Now reverse engineer your analysis to see which of these elements you can also implement into your own project.

Exercises

Exercise 10.1

Write a "meet cute" for a female MC (main character) and an LI (love interest) of player-determined gender (male/female/nonbinary). Setting should be easily created with assets available in most realistic fiction: schools, bars, coffee shops, etc. Make sure there is branching for the LI's gender and at least 3 player choices.

Exercise 10.2

Write two examples of the upsell for a premium date with the characters created above, one for each type of premium.

Samples

Sample 10.1: *Exclusive Scene Upsell*

Brad: Come away with me, Cindy.

Cindy: What are you talking about? You've got Organic Chemistry at 2.

Brad: Forget it. I don't want to be a doctor anymore. I want to make movies. With you. So let's do it.

Text: Your heart starts to beat faster. He's not serious, is he? You were just . . . joking when you talked about being a movie star. Just fooling around.

Brad: My parents have a lake house.

Cindy: Of course they do . . .

Brad: No, it's not like that. It's gross. Creepy. Perfect for a horror film. We'd hardly even need effects.

Text: You let yourself imagine it for a minute. You and Brad . . . The script you've been working on since sophomore year . . . A secluded cabin with a crackling fireplace . . .

Choice

> **Premium Choice 1 (20 Diamonds)**: I'd Love to!
>
> **Choice 2**: It sounds great, but I don't want to be responsible for you flunking Orgo.
>
> **Choice 3**: Whoa, did you read this situation wrong, buddy . . .

Premium Choice 1

Text: Brad's hundred-watt smile immediately tells you that was the right answer.

Cindy: Let's go now.

Brad: Great! I've got the chainsaws and fake blood in my trunk.

Text: Truly the perfect man.

Choice 2

Text: Brad's face falls, but he covers it quickly.

Brad: Scarier than any horror movie, anyway . . .

Choice 3

Text: You back away. It's been fun, but . . . you're not going to a secluded cabin with some guy you met last week. No matter how much it seems like you have in common.

Cindy: I mean, we just—

Brad: Sorry, I guess that was—

Text: You look at each other. Brad takes a step back.

Brad: Maybe just a screening of the new *Scream*, then?

Cindy: Maybe.

Sample 10.2: *"Don't Screw Up" Upsell*

Brad: Wow, that was a trip! I never thought when I showed up for that student film that it would just be the two of us, half-naked in the woods.

Brad (smiles): Or how much fun that would be.

Text: Your heart beats faster, and this time, you know it's from excitement, not fear.

Cindy: I'm glad you didn't *really* turn out to be a psychopath cannibal.

Brad (smiles): There's still time.

Cindy: Oh, yeah? You planning on getting me alone in the woods again?

Brad: Would you come if I asked?

> **Premium Choice 1 (20 diamonds):** Why don't you make me come?
> **Premium Choice 2 (10 diamonds):** Only if *I* get the chainsaw this time.
> **Choice 3**: Once was enough for me.

Premium Choice 1

Text: You sidle closer, letting your hand brush his and hear his sharp intake of breath.

Cindy: No cameras, no crew. There's a lot more we could do together without them . . .

Text: Brad tosses his backpack on the ground.

Brad: I think I'm feeling the need for some reshoots right now . . .

Premium Choice 2

Text: Brad laughs, but you see the gleam of interest in his eye.

Brad: I could be persuaded. As long as you're gentle.

Cindy: Uh-uh, you come with me, we do this on *my* terms . . .

Choice 3:

Text: Brad's face falls and he takes a step backward.

Brad: Okay, uh, maybe I'll see you at the screening, then?

CHAPTER 11

Storytelling in Open-World Games and Games as a Service

Introduction

In recent years, open-world games and games that run as a service have dominated the gaming space. Many games have opted for large worlds or decided to extend their lifetime by adding additional content after their release, thus extending the experiences the players can have.

In this chapter, we want to share some of our experiences when working on these games and how you can apply the techniques discussed earlier to these games.

IN THE CHAPTER, YOU WILL LEARN . . .

- What the different types of open-world dialogue are.
- How to write systemic, nonreactive ambient, and reactive ambient dialogue.
- Additional types of open-world dialogue.
- How casting and voice variety improve a game's soundscape.
- The importance of cross-disciplinary support.
- How to prepare, plan, and maintain your worldbuilding material.
- How to create living worlds that last multiple installments by layering and seeding storylines.
- What character plots and world plots are, how they relate to each other, and how they can be used in open worlds and games as a service (GAAS).

DOI: 10.1201/9781003369332-11

What Is Systemic Open-World Dialogue?

While not all large-scale games involve this type of writing, the crafting of lines and dialogue specific to open-world experiences requires purpose and dedication. Open-world games usually involve large spaces (an entire city, large sections of a country, etc.) that are often populated by speaking characters, of greater and lesser importance. One of the tools that can make these spaces feel lived in and fresh each time the player goes through them is dialogue.

It is, unfortunately, very easy to assume only minimal work is required when creating "background" dialogue for such spaces. Writing for open-world games with a robust living presence is a skill that is often undervalued, if not outright dismissed. And yet, it is an expertise that is essential when working on this kind of game, which requires both creativity and logic (tracking multiple branches of conversations flawlessly, ensuring that ambient conversations fire at the right time, etc.).

Giving proper attention and care to your open-world dialogue will always pay off. The careful layering of these types of dialogue is a delicate matter, but pulling it off will result in a rewarding player experience.

Systemic Open-World Dialogue

The main goal of writing for an open-world game is to add another layer of verisimilitude to the lifescape of the game. Populating a world with people (animations, characters, etc.) is one thing, but what makes the people inhabiting these spaces as real as possible is giving them opinions in conversations players can overhear, giving voice to their reactions to various situations and interactions with the player. These sounds combine to create what is known as a soundscape, adding to the immersiveness of an environment.

Players often rush through an open world. While they may miss seeing the animations of an NPC (non-player character) pointing at them in surprise, they will at least overhear a shout of surprise as part of the soundscape surrounding them. Even if a player does not stop to pay specific attention to what is happening around them, the illusion of a living world is sustained, and any kind of dialogue players overhear will enhance the overall experience of the space you've created. And if a player *does* stop to listen, there are various tools narrative designers can use to create different levels of immersion.

Types of Open-World Dialogue

There are several types of open-world dialogue, from systemic anyplace/time usage to highly customized reactivity conversations

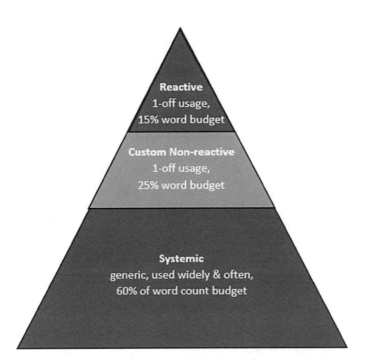

The more generic and commonly used lines require the most budget to implement in a way that lets you offer variety, though there is always the risk of such lines getting overly repetitive. That said, systemic dialogue is meant to be filler noise—heard in the background to give players a sense of life, not always listened to with full attention.

with very specific conditionals attached to them. Ideally, you want to rely on a pyramid system when planning the scope of your open-world dialogue.

More custom lines, which are specific to characters, but may or may not be reactive to player actions or the broader plot, vary in what percentage of the game they make up. They generally follow something close to the proportions in the pyramid above.

Generic Systemic Dialogue

Systemic dialogue relies on narrative designers who can make conversations flow in a way that ensures they make sense in multiple permutations, so players can experience them in any order. Of course, the more permutations you write, the more complicated it can be to make them all flow well—and the more generic they tend to become as a result. Systemic dialogue will invariably be generic, and that's fine— systemic dialogue is the background chatter of your world and doesn't need to be anything more than that . . . as long as it still makes sense. And that's the part that will require focus and attention and a strong ability to puzzle out logic.

Systemic conversations usually do not rely on conditionals (such as, for example, the weather), due to their usage being "at all times" as a default setting. However, one could set light conditionals on the batch if one had the budget and technological support to do so, and then create a batch of subsets for generic conversations about the weather, with variables such as sunny, rain, tornado, etc.

That said, the more generic these conversations are, the more widespread their use, and the more effective they are in filling out the background noise of the world. Each time you add a conditional to what is meant to be generic, the more line budget is required, and the more you slide into "custom" territory.

Below is an example of systemic dialogue that would be used for a hostile faction in a game world. The player could overhear this before either engaging the faction in combat or stealthing past them. Since the player is busy engaging in instant, direct action or just going by quickly, this needs to make sense while not being super informative. Furthermore, the different permutations mean this dialogue can be used frequently, since the variable branching will generate enough variety that it won't strike the player as overly repetitive.

Start (Actor 1)	Middle 1 (Actor 2)	Middle 2 (Actor 1)	End (Actor 2)
Did you hear the latest rumor?	Yeah. Was the boss upset?	Well, I hear someone's in trouble.	Eh, as long as it's not on me, I don't care.
Did you know the new guy decided to get ambitious?	What now . . . ?	Let's just say things are gonna get interesting.	Whatever.
That heist last night? It did not go well.	I don't wanna know.	The boss is upset.	Same old, same old.
I am so glad I was off last night. That robbery . . .	Tell me more.	Half the crew got caught.	Of course.

As you can see in the example above, each variation has to flow together. It is highly recommended to add performance notes in order to help the lines merge better. In the case above, the voice notes would go as follow:

- Actor 1: eager to share bad news, horrified interest
- Actor 2: has seen it all before, "didn't even get a T-shirt" level of bored

Systemic dialogue is generally the line hog in your open-world budget for a very specific reason: voice variety. Having different people and genders speak the same lines is what refreshes your systemic dialogue and makes lines feel new and less repetitive. Hearing the same line said the same way several times will tip your player off to the repetition. That's how human brains and hearing work and why we get ear-wormed—we remember what we hear, and sounds that are always the same can catch our attention. To avoid that, you would rerecord the above permutation several times with different actors to add that vocal freshness/differentiation. As such, what seems at first to be 16 lines in all, spread across 2 actors of different vocal ranges, can actually be budgeted for up to 128 lines if you have 8 voices to fill out the variety and scope. Systemic dialogue is one of the most-used methods to fill an open world—and the line budget goes up fast! It's worth it, of course, but if you're going to spend that much of your budget, you want to make sure that you're using it in the most creative and purposeful way you can.

This is where factions come into play. Civilians won't care about the same topics as a criminal faction. Rich people won't have the same concerns as the middle class. Giving each faction, class, and cultural group in your game their own topics and concerns and having them focus on that in their systemic dialogue, even at the most generic level, will help differentiate areas and groups of people in your world in a nice, subtle way.

If you've already got some good back-and-forths going but need to round out the soundscape further, consider some of the following ways to add lines to just a single character:

- A character can be on a phone in a modern setting, and the player only hears one end of the conversation.
- Characters can be talking to themselves, though that should be used more sparingly.
- Someone can be whistling while walking down the street, or humming a tune they are listening to on a headset.

Custom Nonreactive Dialogue (Ambient Conversations)

Nonreactive custom dialogue is easier and more fun to write, allows for more specific topics to be tackled in a conversation, and can vary in scope. A minimum of 4 lines makes it easier on a writer to craft something interesting, and the maximum honestly is up to your line budget and what kind of conversations you want players to hear. Generally, though, 8 lines is enough of a budget to dig into a subject more deeply if desired.

Keep in mind the following regarding custom dialogue:

- Each conversation should fire only once during a game's entire playthrough, since it will be memorable enough for players to notice repetition.
- You only need as many voice actors as there are characters for the conversation.
- Their line numbers are set, since there are no permutations to worry about.

Good ambient conversations will showcase the lives of the characters: what they care about, things they love or hate, what happens to them in the living world, their inner lives and experiences. They can cover the entire gamut of emotions, sharing stories that are sad, joyous, or funny. The characters also can have any sort of connection: They can be strangers discussing the news, coworkers gossiping about work, friends ribbing each other, or family members grieving together. All of this serves to give your players a sense of the larger world and who is living in it.

While ideally you would use open-world ambient conversations to show the changing state of the world in reaction to the player's actions, sometimes, for tech or scope reasons, that just isn't possible. When that's the case, it is crucially important to remember to *not* refer to specific events in these conversations and keep the topics to things that do not contradict anything in your game's storyline beyond the unreliable nature of gossip or rumors.

Always remember that players are constantly scanning your world for what is relevant to *them*. This means that ambient conversations should never hint at gameplay or missions that don't exist, or actions the player can never undertake. For example, if an ambient refers to Timmie being in danger near the lake, there better be a Timmie in danger near the lake for the player to rescue!

TELLING SEQUENTIAL STORIES WITH OPEN-WORLD DIALOGUE

The term "sequential ambient conversations" refers to times when a player returns to a location and can hear the same characters' conversations continue and evolve. This allows writers and narrative designers to use several custom conversations to build to something bigger narratively, while creating an emotional investment in the location and characters on the part of the player. This can end after a set number of ambient conversations or, if desired, can even open a new side quest, depending on your budget for noncritical content.

If a sequel or new expansion for your game is planned, you can seed ambient conversations that hint at what is coming later to reward attentive players. This is a rare thing to be able to create intentionally, though, as you may not know far enough in advance whether sequels are planned or what they will involve. More frequently, writers of later games and expansions remember small, interesting moments from previous ambient conversations and use them as a jumping-off point for new content.

Custom Reactive Dialogue (Ambient Conversations)

Custom reactive ambient conversations are your primary means of rewarding players by showing how the world changes as a result of their actions. These are the conversations that reflect the things a player did directly, be it finishing a mission, a story arc, killing or saving a character, unleashing monsters or stopping them, etc. Custom reactive ambient conversations should be highly specific and reward (or condemn) player action, and respond to major changes in the world or major story beats. They can build on the lore of the game, offer Easter eggs, etc. They can even lead to bonus rewards if you so wish, but not in such a way that it penalizes players who don't engage in the conversations, at least never in the open-world portion of your game.

REACTIVITY CONDITIONALS VERSUS VARIABLES RULES

There are different ways that the terms "reactivity," "variables," or "conditionals" are used, often interchangeably, but it is a good idea to set clear definitions across your team to avoid misunderstandings. Common definitions would be:

- Reactivity refers to "x thing happened during a mission, and now the world changes to reflect it/this line can fire to acknowledge it."
- Variables are used to allow a line or conversation to fire (or not) depending on factor y and/or x (for example: fire line Y if choice Z *and* B were made).
- Conditionals allow a conversation or line to fire if x condition is met (for example: if a quest is complete, then a reactivity ambient can fire).

As with nonreactive ambient conversations, reactive ambients only fire once, meaning they are lower-budget. They require conditionals to be applied to reflect if or when they trigger. If the tech allows, you may even want to set further conditionals for if they played only the first line or all the way through, allowing more important conversations to repeat if players only heard a little bit of them.

Additional Types of Open-World Dialogue

The above cover the most common methods used to inject life in open-world games. But by no means should you limit yourself to only these if you can think of more ways to widen the breadth and scope of the life in your game. *Spider-Man: Miles Morales*, for example, introduces that Miles Morales knows American Sign Language (ASL). His interactions with Hailey using sign language build on the existing systems of the first *Spider-Man* game in order to broaden the possible interactions. A future sequel could now add sign language and the associated animations to the living world, with characters speaking to each other in ASL rather than using voice.

This does require the support of animation, voice design, tech level design, and programming, however, which brings us to our next topic.

Casting and Voice Variety

A surefire way to add variety to your soundscape is to plan right from the start for a vast range of different types of voices. Male, female, and nonbinary are only the starting point for aural differentials. You can layer on age (young, adult, old). You can plan for accents from different languages. You can even add in different languages!

All of the above will directly impact your budget—sometimes it's better to do some things in custom only and keep some for systemic. Tech (tying voices to specific models) is another consideration too. But if you plan ahead, have the budget for it, and garner the buy-in of your colleagues in other disciplines, there is a tremendous amount of variety that can be introduced in your living world.

Also keep in mind that things you can't do now might be doable later. Sometimes for a first game (even more so if you're using a new engine), you must limit yourself and use what gives you the most variety for the best budget. But planning ahead and building on what you already have in subsequent releases will be truly rewarding as you see your living world grow.

Cross-Disciplinary Support

You can write all the dialogue you want, but if the systems aren't built to trigger it at the right time and place, if the animations aren't generic enough to support a wide range of conversations and emotions, if all the elements aren't in place to make them fire and work properly . . . then it just won't have the effect you intended.

Therefore, it is important to maintain open lines of communication with all your fellow disciplines. If your game is an open-world game, and open-world conversations are an important part of that, then it is vital to communicate this clearly to your colleagues and for them to get on board with ensuring all the proper systems are in place. But be aware that budget, time, and personnel restraints may all require adjustment on your part as well. If there's no time or people to create custom conditionals to trigger an event at a specific time, you may need to cut your favorite highly customized reactive ambient conversations.

Hope for the best, but sit down with your team early to adapt to what can be realistically done, and always plan for the worst. This may mean being ready to let go of a feature or having simpler ways to integrate it just in case something gets cut during a necessary scoping exercise.

ORGANIZING YOUR DATABASE

Let's be real—open-world dialogue eats up a lot of word or line budget. It's usually a huge portion of the overall game budget. And that means you can end up with a complete mess of a database far more quickly than you might expect. Plan your database structure right from the start. There's no way around it; it will end up in a disaster if you don't—once lines are hooked up, some tools cannot handle your ever-moving lines in the database. Don't risk it. You want to make your database as clear and user-friendly as possible, since writers will not be the only people using it. The people hooking up your content (attaching it to NPCs and locations in the open world) will be in there far more often than you once the writing is done, and you want them to be able to find things quickly and efficiently.

Games as a Service (GAAS)

Now that we have covered how to write and develop stories and tell them in open worlds, we want to share a few tips, approaches, and techniques to adapt your stories for games that run as a service and thus constantly change and need to add new experiences to keep their audience entertained and engaged.

Live-service games, another name for games run on the games-as-a-service model, never really end their development until they are shut down. After their initial development and release, a smaller team continues to improve the game and add content. The worlds of these games don't stand still, so our work as narrative designers is never done.

Many of the techniques discussed previously for open worlds apply to live-service games as well, as both face similar challenges, such as uncertainty of the player path (we usually do not know with 100 percent certainty what a player completed and from where they approach the current plot point), unconnected/unrelated plotlines, extensive and complex background lore, etc.

In addition to these challenges, in live-service games, we have something like a "real," ongoing history for our game world as events come and go. Players can join the game at any time, and thus their experience is based on current events, while the world's history consists of the lore we wrote initially *and* the stories the players have already experienced since the game launched. In some cases, this means that a former ending point is now in the middle of a campaign as new stories were added. In others, it may mean that some experiences were removed and can never again be experienced.

For example, *Drakensang Online* today features a completely different beginning than when it first launched, and even before the current beginning, there was another one that was added during its lifetime. The same can be said about *World of Warcraft* (considering the main game and not its classic version). The world you encounter in today's

World of Warcraft is vastly different from what it was when the game first released.

Developing stories for live-service games is like writing a TV show, where viewers can join in season 1, 2, or 5 and still want to be able to understand the world, the characters, the challenges, and the events they face.

So, the first question you need to answer (with the game's direction) is if the game is planned as an open-ended or finite experience. In an open-ended experience, you look at something like the *Forgotten Realms*, with all their stories and their ongoing history that never seems to end. They have continued adding years and years of events and history since it was first created. Finite live-service games are more like a TV series with a finite number of seasons, which will end at some point. Maybe after 10, 20, or more seasons. An example of such a series is *Lost* or *Game of Thrones*. Both had multiple seasons, but also a clear ending at some point. Why is this important? It's important because it will shape how your world develops over time. Is it drifting towards destruction or any kind of end, or is it in a state of permanent existence that goes on and on and on (at least from the perspective of the players)?

Once you have clarified the general idea of the live service and your world, you are ready to plan your initial plots and events.

How to Keep Your Material Updated

An absolute must-have for live-service games is a central, up-to-date source of world/lore documentation. If worldbuilding is ignored, you will quickly run into retcons (see Chapter 3 for details on retcons) and inconsistencies in your events and stories. Make sure that the world documentation is always up to date. It's part of your responsibility when adding new content to check this content for consistency and to add any changes/additions, etc. to the world to the central documentation. This is equally important if you work alone or in a team. In the end, you are building a fictional world and defining its canon for everything that was and is to come.

If you are working in a team, it is always a good idea to have a dedicated team member to act as the loremaster, the keeper of the central documentation. They will ensure that the latest version is always accessible to everyone in the team and serve as the go-to person for everything lore related. Imagine how negative it would be if you wrote a backstory for the player characters where they left their relatives and families happily behind in their village, while someone else changed the world history and now this village was burned down and everyone was killed during the characters' childhoods?

Simply committing to keep your material updated is not enough. You also, from the very start, need to plan for how you maintain your material, how you develop it, and what the points of extension are. The plan can almost be as technical as designing a new API (application programming interface, the stuff your programmers like to develop and work with). It is important to clearly define how your world grows, what the common values are, and how events of global relevance are developed and make it into the lore of your world. Nothing would be more frustrating to your coworkers than if your great new idea means that they must rewrite all their quests and dialogues just to make it happen.

One good approach is to establish story/worldbuilding stand-ups from the beginning of development with your content team, which can be solely narrative designers and writers but may also include level designers, system designers, artists, etc. During these regular stand-ups, each member of the story team updates everyone briefly

TITLE
Sub-Title

Author:	**Tobias Heussner**
Created:	**01/01/2022**
Last Changed:	**01/05/2022**
Status:	**APPROVED**

Executive Summary
TBD

Last Changed
TBD

Contents

Header 1
TBD

Header 1.1
TBD

Header 2
TBD

An example of how to format documentation.

on the recent changes and work they have done. Afterward, the team identifies the main points they need to discuss and decide for this specific stand-up. This meeting then becomes an excellent place to talk about changes to the lore and to decide if they are made or not.

Besides, and as mentioned before, your plan does not only need to include how decisions are made but also what software is used to store the lore of your game and if the individual pages in your lore documentation need to follow a specific format. For example, it is a good practice that all pages in the documentation start with a summary of the most important points of this lore piece followed by a section listing the changes made in each version of the document and by whom they were made. A typical page in your lore documentation might look like Figure 11.2, above.

One last important point will lead you back to the direction of the game you are working on. As early as possible, you want to know as part of your plan how often content will be released to players once the initial version is shipped. It can and will make a big difference if you must come up with new plots and stories every two weeks or every six months. Usually, the more frequent releases are, the more organized you must be with your material, as you will need to be able to quickly and reliably find the information in your documentation that you need to extend the narrative of the game. With less frequent releases come bigger extensions, but also more time to sort through all the available documents and to check everything for consistency.

Having as much of your process as possible defined in the beginning will save you a lot of headaches and discussions later. It will help you and your team to stay focused. And if you work alone, it's good to practice the steps above as well, as they will be a guideline for you during the weeks and weeks and weeks you spend developing your world and plots.

How to Layer Plots

With the foundation laid, we can start talking about developing plots for a never-ending story.

The first and most important consideration is that your plots will be layered on top of each other and intersect with each other. In your planning, you need to avoid a situation where you become strictly sequential; you usually want to have different overlapping plots that help to create the impression of one huge consistent plot instead of many unconnected smaller ones.

So, How Can You Layer Plots?

In a variety of ways. You can, like in the second half of *Lord of the Rings*, have events happening in parallel at different locations and guide the player between these locations or let them choose where they want to continue the story. You can introduce characters and events from the next plotline before the current one finishes. You can spread breadcrumbs of the next plot throughout the current plot, preparing the player and sparking their interest to move forward to the next part. In short, look for ways that feel like natural transitions between the plots and introduce new plotlines with some degree of overlap.

Besides overlapping plots, you also can draw from the concept of "world story" vs. "character stories." In a simplified way, this concept expresses that the story of your world develops independently from your character plots and, while both affect each other, neither is ever waiting for the other.

A world never waits for a hero, even if it needs one. This is what the world story is all about. It is the sum of all the events that form the past and the present of your world. It is also the future of your world if nothing affects it. Think about it as all the what-ifs, possibilities, and the events where the players *couldn't* change the outcome. What if the players didn't defeat the villain? What if the players didn't rescue the merchant from the bandits? Would your world still exist? What kind of place would it be?

The world story is a great tool for live-service games, as so many aspects of the world can't depend on individual characters, but rather on events and characters outside of the control of a specific group. Even if all players go through the same quests/missions, rarely will they do so in the same order or at the same pace . . . all of this changes their view on the world and the impact they had on it. The world story is developed by your NPCs, by characters outside the control of the players, and these events move the world forward. The world story allows you to build a believable history that players can enter at any given time without missing out on anything or feeling like they had to do something specific to get to the point they are at. Their character just enters the flow and becomes part of the greater story through their actions.

The character stories are the point where your world becomes personal to the players. These are the points where they influenced the world story (or at least believe they did) and became central figures in an epic story they might tell around a campfire. Character stories are the sum of what the players experienced in your world when solving quests and overcoming obstacles. These are the stories you design when developing your quests and missions. It is always good to think of each questline (a collection of one or more quests) as a mini story that may or may not be part of the bigger world events told by your world story. Character stories don't have to be related to world events. Often, characters will do things and interact with others without even caring about the bigger world context. Players' heroes may not be saving the world; they may be saving a friend or a love interest, or just exploring an interesting new vista.

Character stories relate to our own experiences and actions we would take. They are the window into heroic acts that give us reasons for heroism that we can understand. They are extremely powerful, but in the context of live-service games, they need to be carefully designed so that players can encounter them in any order they choose (except due to gameplay/balancing/world limitations) and without ever being required to complete all of them. A good character story starts with something the characters can relate to and would be interested in addressing. It takes the characters on a journey to explore themselves and the world they live in.

Eventually, the outcomes of some of these character stories will affect your world story, and so the players become heroes, forever remembered in the history of your world and documented in your lore documentation (that you've been meticulously updating!).

The Problem with Success (or Its Absence)

So, the game you worked on has launched (or you joined an existing game). Congratulations! Now that players from around the world can experience the plots and questlines you wrote, you can sit back and enjoy the stories they share on social media . . . or not!

With live-service games, the work is not done when a game releases; most of the work is just starting! Up to this point, you likely only had to fulfill internal deadlines. Now you must also provide new content for players who play through it faster than you can finish writing.

Working on a live-service game can be quite stressful and demanding but also very rewarding. You don't have to wait years before players can enjoy your newest creation; instead, you can respond to what they already like and incorporate their actions and favorites into your stories. Now is the time when hopefully all your preparations pay off. The moment where your lore documentation becomes the basis for a world people live in and care about, which you must extend with new events faster than you ever imagined.

But this is also a time when you will face one of the biggest issues of live-service games . . . the problem of success.

If the game you are working on is successful, you can end up in a constant race with your fan base and will have to come up with new content on a punishingly fast basis. On average (assuming that it takes two to three weeks of average play sessions to complete a storyline), you will want to release a new storyline every three months or so. While coming up with new ideas is one of the challenges, the other is integrity. Not only must your ideas be new and entertaining but they also have to fit into the existing lore and extend it in a logical way. This is where retcons usually happen. You had to finish one quest quickly and did not have enough time to check the lore documentation, and now, months later, you realize the contradiction that you added to the world. While you can't always prevent this, the best antidote is to always engage an editor before marking your content as ready for release. This editor can be a professional editor on your team, it can be a fellow writer from your writing team, or any other person on the team who is familiar with the lore. It is also a good practice to have review meetings with the development team and to present your newest content so that more people can discuss it before it is released. This is also why we keep hammering on the importance of keeping your lore documentation updated. It will feel like an extra burden, but it will help you with creating new content that fits into your world for years to come.

But what if your game is not a success (or isn't any longer)? That is usually the moment where the time has come to bring your stories to an end. If a title is not successful, sooner or later the service and the addition of new content stop. What you want to avoid is leaving your players hanging with unfinished plotlines, so it will be important to figure out with the project leads what the plans are for the remaining service so that you can redesign your storylines to come to a satisfying end by the time the last update is released. Some live-service games continue to exist beyond this point, so players will be able to enjoy the content; others will be shut off and become a part of the long history of video games. Regardless of the fate of your game, finish well, because these last moments of your game will most likely be what it is remembered for in the future. As you cannot foresee if your title will be successful and for how long, it is always good if your documentation includes some ideas for how everything would end if the stories of your game were to end today. But, until the last player stops playing, we hope that you can tell a lot of engaging stories and enjoy every moment of seeing them experienced by others.

How Can I Practice Writing for Live-Service Games?

As you've seen throughout these chapters, a lot of your journey to become a better writer and narrative designer depends on how much you practice your craft. It is not only about getting familiar with different techniques and approaches but also about finding your style and your approach to solving narrative problems and engaging players. In the past, it was said that you must write ten bad pages to write one good one; this applies to game writing just as much as it applies to books, movie scripts, and so on.

But How Can You Practice Writing for a Live-Service Game If You're Not Working on One?
The best way to practice writing and narrative design for live-service games is by running and developing campaigns for pen-and-paper roleplaying games. As you build your campaign, as you flesh out your world, and as you engage and react to your player group, you can apply a lot of the techniques and approaches discussed above. Roleplaying games aren't that different from live-service games. Yes,

the scope and scale may differ, but so does the team working on the content. You can also attend and help organize live-action roleplaying events and observe how players consume certain content, how they come to certain conclusions and what this means for the plot, and how to move it forward.

Online, you can find a lot of good material on being a successful game master, a role similar to yours when you develop live-service games. Good starting points are the YouTube channels from How to be a Great GM (www.youtube.com/c/HowtobeaGreatGM), WASD20 (www.youtube.com/c/WASD20), and World Anvil (www.youtube.com/c/WorldAnvil).

Also, try finding some like-minded writers with whom you can form a critique group to review each other's material or to work together on a world, fleshing out a series of plots and events.

In the end, just like the material you develop, the writing process is a journey with many obstacles to overcome. We hope that the tips and techniques shared above will help you to get started working on open-world and live-service content.

Exercise

Exercise 11.1

Develop the structure for lore documentation (for a region or part of your world) for a live-service game, considering the elements you will need to track and how you can easily find a piece of specific information if you need it.

Sample

Sample 11.1

Sample Lore Documentation Structure for a Region

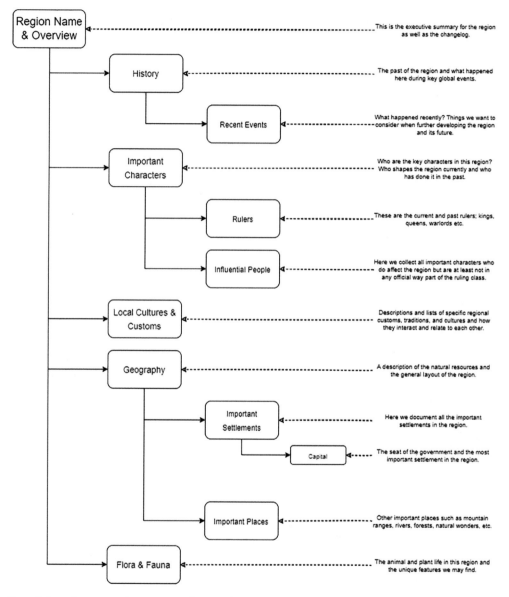

Sample lore documentation structure for a region.

Conclusion

Well done, and welcome to the last chapter (unless you skipped everything and started reading here)! Hopefully, it was a good journey, and you learned a lot from all of the exercises.

IN THIS CHAPTER, YOU WILL LEARN TO . . .

- Build a résumé for narrative design.
- Expand your knowledge of games.
- Consider opportunities you might have to work in games.
- Consider being an innovator in narrative design and an inspiration to players.

You read about concepts, worldbuilding, story structures, dialogue, characters, cinematics, execution, and troubleshooting. Unfortunately, one book is not enough to cover everything about the art of telling interactive stories. It requires a lot of practice and adaptation. The industry just started to explore this ground a little more than two decades ago, and much more progress will undoubtedly follow. We, the authors, hope that one day we will meet you at one of the many industry conferences. Maybe you will have something to share with us, something new that we haven't discovered yet. In the appendix, you will find some links to active game-writing communities that will happily welcome you and walk with you on your journey to tell great stories in games to come.

But before you take your next steps into the wilderness of the game industry, each of us would like to share some parting words about how to work in this creative, chaotic, and demanding industry.

Ann Lemay

Résumé Tips

While traditional job-seeking advice tells you to keep your resume to one page and make it as simple as possible, standing out on paper with game-industry recruiters requires something a bit different than traditional résumé-building techniques.

I had the good fortune to help someone look over her résumé recently, to try and make it shipshape for job applications in the industry. When I say "good fortune," I mean that she'd done everything right. She had academic work focused on games, she'd participated in several game jams, she had several of her games to link to, and much more. She was obviously interested and active in game creation and had already taken on different roles while working on game jams. Even if these were short-term, skim-the-surface projects, her participation stood out as a clear marker of her ability not just to work with others but also to appreciate what other disciplines required of her as a narrative designer. Her earlier initiative and interest in the craft showed that she would go the extra mile needed and that she was well prepared for a career in the industry. Showing that you are willing to go the extra mile and getting prepared before you apply for your first job certainly can be a door opener, just in the same way a good résumé can be.

What to Put in a Résumé

For a game-industry resume, you want to do a lot more than just include your studies and non-game-related employment. This can be hard if you're just coming out of school. Fortunately, there are many tools and options for you to spruce up your résumé, though all will require work and effort and careful review to catch any typos.

To start, if you're going through a design program, make a point of taking a game-design class, a level-design class, an art class. Show an ability—and a desire—to understand how the other disciplines are involved in game-making work and, more importantly, how they work with narrative, and vice versa. Make a note of this in your cover letter. Showing that you have insight not only into game narrative but also other disciplines can only be to your advantage.

Participating in projects where a game is the result will also indicate to a company that you at least have a notion of a production pipeline and what creating a game from start to end might be like, even on a small scale. Linking to the results of said projects will be, of course, a must. Keep the list succinct, but make sure to include a credits section on the website where the game resides (if you have your own website), or on a separate file located in the same folder as the game if you turned in a hard copy. It speaks to teamwork and your appreciation of your cocreators.

Create stories using Twine (http://twinery.org/) or StoryNexus (www. storynexus.com/). Put them online. Get feedback. Specifically, make sure to put your stories/games through a beta test with friends and fellow students. Write a postmortem of your experiences, and make a note on your résumé that one is available upon request. Showing an ability to request constructive criticism and use that to improve your work will tell an employer you can work with others and adjust your work when given feedback. When I applied to BioWare, feedback and iteration on said feedback were crucial parts of the process. They didn't just want to see how my first writing test would turn out; they also wanted to know how I would react to their feedback and how this would impact the revised writing test.

Show that you are interested in game creation as a whole. Create games and stories on your own and with fellow students. Play other games, all kinds of games. AAA, to indie games, to mobile games, to social games—all of them will have something you can learn from. For a creative who is starting out in the industry, it is particularly important to appreciate all forms of games out there and to approach any job opportunity as a chance to learn and improve your skills.

Be prudent with services that charge to tailor your résumé for success, particularly when you're new to the industry. Some of these services (not all but some) will, in fact, lean on obfuscation tactics that can risk setting you up for failure. What does this mean? Instead of finding the experiences, skills, and knowledge you have that can apply to a career in games and making that stand out, some may, in fact, muddle the waters by creating false impressions as to your skill set and capabilities to make you more "saleable" in your resume. This can risk setting you up for failure—if you start a job and it turns out you can't do what you said you could do in your résumé, . . . that might not be a fun time for anyone involved. Also, recruiters and hiring managers are starting to recognize these sorts of doctored résumés nowadays, and it may result in your job application being thrown away automatically. In short—be honest in your résumé, particularly when you're a junior. We know we're hiring a junior, and we expect and want to train you up. The better our understanding of your actual capabilities, the better off we'll all be.

A few more points:

- Be succinct but thorough in listing out everything you have created or worked on, as well as any awards you have.
- Don't be afraid to list what you are currently working on or learning—this also showcases your willingness to keep learning and highlights potential skills a company can help polish when they hire you.
- Make sure your games/stories are available online.
- If you have any hobbies that are relevant to games (particularly if you play tabletop RPGs or board games!), make sure to list those in a hobbies section.
- Make a list of your hobbies, and look at them carefully; see which ones could be applied to games.
- Examples: Photography can speak to how to set a scene, fencing speaks to an understanding of fight scenes for a sword-and-sorcery game, horseback riding speaks to understanding the potential primary locomotion in a Western, etc.

A few interview talking points:

- Be ready to discuss your personal work in a postmortem fashion.
- Be ready to discuss recent games.
- Be ready to discuss games the company you are applying for has produced (I cannot stress this enough), and particularly the game

you are aiming to work on, if that information is available to you during the application process.

- Be ready to talk about why you want to work in the game industry beyond "I love video games!"
- Be ready to discuss how narrative design can support other disciplines and how it should harmonize with game design in particular.
- Be open and interested in learning.

Networking: How to and When to

Since I've got you here, I'm going to share some advice based on my experience in the industry since I started out. Let's start with networking! While the Game Developers Conference and other such events can open up amazing career opportunities and offer you excellent exposure, they aren't always affordable. Social media is an amazing networking tool, though how you approach it can literally shape your career and open (or close) opportunities in the blink of an eye.

I've often expressed this to people—both those starting out and veterans alike—but the article by Tara J. Brannigan cited below perfectly covers online networking and how to approach it as a whole, and I cannot recommend enough that you read it. Right now. And bookmark it or print it out, so you can refer to it now and then as needed. While what Tara discussed may seem like common sense, I've seen people post things online that ensured they'd never be hired at certain companies.

"Game Industry 101: The Power of Online Networking," by Tara J. Brannigan, https://medium.com/@kindofstrange/e59edcdb2f4e

An important note: Remember that almost everything Tara discusses in her article can be applied to in-person interactions as well. In my experience, game-industry folk absolutely love talking about their jobs, about making games, about how to learn. We're a passionate bunch, more often than not. Keeping to the advice Tara gives will make interactions a lot easier on both you and the people you are talking to, however, and will ensure that if your résumé ever comes to their attention, they will have a good word to put in on your behalf.

My social media handles tend to be: @annlemay. While I tend to talk about pretty much everything but my day-to-day job (unless I'm being a horrible person by teasing people with obscure tweets about what I'm working on), I will gladly answer questions if I see them and as time allows. I'm also happy to put eyes on a résumé and help polish it.

Being a Writer in the Game Industry

While most of my colleagues come from many different backgrounds (movies, television, comics, books, tabletop RPGs, journalism, etc.),

I learned on the job while transitioning from one role (game design) to another (writing). Working in the game industry can be hard, frustrating at times, and often exhausting, but it is also infinitely rewarding. To this day, whenever I realize that I'm being paid to make video games, I feel a certain amount of disbelieving delight. What I love the most about what I do and working in this industry is that the medium of game narrative is a highly interactive one. Beyond the creative rush of setting up a plot just right, or finding exactly the right turn of phrase in a dialogue, is the interaction with my teammates at work, the satisfaction of a well-crafted story taking life when the game comes together across all disciplines, and the emotional investment of those who play our games.

Some Advice after over Two Decades of Making Games

Below are some of the most important tips I can give you, which I discussed in my keynote for GCAP (Game Connect Asia Pacific) in Australia in 2019. I hope these serve you well and help you take care of yourself as you start making games.

It's Ok to Walk Away

I'll repeat it: It's ok to walk away. A project, a game, is not worth your health, your happiness, who you become when you're an unhappy person.

Sometimes it's not even anyone's fault—for whatever reason, the human connection just isn't there, the project changed from what it was supposed to be or what drew you to it in the first place. Or the people you wanted to work with have left, for their own valid reasons. And sometimes the project and company culture are toxic and you need to get out. For any number of reasons, it may not just work out anymore.

You do not have to finish a game if it will harm or destroy you in the process. It is not a price worth paying. It's okay to walk away. There are more projects out there. There are always games to be made.

Post-Project Depression

Post-project depression is a very real thing. And we all have or will experience it at some point.

It takes more than a few weeks to process an entire production. Even a normal, nontraumatic project requires downtime so that we can reset our minds and creativity for something new. End-of-project depression is a thing that often devs don't know to watch for. And if a production was traumatic, it's even worse. We need rest and recovery time even more. As creatives, we are indoctrinated by society to believe we should do things because of our passion for our art, dedication to our work. But part of *any* craft or job is to take care of ourselves and to process the impact the act of creating has had on us.

It is hard to do good art when we're tired and depressed.

Choose People, Not Projects

I know, I know. The big IPs are nice and all, and you'll often get people selling you on that point.

But it's the people you work with that will determine your experience. That's it. That's the biggest secret of the industry. If you work with good people who genuinely care about you, that's what will keep you in one piece, no matter how a project actually goes.

I have met amazing people in this industry. Many of whom I stay in touch with to this day, that I call friends, gladly and gratefully so. They have made my life, both in the professional and the personal, better. I hope I've done a little bit of that for them too in return.

As Mr Rogers would say . . . look for the good neighbors. And be a good neighbor too.

You Can Do This

Finally, this: I believe in you. You can do this. Remember that.

Tobias Heussner: Résumé-Building Tips

Not to repeat what was said before, I'd like to give you some résumé tips in case you want to have a stronger design focus and maybe work in the area of story implementation and game design. Certainly, great writing samples will help. As a game designer, you will need to write a lot and be able to communicate clearly. Clear communication is also needed for all of your work as a narrative designer. So, why not sit down for a while and think about how you would communicate a story to a programmer, to an artist, to a sound engineer? Maybe you can create a short document for your portfolio where you highlight how you would approach the different groups, how you would address their needs, and how you would approach solving their tasks. Such a document can be part of your portfolio. At the very least, it can be useful prep for future job interviews.

Another very useful skill to learn for your résumé, especially if you want to look into content design, is to study various level and content editors. Try building your own little map or game using Unreal 4/5, Unity 3D, or Twine, or even the older but still well-known *Neverwinter Nights Toolkit* or *StarCraft II* Editor. Maybe you can include some friends on this project and work together as a team. Try using at least one of these technologies to implement some story into a game or create a small demo. It will not only help you with your résumé but also will help you to understand the challenges of content creation, especially level design. It will give you a chance to learn some scripting as well, which you may need later to implement stories. If you want to look more into game design, then I encourage you to have a deeper look at flow charts and diagrams. Try to visualize your ideas and rules in flow charts. Visualizing and being able to read flow charts is a great and useful skill for every area of game development.

Maybe I've scared you a bit with all the possible things to learn, but keep this in mind: No one expects you to be an expert scripter or level designer. Looking into the required skills from other areas and learning the basics will certainly help when you're trying to break into the industry or advance your career. Becoming the person in charge of a whole fantasy world takes years and lots of different skills. Showing your willingness to learn now can be more of a door opener than you may think. Your work and projects can tell industry vets more about you than any university degree. (This doesn't mean you shouldn't go to a university, but use the projects they offer or your free time to give your résumé this little extra project that shows that you know what your craft involves.)

#1reasontobe

As I said in the Introduction, I've been in the industry now for more than two decades, and in all these years, I have experienced things I like and things I don't like. I remember times when I worked through the night or had a camp bed next to my desk, and times seeing my latest game on the shelf in the nearby electronics store. All the little and big ups and downs between crunch time and finding the idea for the next project. The blank pages and the pages that felt like they had been rewritten a hundred times. The times I looked at my paycheck and wondered if I should do something that paid better, and the times when I first played through the levels I designed.

Why am I still in this industry? Because it is a great place to work with very creative and talented people. It's the joy of working together on something, on looking for and eventually finding these rare jewels that are called "great games." Yes, it can be tiring to sit and work on the same project for years, but it's extremely rewarding to finally see others enjoying it. Also, a great thing that I found among all the game writers and narrative designers of the IGDA Game Writing Special Interest Group is the friendliness, the openness, and the "like a family" spirit among individuals and professionals from so many different backgrounds and places in the world. This spirit of creativity and community unique to game development is what makes me want to be part of it. Unfortunately, I can no longer invite you to our once-famous Ginger Man meetings in Austin for GDC Online, but maybe one day we will meet at GDC San Francisco at the new famous writers' hangout.

NETWORKING AT GDC AND SIMILAR CONFERENCES

If you're planning to head to GDC or any other professional conferences, here are a few tips for networking as a narrative designer or game writer:

"How to Get Your Story-Oriented Hustle on at GDC (a.k.a. Networking for Game Writers)," by Toiya Kristen Finley PhD, http://gamewriting.org/2014/03/how-to-get-your-story-oriented-hustle-on-at-gdc-a-ka-networking-for-game-writers/

GDC Write Club. This image was made by Alexander Bevier and is protected by United States and international copyright law. © Alexander Bevier.

Toiya Kristen Finley: Evolving as a Storyteller

You've learned a lot about the building blocks of narrative design and how they work with game design to create great stories in a variety of game genres. You've had the opportunity to expand your portfolio, generate new samples, and create documentation types you may never have worked on before. But now what? Are you looking for that next job, or are you looking for your first? No matter where you are in your career, there are always opportunities to improve your skills as a narrative designer and gain insight into the process that will be unique to you.

Don't just play games—analyze them. Games look and play differently when you experience them as a narrative designer. If you enjoy something about the story and narrative design, take a note of that. If you don't, take a note of *that*. Go beyond making observations.

Ask yourself *why* something isn't working. Is it confusing? Not clear enough? Were there missed opportunities? Ask yourself how you might have done something differently. Of course, focus on strengths too. Just as a problem can take you out of a game, what's great about it can be thrilling. Why were you so impressed? How did the narrative design and story engage your emotions? What clever ways did the narrative design tie the story into the gameplay?

Keep in mind that, as a narrative designer, you might work on games you wouldn't choose to pick up yourself. However, there are players who do enjoy those games, and you want to give them the best possible experience you can. Start paying attention to games you might not normally play. You can learn just as much from them, if not more. Also, every once in a while, note how other people play games. Watch your friends play, and ask them to tell you what they like and don't like. Watch Twitch streamers and Let's Play videos on YouTube. The best LPers (Let's Players) and streamers can verbalize their observations and make astute comments about story as they're playing. It's always important to get other perspectives, especially since tastes can widely vary. Something that might make you cringe could make other players throw their hands up in exhilaration. Both your response and theirs are valid—as are the storytelling techniques and narrative design that elicited the blahs in you and excitement in them.

Storytelling has existed for millennia. As media evolves, the platforms in which we tell our stories have changed, but many of the techniques have stayed the same. There's a reason for that—the ingredients of a good story work. They're similar among all cultures and enjoyed by people of all life experiences. Don't be afraid to analyze stories in other media. Just because they're not games doesn't mean you can't apply what you see in prose, comics/manga, animation, film, music, and TV to your narrative design. All stories have their weaknesses and strengths. How would you avoid them or apply them to your work as a narrative designer? Much of what I understand about narrative design is a culmination of my experiences writing and editing other media, being a consumer of stories, and working as a narrative designer. I continue to learn, and I encourage you to think about and absorb whatever you can from wherever you can.

With the growth of social and mobile gaming, apps available on a variety of platforms, programs that require little to no coding, and the rise of the indie developer, you have more opportunities than ever to work as a narrative designer. There will still be competition as you look for work, but remember that narrative design is a discipline many in the industry are still learning about. You have chances to innovate narrative design in new media and on new platforms. Combine the strengths of storytelling handed down through the ages with narrative-design techniques that are unique to games' interactive medium.

Jennifer Brandes Hepler:
Ten Thousand Hours

There is no easy road to become a narrative designer. Of all game industry disciplines, it claims perhaps the smallest numbers, and since it doesn't require a lot of specialized training, there are often the greatest number of inexperienced people trying to break in.

We hope this book helped you start the portfolio that will raise you above the crowd. But don't stop there. The best way to be a better writer is to write, continuously, about anything that interests you, and some things that don't. The best way to become a better game writer is to write games.

Any practice writing and designing games will help you strengthen both your skills and your résumé. Tabletop game design is a great way to get your feet wet. Writing for tabletop RPGs gives you tremendous practice in worldbuilding and character creation, as well as training you to design stories in which the protagonist is left blank. Board-game and card-game design help you understand game systems and appreciate the strange mix of creativity and obsessive-compulsiveness that motivates designers. If you can't design tabletop games, play them a lot. GMing tabletop RPGs lets you see players react to your stories in real time—there's no better training for keeping the player in mind than having to anticipate the reactions of your gaming group to the latest adventure you're planning. GMing is one of the best ways to practice and improve the skills a narrative designer requires.

Beyond tabletop, many PC games have a modding community, a group of fan designers who create their own assets and stories for their favorite games. The last project I worked on at Pixelberry Studios is a visual novel tool called Storyloom, which allows even novice writers to create their own visual novels using professional art assets, with tips on story creation from the great team of Pixelbrry writers. Someone who has successfully planned a story arc, designed it, written it, and sent it out for the community to play will always get taken more seriously by game companies than someone who has only daydreamed about it.

Any kind of published writing will definitely get you past the gatekeepers, so be open to all writing opportunities that come calling. At BioWare, we had writers with backgrounds in film, television, comics, tabletop games, playwriting, novel and short-story writing, and even newspaper reporting. Scriptwriting and playwriting are both dialogue driven, just like games, so they are a great way to train your ear to write speakable lines. Screenwriting and comics both marry dialogue to visuals and help develop your inner artist. And any project in which you have to work with artists, actors, or other creative disciplines is a good way to learn whether you have the temperament to work in an interdisciplinary team.

Ten thousand hours is the number currently floated as how long someone must practice to reach a level of expertise. It sounds like a lot, but the great part of working in a creative field is that those hours will be *fun*. Not fun in the same way as playing a game—writing can be hard, and no one enjoys having to be creative on command—but creative work is *meaningful* work. There is nothing that feels as good as taking a blank page—or a section of undifferentiated gameplay—and giving it meaning and context by making it a story.

Games are the new art form of our generation. They are the forefront of a new kind of interactive entertainment that is just coming into its own. Schoolchildren now grow up playing games; when they want more sophisticated stories and deeper characters, they will look for them *in games*. As writers in this field, we do more than provide the words; we provide depth and longevity, to allow game stories to linger in people's minds and affect their lives.

When I was working on *Dragon Age II*, the team made the decision to have all romance characters be able to fall in love with players of either gender. This decision met with some very publicized homophobic backlash, but what will always stay with me is the letter we received from a young man who was struggling with the decision of whether to come out of the closet. He was from an intolerant family in an intolerant town, and he said it had never occurred to him that gay men could actually *love* each other, not just have meaningless sex. He was on the verge of killing himself, rather than accept a future without love. Then he played the *DAII* romance with my character, Anders. When he saw that portrayal of a love story between two men, he decided to live and to devote his life to trying to find that level of passion and romance in real life.

So, if you ever wonder whether writing for games actually matters, I can tell you—yes. You never know when your words will be the exact lifeline someone needs at their loneliest time.

When the first motion picture aired in 1895, no one knew that 1942 would bring them *Casablanca*. That's forty-seven years. *Pong* came out in 1972. Have we seen our *Casablanca* yet?

Casablanca.

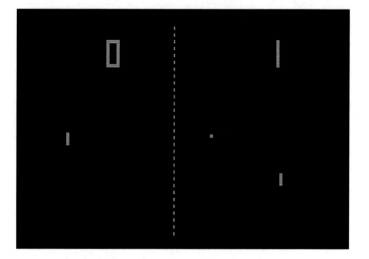

Pong.

We wish you all the best and blessings for your journey. We hope that you'll enjoy it as you start creating stories and games, facing all these challenges that make the game industry unique.

Resources

Recommended Reading

The following resources were of great benefit to us, and we hope they're helpful to you:

Brannigan, Tara J. "Game Industry 101: The Power of Online Networking." *Medium.com*. Last modified May 11, 2014. https://medium.com/@kindofstrange/game-industry-101-the-power-of-online-networking-e59edcdb2f4e.

FILM CRIT HULK. *Screenwriting 101 by Film Crit Hulk!* Austin: Badass Digest, 2013.

Freed, Alexander. "Branching Conversation Systems and the Working Writer, Part 1: Introduction." *Game Developer*. Last modified September 2, 2014. www.gamedeveloper.com/design/branching-conversation-systems-and-the-working-writer-part-1-introduction.

McDevitt, Darby. "A Practical Guide to Game Writing." *Game Developer*. Last modified October 13, 2010. www.gamedeveloper.com/design/a-practical-guide-to-game-writing.

Megill, Anna. "FAQ of Game Writing." *Annamegill.com*. Last modified January 1, 2013. www.annamegill.com/game-writing-faq/.

Skolnik, Evan. *Video Game Storytelling: What Every Developer Needs to Know About Narrative Techniques*. New York: Watson-Guptill, 2009.

Recommended Viewing

You can find several narrative-related talks, including Murray's below, at the Game Developers Conference free video archive:

www.gdcvault.com/free/.

Murray, Jill. *Binders Full of Women: Diversifying Feminine Archetypes in Games*. Video. GDC Next, 2013. www.gdcvault.com/play/1019720/Binders-Full-of-Women-Diversifying.

Murray, Jill. *Diverse Game Characters: Write Them Now!* Video. GDC, 2013. www.gdcvault.com/play/1017819/Diverse-Game-Characters-Write-Them.

Heather Albano's lecture and the LudaNarraCon panel focus on designing and structuring branching narratives:

Albano, Heather. "Vermont Game Developers #7: Narrative Design and Player Agency Are Friends by Heather Albano." October 5, 2015, YouTube video. 45:01. www.youtube.com/watch?v=NN7zKPSGfOU.

Reznick, Graham, Sam Maggs, Karin Weekes, Sam Barlow, and Christian Divine. "Developing Branching Narratives: LudoNarraCon 2020 Panel." April 25, 2020, YouTube video. 48:05. www.youtube.com/watch?v=mgD81pQlu1o.

Books by the Authors

In addition to *The Game Narrative Toolbox*, we have additional books on narrative design and game writing and the game industry at large.

Jennifer Brandes Hepler, ed. *Women in Game Development: Breaking the Glass Level Cap*. Boca Raton: CRC Press, 2017.

Tobias Heussner, ed. *The Advanced Game Narrative Toolbox*. Boca Raton: CRC Press, 2019.

Toiya Kristen Finley, *Branching Story, Unlocked Dialogue: Designing and Writing Visual Novels*. Boca Raton: CRC Press, 2023.

Toiya Kristen Finley, *Freelance Video Game Writing: The Life & Business of the Digital Mercenary for Hire*. Boca Raton: CRC Press, 2022.

Toiya Kristen Finley, ed. *Narrative Tactics for Mobile and Social Games: Pocket-Sized Storytelling*. Boca Raton: CRC Press, 2017.

Organizations and Groups

International Game Developers Association (IGDA)
Website: www.IGDA.org/
Twitter: @IGDA

The IGDA is a non-profit membership organization for game-industry professionals, students, and individuals interested in the industry. The IGDA has local chapters worldwide, where developers from the community get together to discuss game development and issues that affect game developers. IGDA meet-ups are great places to network and share ideas.

IGDA Game Writing Special Interest Group (SIG)
Websites: https://igda.org/sigs/game-writing/
Google Group: https://groups.google.com/d/forum/wsig-main
Facebook Group: www.facebook.com/groups/119570501396639/
Twitter: @IGDAWritingSIG
Discord: https://discord.gg/qx3RrDp

The Game Writing SIG is a community of narrative-design and game-writing professionals, students, and individuals interested in evolving and promoting narrative within the industry. Anyone can join the SIG; you don't have to be a member of the IGDA. The Game Writing

SIG discusses game-writing and narrative-design theories and best practices, shares diverse personal experiences, and chats informally about favorite stories in games.

Online Communities

GameDev.net
Writing for Games Forum: www.gamedev.net/forum/32-writing-for-games/

GameDev.net serves game developers at all stages of their careers with news, developer journals, informative articles, and community forums. This is a good place to network, share ideas, collaborate, and look for feedback.

Other Communities

Coding programs and languages like Unreal Engine, Unity, ink, Twine, Yarn Spinner, Ren'Py, RPG Maker, and GameMaker have their own community forums. Like the GameDev.net forums, these are great places to connect with other game developers, discuss narrative techniques, and get feedback.

Game Conferences

Game Developers Conference (GDC)
Website: www.gdconf.com/
Game Narrative Summit
Website: www.gdconf.com/conference/gamenarrative.html

There are several GDC conferences worldwide, but the largest is the five-day event in San Francisco during early spring. GDC in San Francisco is also home to the Game Narrative Summit, held the first two days of the week. A large community of narrative designers and writers meet at GDC each year. Attending the conference is a great way to become a part of the community. The community is friendly, welcoming, and always looking to support new members.

East Coast Game Conference (ECGC)
Website: www.ecgconf.com/
Narrative Track: www.ecgconf.com/tracks/

ECGC is held in Raleigh, North Carolina, during the spring. It's a two-day conference that also features a Narrative Track dedicated to game writing and narrative design, and it has its own narrative community. While ECGC is a much smaller conference than GDC, its passes are more affordable.

PAX
Website: www.paxsite.com/

PAX, short for "Penny Arcade Expo," has several year-round events in the United States and Australia: PAX East (Boston, Massachusetts in April), PAX West (Seattle, Washington over Labor Day weekend in August/September, PAX Aus (Melbourne, Victoria in October), and PAX Unplugged (Philadelphia, Pennsylvania in December). While PAX is fan oriented, game developers organize panels on topics of interest to both players and devs. Panels on writing and storytelling in games are popular. You might consider attending PAX as a fan or submit your own panel. Speaking at events is networking, and it's a way to get yourself, your work, and your ideas known. Additionally, PAX Unplugged is specifically for tabletop gaming. Story and narrative design is just as important in tabletop as it is in video games, and speaking and networking at Unplugged could open up more opportunities for you.

Glossary

AAA (also triple-A): A game that aims for the highest market and industry standard, similar to a blockbuster in Hollywood. Also refers to the developer of such games.

Animatics: Still images with text, voice-over narration, and/or a soundtrack, or comic book panels appearing in sequence.

Branching narrative: A narrative in which players make choices that affect individual sections of plot and gameplay.

Cinematics: Fully pre-rendered in-game movies with high production values and no player interaction.

Core leads: Directors and leads of various disciplines within the project. People like the technical director, lead game designer, art director, producer, etc.

Critical path (also critpath): The collection of all the missions, narrative, and gameplay elements that are required to complete the game.

Cutscene: A non-interactive scene, scripted by narrative and usually done "in-engine," which does not allow dialogue options to the player.

> **Interactive cutscene**: An interactive scene, scripted by narrative and usually done "in-engine," allowing the player dialogue options.

Dialogue: Words or utterances spoken in the game.

> **Ambient dialogue**: Dialogue during gameplay spoken by players, AI companions, voice over a radio headset, or any characters players pass at locations.

> **Banter**: A few lines of dialogue spoken between two or more characters.

> **Combat barks (also soundsets)**: One-liners spoken in combat situations.

> **Interactive dialogue**: Any game system in which the dialogue pauses the action to allow players to select responses from a list, wheel, or any other presentation of multiple options.

> **Onomatopes (also grunts)**: Sounds with no words involved.

> **Voice-over (also VO)**: Auditory narration not accompanied by a visual of the speaker.

Downloadable content (also DLC): New game content offered in downloadable formats after the initial game has been released.

Dynamics: Players' applications towards the game's mechanics and how they try to optimize or use the mechanics to maximize their chance to win.

Environmental narrative: Audio, visual, and design techniques in the game's world used to intentionally communicate information regarding the world, its story, and its characters.

Eye dialect: Nonstandard spelling to mimic a character's pronunciation, accent, or regional dialect.

First-person shooter (also FPS): A genre where the player sees the game world through a first-person perspective and where the core mechanics are built upon weapon usage.

Flavor text: Functional in-game definitions given a fictional spin.

Full motion video (also FMV): A heavily scripted scene in which the player is offered a limited range of options by pressing buttons at the right time, or other similar game systems.

Game bible (also story bible or universe bible): A document detailing all of a game's worldbuilding and lore, including information covering character development, storylines, and missions/quests.

Game design: The rules and mechanics of the game.

Game design document (also GDD): The technical documentation of the intentions of the game design team; not the same as the game bible.

Game narrative design (also narrative design): The art of telling a story in a video game using the techniques and devices available, including gameplay and the sum of visual and acoustic methods to create an entertaining and engaging experience for players.

Game narrative designer (also narrative designer): The champion of an interactive story, working in the field of narrative design, combining the roles of a writer with that of a game designer.

Gameplay: The set of mechanics, challenges, and story by which players interact with the game.

Geopolitical services (also GeoPS): "Deep localization" review of dialogue and situations to eliminate what may be taboo to a specific people or country by exploring how people think or interpret what they see, and regional, cultural, religious, or other variables that may affect players' reactions.

GM: Game master, the person who leads the storytelling in a traditional roleplaying game.

Graphical perspective: The in-game camera view (first-person or third-person perspective).

High concept (also tagline): The game idea condensed into one or two sentences.

Intellectual property (also IP): A legal term that describes creations of the mind, such as artistic and creative works.

Iterate: A process of revision and improvement that leads from one status of a project to an improved status.

JRPG: Japanese roleplaying game, defining a specific style and subgenre of roleplaying games.

Linear narrative: A narrative in which every player experiences the same events in the same order every time the game is played.

Living document: A document, such as a game bible, whose content is continually revised, edited out, and added to.

Lore: All material that describes and defines a fictional world and its history.

Massively multiplayer online (also MMO): A group of genres where hundreds of players play together in the same game world/scenario while being connected via online functionalities.

Mechanics (also game mechanics): The rules of the game.

> **Core mechanics**: The mechanics that define the core idea of the game.

Merits and flaws: Benefits, such as superiority in a certain field, and undesirable weaknesses used in character creation.

Mission: A task or group of tasks composing a single part of a linear story.

Multilevel storytelling: Interactive stories occurring on at least two levels, the player story (players' experiences through their actions and imaginations) and the world story (everything created by the designers to support the players' experiences, including the environment, enemies, plot, and dialogue).

Narrative space: The amount of time players allow for a story to be told in a game, based upon their attention span.

Narrative type: The way a story is told through the game, as through quests (quest-based narrative), through missions (mission-based narrative), environment (environmental narrative), etc.

Non-disclosure agreement (also NDA): A legal contract between two parties, which regulates the kind of information these parties can share with third parties and what information cannot be shared.

Non-player character (also NPC): A character within an interactive story that is not controlled by any player.

On-demand storytelling: Player-controlled narrative content that is not a required part of the gameplay and/or story. Players can decide how much or little of this content they want to experience. Example: Audio logs players find in the world, which they may or may not decide to play.

One-liner comparison: A short description of the game, including elements such as genre, protagonist, comparable game, goal, and type of game world.

One-liner description: A one- or two-sentence description of the game's core idea that does not compare the idea with an existing one.

Open narrative: A narrative in which players can choose their own order to complete any content.

Player agency: The players' beliefs that their choices and actions are what drive the events of the story.

Player versus player (also PvP): A game activity where at least two players compete against each other within the set of game rules.

Postures: Short animations using NPCs, creatures, or the environment that help set a scene and can be reused across levels to bring the game world to life.

Producer: A project manager overseeing the business part of the development process. Responsible for the project's schedule and available resources.

Quest: A task or group of tasks composing a single, self-contained storyline that may be a part of, or alongside, a larger plot in a non-linear story.

> **Side quest**: An optional quest in the game, which do not have to complete to advance the story.

Quest texts: Structured text boxes that include a short dialogue, a description of the task, a summary of the task, and the rewards players will receive upon the task's completion.

Railroading: The forcing of players into narrative choices that are inconsistent with the players' choices, or forcing gameplay situations despite anything players may have access to in terms of skill sets or available mechanics.

Real-time strategy (also RTS): A genre where the player has to make decisions in real time and not in turns.

Retcon (also retconning): The process of making a change to a game's world or story in a way that strives to be true to what's already published about that game.

RPG: Roleplaying game, a genre where players act out the roles and take on the responsibilities of characters within the game.

Sequences: Very short scenes, sometimes with repeatable dialogue, that can be looped.

Stereotype: A cliché based on a single concept to provide superficial character development.

Storyboards: Illustrations and/or images displayed in sequence as part of the preplanning process for animations or other interactive sequences.

Subtext: An underlying sentiment or meaning, such as in dialogue, not explicitly expressed.

System designer: A subgroup of game designers often just referred to as "game designer." Responsible for the rules and mechanics of a game.

Task: Any goal a player needs to accomplish through gameplay.

Testing plan: A document outlining all of the ways to play through the content of the game, for purposes of ensuring that every branch is tested.

Tokens (also strings): Tiny bits of code that let the game know when to refer back to something players chose about their characters.

Transmedia: The telling of several or many stories from the same fictional universe/world in various media, including prose fiction, comics/manga, film, animation, and games.

Trope: A popular, known concept which is a part of cultural knowledge.

Visual novel: An interactive narrative heavily focused on narrative choices with little to no further gameplay; frequently used for interactive romance stories.

Wireframing: The process of structuring the hierarchy of information flow.

Worldbuilding: The development of details of the world where a story takes place, including its history, geography, peoples/races, governments, science/technology, religions, and languages.

Index

Note: Page numbers in *italics* indicate a figure, and page numbers in **bold** indicate a table on the corresponding page.

Index

interview with Cori May, 226–227
iteration process, 5, **12**, 12, 13, 18, 20, 41–42, 64, 116, 117, 193, 301
making revisions, 215–217
25 percent more awesome, 220–221
working with QA, 218–220
Final Fantasy franchise, 35, 111
Finley, Toiya Kristen, xxii–xxiii, 6–7, 290–291
first-person shooter (FPS), 30, **31**, 37, 44, 48n4, 51, **145**, 300
flavor text, 67, 300
fluff text, 39, 46
focus tests, 220–222
Food of the Gods, 72
Forgotten Realms, 274
"Frankenstein Method," 90–91, 100n3
free-to-play games, tutorials in, 181
Frogger, xxiv
full motion video (FMV), 192–193, 300
Fungus add-on, 224

G

game bible, 132–135, 300
game design, 2, 3, 6–11, *7*, 300, 303, *see also* gameplay
game design document (GDD), 37, 161, 222, 300
Game Developers Conference (GDC), xxvi, 23, 289–290, *290*, 295, 297
game development and production, xxi, 143, 156–160, *see also* cutscenes and cinematics; documentation; narrative design
AAA (triple-A) games, 4–5, 68, 114, 136, 156, 199, 223, 299
downstream vs. upstream teams, 157–159
feedback and troubleshooting, 211–228
glossary of terms, 299–303
implementation and production, 143–163
localization, 184, 185–186, 201, 202, 300
narrative design and team dependencies, 156–160
quality assurance, 159–160
resources, 295–298
game logos, 259, *259*
GameMaker, 224

game masters (GMs), 59, 77n5, 280, 292, 300
game narrative design, *see* narrative design
game narrative designers, *see* narrative designers
Game of Thrones franchise, 72, 77n6, 138, 167, 178, 274
game pitch
alternative techniques, 36
exercises and samples, 43–47
the game pitch doc, 37, 38–39
high concept one-liner (logline), 31–35, **31**
making the pitch, 36
the narrative pitch doc, 39–41
one-liner comparisons/descriptions, 32–34
presenting your pitch, 35–36
writing your, 36–39
gameplay, *see also* combat; missions; narrative design; quests
core mechanics, 26–28, *29*, **31**, 157, 301
dynamics, 27–28, 300
"gameplay loops," 157
tasks, 14–16, *17*, 17, *115*, 116, 118, 192
games as a service (GAAS), 265, 273–280
exercise and sample for, 281, *282*
keeping your material updated, 274–276, *275*, 281
layering plots, 276–278
practicing writing for live-service games, 279–280
the problem with success (or its absence), 278–279
Generation Kill miniseries, 117
geopolitical services (GeoPS), 185–186, 300
Grand Theft Auto franchise, 94, 126
graphical perspective, 143, 144, 145–146, 163, 301

H

Half Life franchise, 44, 80
HBO, 117
Hepler, Jennifer Brandes, xxii, xxiii–xxiv, 2–5, 292–293
Heussner, Tobias, xxii, xxv–xxvii, 7–8, 18–19, 22–23, 288–289
high concept, 2, 30–32, 38, 216, 222, 232, 301

I

Iglesias, Karl, 32
Incarnō: Everything Is Written, *256*
Independent Game Developers Association (IGDA), xxvi, 99, 223, 289, 296
indie games, xxii, 13–16, 16, 36, 130, 291
inFamous franchise, 199
Inform, 224
inklewriter, 224
Insecure: The Come Up Game, xxiii
intellectual property (IP), 301
new IPs as investment risk, 58–59
original, 52
research and, 56–57, 58
retaining your, 225
working with existing/licensed, 68–70, 81, 98–99, 253
iteration process, 5, **12**, 12, 13, 18, 20, 41–42, 64, 116, 117, 193, 301

J

JRPGs, 35, 43, 44, 48n11, 301
Jubert, Tom, 136–137
Jung, Carl Gustav, 89

K

Kindregan, Brian, 202–204
KingsRoad, 14, *15*
KOTOR, see Star Wars: Knights of the Old Republic (KOTOR)

L

L.A. Noire, 54, 56
lead artists, 4
lead designers, 4, 72
Left 4 Dead, 154
Legend of Zelda, The, 81
Lemay, Ann, xxii, xxiv–xxv, 5–6, 283–288
Letter, The, 259, *259*
level design, 2, 3, 8, 10
environmental narrative and, 114, 148, 150, 151, 152–153
initial, 157, 158
tools for, 8, 288
worldbuilding and, 59–60
level designers, 4, 5, 8, 11, 18, 59–60, 132–133, 158, 275, 289
licensed IPs, 68–70, 81, 98–99, 253

Index